CRITICAL THEORY OF
THE FAMILY

Mark Poster

CRITICAL THEORY OF
THE FAMILY

A Continuum Book
THE SEABURY PRESS   NEW YORK

1978
The Seabury Press
815 Second Avenue
New York, New York 10017

Printed in the United States of America

Library of Congress Cataloging in Publication Data

Poster, Mark.   Critical theory of the family.
(A Continuum book)
Includes bibliographical references and index.
1. Family.   I. Title.
HQ734.P79   301.42   77-28487   ISBN 0-8164-9343-X

FOR JUNE

CONTENTS

PREFACE

TODAY the family is being attacked and defended with equal vehemence. It is blamed for oppressing women, abusing children, spreading neurosis and preventing community. It is praised for upholding morality, preventing crime, maintaining order and perpetuating civilization. Marriages are being broken more than even before and being constituted more than ever before. The family is the place from which one desperately seeks escape and the place to which one longingly seeks refuge. To some the family is boring, stifling and intrusive; to others it is loving, companionate and intimate. And so it goes with the family, back and forth with no sign of agreement on the horizon. Just at a time when public concern for the family is widespread, social scientists have little theoretical clarity to offer. People are intensely interested in finding out how the family is faring, how it has evolved from the past and what forms it may take in the future. Yet social science does not have an adequate definition of the family, or a coherent set of categories from which to analyze it, or a rigorous conceptual scheme to specify what is significant about it. The purpose of this book is to demonstrate the weaknesses of existing theories of the family in the fields of history, sociology and psychology and to offer at least the beginnings of a more adequate theory.

Family history provides an example of some of the theoretical deficiencies. With a dominant empiricist tradition, historians have come to the field of family history without a clear sense of what the significant questions are. They have not

self-consciously theorized the family as a field of investigation.
Instead they began by adopting the conventional wisdom of
sociology which, going back to Frédéric Le Play,[1] saw a broad
change in the family from an extended form of the Middle
Ages to a nuclear form of modernity. This position maintained that before industrialization the family was composed
of numerous kin living together in cohesive solidarity. Only
the irresistible pressures of modernization could tear apart
these bonds. This tradition of sociological history assumed
that the family was defined by the quantity of kin relatives in
a household.

Over the past several years the thesis of a premodern extended family was challenged by a group of Cambridge
demographers led by Peter Laslett. Analysing English parish
registers from the sixteenth century on, Laslett discovered no
extended family at all.[2] On the contrary, the family was amaz-
ingly stable in size, consisting of the conjugal unit with a small
number of children. There had been a significant demographic
shift from a pattern of high fertility/high mortality in the old
regime to one of low fertility/low mortality in the modern
period. Some historians could claim that the change in demographic pattern, while not affecting family size, had considerable impact on the daily life of the family. Such factors as the
length of interval between births seriously affects the condition of women, and high mortality among children has deep
consequences for parents' attitudes toward their progeny. Yet
for Laslett the stability of family size over the past four hun-
dred years was the major finding, one which led him to question the family as a suitable object for historical investigation
since it seemed impervious to change.

Laslett's conclusions were criticized effectively on several
counts. Lutz Berkner pointed out that Laslett had done his
counting in a static way, forgetting that the family has a life
cycle.[3] If families of the old regime are studied over the course
of time, it becomes clear that in a significant number of cases
in the regions studied by Berkner the grandparents live with
the conjugal unit. Hence the family begins to resemble the

extended model more than the nuclear one. Numerous instances were also found, in southern France for example,
where brothers banded together with their families apparently for reasons of economic survival. A more complex picture than Laslett offered of family size thus emerged for the
premodern European peasantry. Although the finding of Laslett and Louis Henry, the French demographer, of the late age
of first marriage (apparently unique to premodern Europe) has
not been challenged, the notion of a stable nuclear pattern
cannot be maintained.

Yet another blow to the Laslett thesis came from Roland
Mousnier and Jean-Louis Flandrin, who faulted Laslett for his
aggregate figures.[4] If the national figures were broken down,
it became apparent that certain groups, especially the nobility,
did not conform to the general nuclear pattern. These high-
ranking families consisted of large groupings of from 20 to 200
souls. While the members of these households were not all
blood relations, and their composition was not at all stable,
they did constitute "families." Flandrin reminded Laslett that
the word family in the old regime included all members of the
household. Hence Laslett's picture of a baker's family in *The
World We Have Lost*, consisting of thirteen people (parents,
children, servants and workers),[5] was closer to premodern
reality than the statistics of small family size.

The theoretical question intervenes at this point. Laslett and
many other family historians simply assumed that family was
defined by size and by blood relations. The criticisms of Laslett's work make it clear that this definition is sorely inadequate. While quantitative, demographic studies are needed,
they cannot provide historians with a concept of the family
that can pose the important questions and render the family
intelligible in premodern and modern Europe. The nuclear
family that emerged in the transition to modernity is a unique
configuration of behaviors and attitudes, decisively different
from what existed before it.

A superior beginning was made by Philippe Ariès in his
classic study *Centuries of Childhood*.[6] On the surface, Ariès was

concerned only with the idea of childhood and how it changed from the old regime to the modern era. He studied an uneven mass of evidence, from portrait paintings to village games, to prove his thesis that there was no concept of childhood under the old regime. One important consequence of his work was that it showed how historians of the family might make use of evidence like portraits, which are normally employed in other fields of study. Hence the old bugbear that there exists no evidence for a history of the family was put into doubt: the family could be studied by the use of indirect evidence. More significantly, however, Ariès' book opened up questions well beyond the confines of the intellectual history of childhood. He concluded that the modern family brought with it a new set of attitudes toward children. Bourgeois types in mid-eighteenth-century France began pulling away from wider networks of sociability, as Ariès termed it, by separating their workplace from their home, creating their home as a private world and initiating new forms of intimacy, especially between parents and children. The important question raised by Ariès is that family history ought to concern itself not simply with family size but with the emotional qualities of family relations. He implied that family history can raise questions about intimate life, the "private" world, and that perhaps changes in family structure lead to changes in emotional or psychic structure. Without any theoretical discussion of the object of family history, Ariès suggested a most fruitful line of investigation. In broaching the question of the forms of intimacy between parents and children, Ariès' book led directly to the route of psychological theory. For only psychological theory can enable the investigator to explore the rich set of meanings surrounding feelings between parents and children. This study will examine several traditions of psychological theories of the family in order to construct a theory of the family which can approach the problems opened by Ariès.

In addition to Laslett and Ariès, a third framework or general orientation for family history was proposed by Edward Shorter in *The Making of the Modern Family*. Influenced deeply by the Parsonian theory of Fred Weinstein and Gerald Platt, Shorter wrote the first comprehensive history of the family in Europe. He argued that the bourgeois family emerged as a nest of domesticity, as a private world withdrawn from society, when the capitalist economy liberated individuals from community constraints. The capitalist market eroded the collective authority of the village and other corporate bodies over the intimate affairs of the individual. Shorter claimed that love and sex based on spontaneous and empathic emotions replaced relations based on calculation and interest. In Parson's words, the expressive function replaced the instrumental function. Once capitalism gave individuals the opportunity to escape from parental restrictions and to choose mates freely, nothing could hold back what Shorter termed "the surge of sentiment." The nuclear family was established, he continued, when couples paired on the basis of romantic love and regarded the intrusions of the community as unwarranted interference with privacy. Domesticity, romantic love and maternal love, all built around privacy and isolation, were the cornerstones of the nuclear family to Shorter. One basic problem with Shorter's presentation is that he regarded these features of the modern family as *natural* impulses which arose inevitably once individuals had any say in the matter, once, as he said, capitalism fulfilled the "wish to be free."[7]

Historically, there are many errors and dubious generalizations in Shorter's account. For example, he asserts that a sexual revolution began in the nineteenth century along with the rise of domesticity, romantic love and maternal care. He makes this argument on the basis of his view of the peasants as sexually repressed. Hence only in the nineteenth century do we find, according to him, an explosion of sexual exploration. Even if Shorter's view of peasant sexuality is correct, which by no means should be conceded, he can make his claim only by offering a series of outrageous secondary arguments. First, he ignores the aristocracy completely. This is a class which is characterized by libertinage and extra-marital affairs—certainly not a repressed group. If there was a sexual revolution in the nineteenth century it hardly outdid the aristocracy of the old regime. Second, Shorter fails to make crucial class distinctions. In the early nineteenth century, the rise of romantic love, domesticity and maternal care were *bourgeois* phenomena. But this group certainly did not participate in any sexual revolution; if it did it was a "revolution" toward frigidity for women and perversity for men, as Freud demonstrated. The sexual revolution of which Shorter speaks, based on a rise in illegitimacy figures, was if anything confined to the early industrial working class. The "promiscuity" of this class, so bemoaned by nineteenth-century moralists, can hardly be considered part of the same phenomenon as the rise of domesticity. The latter was associated with the emergence of the bourgeois nuclear family. Hence to claim, in a blanket way, that the sexual revolution was part of the same process of "liberation" as the rise of romantic love obscures the fact that the two things went on separately at different levels of society. Finally, Shorter uses sexist arguments which distort the history of women. He actually claims that prostitutes were participating in the "sexual revolution." For bourgeois women who were experiencing the new feelings of romantic love, maternal care and domesticity, Shorter suggests a criterion of a "sacrifice test" which these women pass; they thus receive a diploma of modernity. While it is true that bourgeois women devoted themselves to maintaining their homes as a nest and refuge, the use of the phrase "sacrifice test" to account for the phenomenon obscures the confinement of women in the nuclear family and makes their protest against it appear as a failure to pass a moral exam. In all these ways, Shorter's account and conceptualization of the sexual revolution fails the "historical test" of intelligibility and adequacy.

The main question raised by Shorter's book concerns the theoretical problem of defining the bourgeois family. If one views this family structure as the spontaneous consequence of "freedom" which wells up from deep within each individual rather than as circumscribed by social structure, one is essentially presenting it as natural to mankind. Therefore one is presenting it as the fulfillment of human needs, as an ideal social arrangment. This is of course ideological, justifying a given social structure on the basis of a metaphysics of human nature; more specifically it is a theodicy, justifying the ways of the bourgeoisie to all humanity. For Shorter, society today has attained a family structure which allows human beings the freedom to experiment with their personal lives, which guarantees them a free quest for individual development, and which supports their basic needs for spontaneous, intimate relations. But Shorter recognizes the crisis of the bourgeois family of the past few decades, although he has no adequate explanation for it. Speaking of the loss of communal sociability, of the tragic rise of divorce rates, of the communication gap between parents and children which beset the bourgeois family, he can state only this: "It's just like my mother said: nothing comes free in this world."[8] I would not repeat this remark, which accepts social irrationality as a product of fate, except that it marks the collapse of Shorter's whole position: there can be no historical view of the bourgeois family structure in his account, no critical assessment of its limits and its changing features, no prescription of its weaknesses and needed transformations.

In addition to the ideological weakness of Shorter's view, another difficulty stems from his lack of a psychological theory. The advantage of a position which includes a psychological theory can be seen best through examining Shorter's inability to show the mediations between society and the family. Without a psychological theory of family structure the relative autonomy of the family disappears in his argument and the intelligibility of family history is lost. He is unable to present the nuclear family as a structure in its own right and indicate properly just where the economy determines it and where it determines the economy. Confusions abound when he claims that the capitalist market requires an "egotistical economic mentality" to "spread into various non-economic domains of life."[9] In Shorter's account, the market *forced* individuals to look out first for themselves and this individualism extended to the family as romantic love and maternal care. There are three errors here: (1) How was it possible for the economic system to rely on individualism when there was no psychic or emotional preparation for it, no emotional structure of the family that would internalize values so deeply within the individual that he would appear to be an autonomous agent? (2) Individualism was not supported by the economic realities of the working class because there was little chance of upward social mobility for them, little chance for them to squeeze pennies and accumulate capital. Yet Shorter sees the working class as the vanguard of sexual innovation, the standard-bearers of modernization, just that group which was most "individualistic" and "spontaneous" in sex. How could capitalism be the cause of these sexual changes among the working class when it did not produce parallel changes in the group's economic life? (3) Shorter confuses a determinist explanation based on market forces and an individualist explanation based on personal wishes to be free. If the market is forcing people to be individualists, then they are not free to do so. But this is a basic problem in much of liberal theory, an irresolvable antimony of determinism and freedom. At the level of family history, it means that Shorter presents large-scale social actions as if they were undertaken by individuals in multiple, separate, accidentally contemporaneous decisions: women all over Europe suddenly decided to give loving care to their infants, boys all over Europe suddenly decided to resist their parents' wishes and marry the girls of their dreams. But the task of social history is to avoid the obscurity of presenting change as the simple, private decisions of millions of people. Instead its aim is to depict the conjuncture, to analyze the social structures leading in one direction or another, to present the choices of individuals not as arbitrary coincidences on a massive scale but as occurring in a concrete, definable situation.

The Making of the Modern Family is a central book for family history. It brings together and summarizes studies of the European family by historians from Europe and the United States.

It outlines the kinds of documents that are available to historians. Above all, it pioneers many compelling questions about the change from premodern to modern family forms. More than any other study so far, it courageously poses basic questions for historians to pursue. Yet Shorter's theoretical confusions detract seriously from his advances, discrediting in many ways the very questions he so boldly proposes.

I want to argue in these pages that we must redefine family structure away from issues of family size and toward issues relating to emotional patterns. The significant questions that can be posed in family history do not concern the number of people in the household or in the kin-group residence unit. Instead, family history can contribute to the knowledge of social history by looking at the emotional structures in the daily life of various family types. Such historical investigation will enable social science to shed light not only on the past but also on the present dilemmas of family life which concern, to a great degree, feelings, sexuality and psychic stability. In this way, family history can contribute substantially to our understanding of current discontents as they relate to the isolated, conjugal family type. This study will also suggest that historians and social scientists in general have gone astray by viewing the family as a unitary phenomenon which has undergone some type of linear transformation. I will argue in the concluding chapters that the history of the family is discontinuous, involving several distinct family structures, each with its own emotional pattern, and that these family structures cannot be correlated, in their development, with any single variable, such as modernization, industrialization, patriarchy, capitalism, urbanism or empathy. In all these ways I hope to contribute to a reconceptualization of family history, to aid in redefining the important questions raised by studying the family, and to outline the future tasks of family studies.

The question of family history extends to major issues of contemporary life. It raises the problem of women's liberation —although feminists, with the exception of Juliet Mitchell in *Women's Estate,* have in general not shed much light on family theory. It raises the problem of the class consciousness of the proletariat, since workers at all levels give much support to the social system in part because it allows them, or so they think, privacy with their families. If the worker himself cannot get ahead socially, at least his children can; if work itself is alienating and exploiting, leisure time in the family compensates for it. In addition to the types of domination generated to a large extent within the family—those of age and sex—the family plays an important ideological role in the stability of the social system.

The tendency of Marxist social theorists is to view the family as a dependent variable, a secondary structure, unintelligible in its own right, which will change after the revolution. There are two problems with this position: (1) the family generates precisely those needs which make radical consciousness difficult in the first place, and (2) there are inequities and sources of oppression within the existing family form which are overlooked. Marx saw the proletariat as a radical class because workers had no interests which they would bring to the revolution as a basis for a new class society. Workers had no property; hence, Marx reasoned, they formed a universal class. But even the degraded and propertyless proletariat did have interests in domination: workers had interests in dominating their women and children. This made workers—and still makes them—something less than "universal." Only a theory that can account for the specific coherence and relative autonomy of the family will overcome Marx's mistake.

The book is organized into two sections. The first reviews critically what I consider the major theories of the family. There are discussions of Freud, of Parsons and Erikson, of Engels, of Reich and the Frankfurt School, of Lacan and of the family therapists. Some might dispute my choices, like the omission of LePlay, of anthropological theories, and of the psychological theories of Piaget or Adler, but I believe that a critical study of the theories I have chosen raises the important questions. I am convinced that the major questions of the family concern the psychological level, the types of emotional structure which change as the family changes, generating changes in the deepest needs of individuals. I also think that emotional restrictions have been the most overlooked aspect of our recent history, that aspect very much in need of critical investigation. Because of the importance of Freud I have been most critical of him, pointing out more sharply than elsewhere the deficiencies of his position.

The second section offers my own suggestions on family theory and outlines models of family structures from the early modern period to the present. I call my theory critical, as opposed to ideological. By this I mean that a theory must account for its object as historical in nature and must fix the location of the object socially, defining the limits of the structure in terms of the freedom of people to regulate their lives collectively and democratically. A critical theory, as I see it, is "normative," providing a basis for reform of the structure in question. Theories which do not accomplish these ends I call ideological. By this I do not mean that they have political overtones, since a critical theory is itself political; I mean instead that ideological theories present the social structure ahistorically, as a natural, inevitable, unchangeable or universal feature of human existence. Any theory that tells us that what we have is what we must have is ideological. It serves to legitimize and reinforce the given system, regardless of that system's deficiencies. I contend also that there is no basis epistemologically for ideological theories, since human beings have no ground for saying that a given social arrangement cannot be changed. If every human being had the right and capacity to participate equally in determining the nature of the social system, then perhaps the problem of ideology would be reduced considerably. Ideology always implies that some groups of people cannot or should not attempt to remove some obstacle to their freedom. This notion of critical and ideological theory stems from the Marxist tradition, especially that of the Frankfurt School and Sartre's existential Marxism.

With these requirements in the foreground, the goal of the final chapters is to present a theory, or the rudiments of one, that can make the family intelligible as a structure.[10] I use the term structure somewhat loosely to designate a coherent configuration of behaviors and attitudes. The study of the family is not yet at the point where structure can be defined very precisely, though I hope this book contributes to that end.

I want to thank those who read all or parts of the manuscript and offered me their critical (not ideological) suggestions. I presented the first chapter to the Shelby Cullom Davis Center at Princeton University, to the editors of *Social Text*, and to the Friends of Clio of the History Department at the University of California, Irvine—and was duly met with numerous suggestions for revision. In Paris, Maud and Octave Mannoni, Luce Irigaray, Cornélius Castoriadis, Joseph Gabel and Bertell Ollman all graciously spoke with me about my study. My trip was made possible by a Summer Humanities Fellowship from the Regents of the University of California. My colleagues and friends offered invaluable criticism and support, especially Jon Wiener, David Carroll, Eli Zaretsky, Maria Ruegg, Patricia O'Brien, Stanley Aronowitz, Francesca Cancian, Fredric Jameson and Michael Johnson. Parts of Chapter 1 and the Preface have appeared in *Telos*. Parts of chapter 7 appeared in *Center Magazine*. Peter Loewenberg graciously permitted me to attend sessions of his class at U.C.L.A. on family therapy. Justus George Lawler of The Seabury Press was also of great help to me.

CRITICAL THEORY OF
THE FAMILY

Chapter 1

FREUD'S CONCEPT OF THE FAMILY

> *Freud discovered the subjective nature or abstract essence of desire, just as Ricardo the subjective nature or abstract essence of labor . . .*
>
> DELEUZE AND GUATTARI

FREUD does not theorize self-consciously about the family. He speaks of the family at many points and in various modes of discourse: in case studies, in technical papers on psychoanalysis, in studies of metapsychology, in interpretive works on history, society and culture. But everywhere his dominant concepts are the individual personality and the psychoanalytically reduced social totality. Freud states that the structure of the psyche receives its final form during childhood, specifically at the time of the Oedipus complex. Yet childhood is never conceptualized as a social experience of a structured nature, mediated by and mediating a larger social system.

There are three major blocks that prevent Freud from conceptualizing the family: (1) a therapeutic practice based on curing an individual; (2) a miscomprehension of the individual and his relation to society; (3) a false concept of society. Freud's problem is not that he is concerned with the inner as opposed to the outer, with the imaginary and not the real, with the psychological and not the sociological. These dualisms are already ideological constructions that derive from fundamental liberal postulates about the nature of society. Freud presents the rudiments, but only the rudiments, of a psychologi-

cal theory of capitalist social relations through an analysis of
family interactions which are determined by and determining
of extra-familial relations. Hence the task must be a reading of
Freud's texts in which his own words reveal the specific contradictions which obscure the family as an object of psychoanalysis.

At first glance the family appears to play an extremely important role in Freud's theory. As Freud himself maintains:

It follows from the nature of the facts which form the material of
psycho-analysis that we are obliged to pay as much attention in our
case histories to the purely human and social circumstances of our
patients as to the somatic data and the symptoms of the disorder.
Above all, our interest will be directed toward their family circumstances.[1]

The family is the nexus of the experiences with which
psychoanalysis is concerned. Freud seeks to decompose the
individual into his essential (but unconscious) family relationships. The achievement of psychoanalysis is to unmask the
illusion of individualism, of the self-contained, autonomous
nature of personal experience and motivation. As an isolated
unit, the individual is unintelligible to the analyst. The most
personal and particular characteristics of the individual's
inner life remain obscure, only becoming meaningful signs
when they are traced back to the medically significant body of
the family. Hence, the family is the secret of the individual.

Although the family assumes an importance rarely accorded
to it before in scientific thought, Freud is unable to develop a
social theory adequate to account for this object of psychoanalysis. Instead, every time he seeks to comprehend some aspect
of social reality Freud displaces the analysis either to a biological level of the racial unconscious or, more importantly, to an
individual level. In the case studies Freud's thought proceeds
from the presence of the analysand back to the unconscious
family; in the studies of social questions *(Totem and Taboo,
Group Psychology and the Analysis of the Ego, Civilization and Its
Discontents, Moses and Monotheism)* it moves to the individual or

to biology, as I will show below. We are thus faced with a circle, a circle of incomprehension, a circle that reduces and distorts the explanatory power of psychoanalysis, ultimately calling into question its advances in its stronghold of personality theory.

The fundamental principle of Freudian psychology is that the structure of the mind is formed in childhood. The mind is not, therefore, pre-given, but built up through a process. Two questions are raised by this principle, neither of which Freud deals with properly: (1) the degree to which this *process* is universal and necessary, and (2) the degree to which it is a purely psychological as distinct from a sociological process. (A third question, which I will discuss in Chapter 3 in relation to Erik Erikson, is the degree to which the structure of the mind is subject to further development and also to structural change after childhood.) The strength and power of Freudian theory derives from the way in which Freud is consistent with the fundamental principle and explores its ramifications in depth. The focus on childhood allows Freud to get beyond the normal structure of the consciousness of his day, beyond its rationality and its defenses, and allowed him to explore the realms of the unconscious, of sexuality, of dreams, slips and jokes, to analyze the logic and the mechanisms of non-rational consciousness and to demonstrate its importance and ubiquity. At the same time these advances of Freud are the source of his weakness, indeed of his misleading and ideological positions. For Freud is unable to set the body of his advances in a wider context of historical and social theory. The concept of childhood mental formation is left without a proper elaboration of *the conditions of its possibility*, and this lack comes back to haunt and to qualify Freud's insights. Although these questions arise at the periphery of the psychoanalytic object, at the horizon of its field where it intersects with history and social theory, nonetheless they compel Freud to advance inadequate propositions to cover up and mask his omissions. In the end he will defend the bourgeois family as a universal and necessary institution, he will hypostasize his psychological model into an eternal one, he will reduce the complex processes of social systems to their psychological meaning, and he will present his own theory as a science divorced from the historical field in which it arose. In the last instance, the praxis (therapy) that derives from his theory will end up as an accommodation to the existing ruling powers, not only to the groups that dominate the economy and politics but also to the groups that are in dominant positions in those places where the psyche is constituted, in the family where the male rules the female and, most significantly, where parents dominate children.

We must now uncover the points in Freud's theory where the science of psychoanalysis becomes the ideology of parentism. There is a recurrent, systematic way in which Freud distorts the exchanges that occur in the family. He represents the transactions through which the child's libido begins to take its characteristic shape as *the choices of the child*, albeit unconscious choices. He distorts the fundamentally hierarchical reciprocity of family communications, masking the manner in which the parents constitute the child as their object by structuring an environment in which objects can be cathected and can be cathected only in certain ways. Freud does this by pretending to represent the child, pretending to give us insight into the family through the eyes of the child and then pretending that the child has "needs" which are natural and given prior to family interactions. In truth, Freud is representing the child as the parents see him, only *after* he has been constituted by them as a being with certain "needs." In Freud's words,

The same thing occurs in men's social relations as has become familiar to psychoanalytic research in the course of the development of the individual libido. The libido attaches itself to the satisfaction of the great vital needs, and chooses as its first objects the people who have a share in that process.[2]

And again:

Direct observation leaves no doubt . . . in what a fundamental way the child makes the person it loves into the object of all its still not properly centered sexual trends.[3]

Freud proposes a being with "needs" and a mechanism through which the satisfaction of the needs leaves as a residue an attachment not to the satisfaction of the needs but to the beings who made the satisfaction possible. Thus the "people who have a share" in the satisfaction of the child's "needs" are simple mediators for Freud. They are not active in shaping the needs or the manner in which the needs are satisfied. The fact that children become attached to their parents is simply a by-product of their individual quest to satisfy needs. Freud recognizes that the child's "sexual trends" are not yet fixed or "centered," and this is a good basis for a critique of family structure since it sets up a tension between human needs and family needs. Instead of seeing this as the opportunity for those trends to become set by the action of the parents, instead of seeing the dominant role they play in shaping the amorphous sexual energy of the child, he slips in the word "properly," leaving the parents out of the picture and fixing the process in a natural space that the individual will fill in by himself. But the child at first presents its "needs" pre-linguistically (they are only "needs" to the parents); the parents are the ones who label and give meaning to the child's actions. The child will "center" its sexual trends not simply to form attachments to the parents but by internalizing the meaning (conscious or unconscious) that the child's behavior has for the parents. As soon as one begins to impute needs to the child that it has at the beginning, in some natural state, one is misrepresenting the case. The child has no needs, properly speaking, until it interacts with its parents, and in this interaction the parents, by responding to the child's behavior, determine the existence and the character of the child's needs.

The communication model that goes on in this situation is

distorted seriously by Freud. Let us take the boy's masturbation and the castration threat as an example. Freud writes:

> When the (male) child's interest turns to his genital organ, he betrays
> this by handling it frequently, and then he is bound to discover that
> grown-up people do not approve of this activity. More or less plainly
> and more or less brutally the threat is uttered that this highly valued
> part of him will be taken away. Usually it is from women that the
> threat emanates; very often they seek to strengthen their authority by
> referring to the father or the doctor, who, as they assure the child,
> will carry out the punishment. . . . Now the view we hold is that the
> phallic stage of the genital organization succumbs to this threat of
> castration.[4]

The contemporary reader often smiles at passages such as this,
musing at how quaintly Victorian Freud can be. Surely one no
longer threatens children with castration. The sophisticated
critic will add that the threat itself, not its specific object, alone
is important. To Freud, on the contrary, it is specifically the
castration threat that was fundamental to his theory, being the
pivotal point in the Oedipus complex. There can be little
doubt, furthermore, that in bourgeois families of the period
castration threats were commonplace.

But Freud does not attach this scene to the particular circumstances of his era and class. He regards as inevitable the
fact that all adults repress children's gential activity. In this
universality Freud is not simply time-bound; he also distorts
the exchange, making it appear as an inevitable event. The
only active role the child plays in the whole process is the
touching of his penis. This touching then becomes interpreted
by the parents and internalized by the child. The parents
repress the activity *and at the same time give to the penis its
extraordinary significance.* There is no reason to assume that the
child placed any particular significance on its genitals except
that they give pleasure when they are touched, like many other
parts of the body. The parents transform this activity into a
major violation of good conduct. It becomes part of the deep
repression of sexuality in the bourgeois Victorian home. They

also give significance to the penis as the symbol of the child's sexuality and as the source of its future power or, in the girl's case, lack of power. The parents teach the child to be phallocentric and to keep this phallocentrism out of his consciousness and behavior. Because the threat is so ultimate the child learns the value of the penis to his parents and to society. To Freud, however, the value of the penis was somehow already there for the child. The penis is *naturally* a superior organ to the clitoris; it is *naturally* an organ with absolute value. It is *natural* that the parents suppress the presence of the penis and it is *natural* that the father is the final authority in this repression. In this crucial stage of the child's development, when "the phallic stage of the genital organization succumbs to this threat of castration," the parents, in Freud's theory, had little to do with what happened. To Freud, it is necessary that human sexuality should undergo this transformation. Yet obviously the *parents* were the ones who were threatened by the child's masturbation; and their emotional response charged and structured the situation. With his parentist ideology, Freud does not see this and displaces his explanation to the level of the child's sexual fantasy.

In the case of Little Hans, which concerns a child's animal phobias, Freud is unable to recognize the parent's role in the masturbation threat. The case was unusual because Freud supervised the child's therapy from a distance, through the intermediary of Hans' father. Freud did nothing to prevent the situation of the father as therapist. In fact Freud applauded the methods of the parents in the sexual enlightenment of their child. Yet child and family therapists now recognize that the psychic bond between parent and child is so deep that the parent could not possibly serve as therapist because he is implicated fundamentally in the problem. Hence in this case one can demonstrate conclusively that Freud was blinded by parentism, that he consistently misinterpreted the defensive communications of the parents as the inevitable psycho-sexual development of the child.

With the typically bourgeois need to control and repress the sexual activity of the child, Hans' supposedly enlightened mother[5] persistently inquires into the boy's masturbatory activity and repeatedly threatens him with castration and loss of love. Freud reports that "his mother asked: 'Do you put your hand to your widdler [penis]?' and he answered: 'Yes. Every evening, when I'm in bed.' The next day, January 9th, he was warned, before his afternoon sleep, not to put his hand on his widdler."[6] And again, Freud notes scientifically: "When he was three and a half his mother found him with his hand to his penis. She threatened him in these words: 'If you do that, I shall send for Dr.A. to cut off your widdler. And then what'll you widdle with?' "[7] And one more example just to show how sexually "mature" the parents are and how the child is the one who has a deep problem: "This morning Hans was given his usual daily bath by his mother and afterwards dried and powdered. As his mother was powdering round his penis and *taking care not to touch it,* Hans said: 'Why don't you put your finger there?' Mother: 'Because that'd be piggish.' "[8]

Freud cannot see that sexuality is at first the parents' problem, not the child's; that the child's anxiety of losing his mother and his penis is not a fantasy natural to the development of human sexuality, but one typical in the bourgeois family. In the case of little Hans the parents' role in the child's phobias goes completely unnoticed by Freud. Yet the child's fantasies really cannot be understood without relating them to the actions and communications of the parents. In truth there is no *natural* sexuality, no *natural* stages of sexual fantasy; sexuality is defined for the child through his interactions with his parents, who are themselves unconscious agents of their class, society and emotional economy. As Laplanche and Pontalis, themselves Freudians it must be said, put it, "it is from the *other* that sexuality comes to the subject."[9] By failing to analyze the parents' eroticism Freud is incapable of explaining psychic phenomena through their properly social dimension. He is left with the eternal individual-biological level of intra-psychic fantasy, and psychoanalysis becomes ideology.

In the discussion of primary narcissism Freud repeats the

same distorting mechanisms. In the stage of narcissism the child cathects pleasureful impulses to its own ego. These will later be displaced into the ideal ego. As part of this "inevitable" process Freud depicts scenes from the family:

> If we look at the attitude of fond parents toward their children, we cannot but perceive it as a revival and reproduction of their own, long since abandoned narcissism. Their feeling, as is well known, is characterized by overestimation. . . . They . . . ascribe to the child all manner of perfections which sober observation would not confirm. . . . The child shall have things better than his parents. . . . He is really to be the center and heart of creation. "His Majesty the Baby," as once we fancied ourselves to be. He is to fulfil those dreams and wishes of his parents which they never carried out, to become a great man and a hero in his father's stead, or to marry a prince as a tardy compensation to the mother.[10]

Here Freud does appear to recognize the active role of the parents. These parents have rather specific feelings toward their child, feelings that are recognizably bourgeois. The first step in Freud's distortion of this scene is to attribute these feelings not to the specific emotional, social and economic needs of the social-climbing bourgeoisie but to refer them back to the parents' "long since abandoned narcissism"—they are inevitable feelings of parents, and hence of the child. These feelings, like those in the masturbation scene, are fundamental aspects of nineteenth-century bourgeois experience. (They might also apply to upper sections of the working class in advanced industrial societies.) The feeling of being the center of creation is typical of the ego-structure of the bourgeois male. It has not been found among nineteenth-century workers nor among peasants of earlier centuries. In fact, a French aristocrat in the eighteenth century wrote, "One blushes to think of loving one's children."[11] Where is his primary narcissism revisited? Even for the bourgeoisie in Renaissance Italy, the practice was to send the child out of the house to a wet nurse until the age of two, where it was unlikely that the child would be coddled in this way.

Another central feature of family life that Freud uncovers is the seduction scene. In treating hysterical women Freud traces the source of their neuroses back to an early childhood situation in which the patients claimed they were assaulted sexually by their fathers.

It must be noted that Freud had great difficulty simply discussing incest, so great that he intentionally prevaricated in reporting two cases of incest in *Studies on Hysteria* by blaming the fathers' acts on the uncles. We are dealing with experiences about which the scientist himself cannot utter objectively the simple facts of the case. Not until thirty years after the book came out did Freud add footnotes revealing the truth. It must also be noted that Freud is here in the midst of a quest for the "cause" or "origin" of a disease. The medical model dominates his methodology. He is searching to isolate an event (seduction) and he wants to attribute the event to an agent. He is misguided in both respects. He should be looking for a structure in which individual agents cannot be analytically isolated. Because he looks for a "devil" and because incest was in his day so forcefully condemned, he cannot bring himself to blame the father. Hence he is unconsciously prepared to find the daughter at fault.

In 1897 he wrote to Fliess that the seduction scenes were *not actual events* but fantasies of the daughters:

Let me tell you straight away the great secret which has been slowly dawning on me in recent months. I no longer believe in my *neurotica*. . . . There was the astonishing thing that in every case blame was laid on perverse acts by the father . . . though it was hardly credible that perverted acts against children were so general. . . . There was the definite realization that there is no "indication of reality" in the unconscious, so that it is impossible to distinguish between truth and emotionally-charged fiction. (This leaves open the possible explanation the sexual phantasy regularly makes use of the theme of the parents.)[12]

Again, in a later formulation where the problems emerge more clearly:

In the period in which the main interest was directed to discovering infantile sexual traumas, almost all my women patients told me that they had been seduced by their father. I was driven to recognize in the end that these reports were untrue and so came to understand that hysterical symptoms are *derived from phantasies and not from real occurrences.* It was only later that I was able to recognize in this phantasy of being seduced by the father the expression of the typical Oedipus complex in women.[13]

In these passages Freud's theory has undergone a fundamental and fateful change. He has given up his "belief" in the patient in favor of the "credibility" of the parents, thereby instituting a duality of fantasy and reality in which the child's experience is fanciful and the parent represents reality. But this is surely inadequate. There can be no doubt that the sexually repressed parent, who believed in the total "innocence" of the child, had engaged in *unconscious* sexual behavior with the child. Even if the child had not been literally seduced, the extreme sexual sterility of the Victorian home is an emotional structure in which sex can only appear in a repressed and indirect form. Freud is unwarranted in asserting that the father cannot be blamed. Although it is not a question of moral blame, the "cause" is the structure, largely unconscious and very intense, through which sexuality emerges and in which the father participates. By exonerating the father, Freud is forced to "blame" the daughter and seek an etiology of neurosis at the purely intra-psychic level of individual fantasy. Thereby psychoanalysis participates in and legitimizes the seduction of the daughter.

The distinction between real events and fantasies is basic to Freud's theory. It goes back to the difference between the pleasure principle and the reality principle, in which the former governs the libido and the latter the ego. Such a sharp duality leads Freud against himself to the position that there are no fantasies in the external world and there is no reality to the libido, to the internal fantasy world. It compels Freud to remove psychic reality from social reality and makes it impossible for him to see their interrelation and to analyze it.

In *Totem and Taboo* he writes, "Only *psychic* realities and not *actual* ones are at the basis of the neurotic's sense of guilt."[14] And this either/or forces him to retreat from his general position that the repression of sexuality is the basis of neurosis. Clearly fantasies are *real,* and "external" reality is full of *fantasy.* In order to sort this question out properly Freud needed a social theory that would focus on the structure of interactions, that would seek to specify the mutual interrelatedness of agents who communicate at several levels of fantasy and reality, and that would be able to map the coordinates that differentiate one structure from another. This is precisely what Freud does not have, and, trapped in a skin theory of individuality, he is unable to conceptualize the family as a psycho-social structure.

When Freud discovers that actual rapes had not occurred— conveniently repressing those cases where there are rapes—he displaces the cause of neurosis from the social reality of family structure to biological or mythic reality. He then maintains either that the girls had hereditary weakness or that their illness was due to the nature of sexual development. He makes a false division between an external, real world with events versus an imaginary world rooted in phylogenetic, biological unconsciousness.

In other places Freud gives us information about family life that is more than adequate to explain why girls might have fantasies of incest. He gives us a very clear picture of the emotional and sexual life of the family and its historical development. In both his early writings and his late writings Freud recognizes that the contemporary family embodied an extreme degree of sexual repression: the family in Western Europe practiced a "high water mark" of sexual repression.[15] Freud states explicitly that it was the bourgeois family in particular and the process of urbanization that contained the key to neurosis and sexual repression: "Neurosis attacks precisely those whose forefathers, after living in simple healthy, country conditions, offshoots of rude but vigorous stocks, came to the great cities where they were successful and were able in a short space of time to raise their children to a high level of cultural attainment."[16] Here Freud is suggesting that the recently urbanized *nouveaux riches* suffer most the burden of Victorian morality. This rudimentary sociology of neurosis claims that the morality is too repressive and that the effort to assume this morality *too quickly* has disastrous effects. Instead of drawing the conclusion that repression is connected with the economic needs of the socially mobile bourgeois, Freud lets his explanation rest at the level of the general requirements of civilization and turns to the relations within the family.

Freud always deplores the extreme suppression of sex in the family. Among Victorians, women and children were thought of as asexual, and sexual behavior was limited to the purpose of procreation, sanctioned only between legally married, lifetime partners. Children were not given proper sexual education.[17] As a result, Freud observes, when men and women enter marriage they are unprepared to have fulfilling sexual lives. The poverty of their sexual lives leads them to great unhappiness:

The result is that when the girl is suddenly allowed by parental authority to fall in love, she cannot accomplish this mental operation and enters the state of marriage uncertain of her own feelings. As a result . . . the love-function provides nothing but disappointments for the husband. . . . Psychically she is still attached to her parents . . . and physically she shows herself frigid. . . . I do not know whether the anaesthetic type of woman is also found outside the range of civilized education. . . . This type is directly cultivated by education . . .[18]

Given these general conditions of the nuclear family, what will be the effect on the child? What will be the nature of the relations between parents and children? Again, Freud is remarkably clear and precise:

Such a marriage will increasingly affect the only child—or the limited number of children—which spring from it. . . . As a mother the neurotic woman who is unsatisfied by her husband is over-tender and over-anxious in regard to the child, to whom she transfers her need for love, thus *awakening in it sexual precosity.* The bad relations between the parents then stimulate the emotional life of the child, and cause it to experience intensities of love, hate and jealousy while yet in its infancy. The strict training which tolerates no sort of expression of this precocious sexual state lends support to the forces of suppression, and the conflict at this age contains all the elements needed to cause lifelong neurosis.[19]

In this remarkable passage Freud recognizes the parent's unfulfilled needs as direct causes of the child's sexual fantasies. Hence the father would not have to attack his daughter overtly to instill intense feelings in her that later she might recall as incest.

Freud even recognizes the most distinguishing feature of the bourgeois household, a feature that is as pertinent to its emotional life as to its sexual constraints. This is its relative isolation from any wider community, the *private* quality of family experience. Freud remarks: "The more closely the members of a family are attached to one another, the more often do they tend to cut themselves off from others, and the more difficult it is for them to enter into the wider circle of life."[20] Positively stated, the nuclear family emphasizes intimacy, privacy and companionship; negatively stated, the intensity of family relationships are multiplied and the child must find all its emotional needs expressed in terms of the narrowest possible circle of people. The general result of these conditions, Freud states, is men who are sexual perverts and women who are neurotic. But Freud attributes these results to bourgeois *attitudes,* not to social structures and practices: "It is one of the obvious injustices of social life that the standard of culture should demand the same behavior in sexual life of everyone . . ."[21] Hence it is "sexual *morality*" that "promotes modern nervousness."[22] At this point one might ask, since Freud has named the traits of the nuclear family as "causes" of neurosis, how it can be argued that he has no social theory. The response is that Freud notes the social conditions only in passing, neither clarifying sufficiently the structural conditions of the psyche nor integrating what he does describe into his theory of psychoanalysis. Family structure remains either a vague, peripheral background of psychoanalysis, without explanatory power, or, in Freud's works on society, an ideological defense of the nuclear family.

Another aspect of family life that plays an important part in Freud's theory is the dependency that he ascribes to childhood. The idea of the child's dependence served many ideological purposes for Freud and reveals the way he masks the social reality of the family. Dependency is to him first of all a justification for the bond developed between parents and children. "The child . . . is taught that his security in life depends on his parents . . . loving him and on their being able to believe that he loves them."[23] To Freud a child must develop deep attachments to its parents because its survival is at stake. Once again the parents are innocent, passive mediators in the emotional need that the child has for them. Freud rarely questions whether parents accentuate their role in the child's survival to insure that the child will develop a sense of being dependent on them. One could, of course, just as easily say that the parents are dependent on the child for their own survival, for the continuation of their line, and that this motive is stronger in them than the sense of dependence is in the child. Furthermore, Freud regards this dependence as a biological necessity, indeed as the hallmark of the species. "The human child's long dependence on its parents [is] an immensely important biological fact."[24] The fact of neotony (incomplete biological development at birth) is used by some theorists to explain the immense importance of *society* in the formation of the human individual, since the child can learn new behavior before it is biologically determined or fixed. Neotony has also been used against conservative social theories to argue that changes in early childhood experience can be the basis for altering hierarchical institutions. But Freud reverses the perspective and argues from the simple link between generations (a link that compels one generation to play a role in the experience of the next generation) that children are biologically dependent and therefore psychically dependent. The domination of the old generation over the new is thus sanctioned. He presents parental authoritarianism as an inevitable necessity of human experience. But there is a difference between the need for new generations to be fed, loved, spoken to and introduced into the world by older generations, and the control and domination of the older generation over the younger. Freud grants the excessive domination in contemporary families where children were to be seen and not heard. He warns: "There are only too many occasions on which a child is slighted . . ."[25] But this is forgotten (or repressed) when his theory is constructed and the degree of dependence of the child in bourgeois families is taken as a norm of nature. Given Freud's model, there is no way to account for variations in the quality and degree of the child's dependence in different eras and social classes.

The conclusions drawn by Freud from the alleged dependency of the child, conclusions which are central to his theory, drastically obscure family experience. For nothing less than the Oedipus complex is at stake. The dependence of the child is, according to Freud, the primary (non-psychic) condition for the Oedipus complex.[26] Since the Oedipus complex is the matrix which forms the psyche into its permanent state, the alleged dependence of the child is more than an innocent, secondary assumption. In addition, the tension induced in the child by its dependence conditions its entire psychic development. Freud estimates the importance of dependence in this way: "The danger of psychical helplessness fits the stage of the ego's early immaturity; the danger of loss of an object (or loss of love) fits the lack of self-sufficiency in the first years of life . . ."[27] In other words, the sense of emotional scarcity, the sense that there are few objects to love and that children must struggle to hold on to love objects, the damage that separation from one of these objects can cause—all these fundamental aspects of emotional life have nothing to do, for Freud, with the emotional structure of the family. But indeed a sense of dependence in the child is induced by the scarcity of love objects.

The power of parents to bestow or withhold love coupled with their own peculiar needs for love is the condition that creates dependency as the basic feature of the child's existence.

All these inadequacies in Freud's discussion of family experience are best revealed and have their most serious consequences for psychoanalytic theory in the concept of the Oedipus complex.[28] The Oedipal theory is mentioned by Freud as early as 1897 in a letter to Fliess discussing Freud's self-analysis. Even at this point, before the general psychological theory was developed, Freud argues for the universality of Oedipus. If the theory of Oedipus was with Freud practically from the beginning of psychoanalysis, it also played a central role in his thought. Oedipus is not only at the heart of all neurosis to Freud; Oedipus is also the chief structuring experience of the psyche. "The relation to the parents instigated by incestuous longings is the central complex of the neurosis."[29]

The main elements of the Oedipal situation are the child's sexual feelings for the parent of the opposite sex, the child's profound feelings of ambivalence toward the parent of the same sex and the child's profound feelings of anxiety in relation to threats against its genitals by the parents. Freud believes that these elements are not rooted in any specific family or social structure. Oedipus is universal. There are two critical questions that must be pursued: (1) Is the Oedipus complex and the resulting psychic structure a consequence of these "universal" elements or can it be connected with a specific family structure? (2) Is Freud attempting to illuminate a universal aspect of psychic experience with his concept of Oedipus or is he in fact explaining particular psychic experiences? By analyzing these questions it can be demonstrated that Freud's Oedipus complex explains psychic formations specific to a limited family structure and, because he is unable to conceptualize Oedipus from the perspective of social theory, he falsely expands the explanatory power of Oedipus to cover all situations, thereby disfiguring a critical concept into an ideological one.

It should be noted from the beginning that Freud's discussions of the Oedipus complex usually refer to male children. The case for girls is explained later and most often Freud admits humbly that he is not happy with his analysis of the female Oedipus complex. One could argue, therefore, that Oedipus is far from universal since it applies only to men.[30]

When the child is in the third or genital stage of libidinal development, about the age of five, it begins to receive threats from its parents for handling its genitals. The situation is exactly the same for the child as it was during the oral and the anal periods: its erotic pleasure brings it into confrontation with its parents, and it is forced to choose between bodily gratification and the love of its parents. The unique feature of the gential stage, however, is that the child has sexual fantasies about the parent of the opposite sex and these too must undergo repression. The boy must give up his mother as a sexual love object in addition to giving up his penis as a source of overt pleasureful behavior. In exchange for this, the boy internalizes the father and achieves satisfaction of both the penis and the mother *at the fantasy level.* More accurately, the child defers these gratifications to a later point while identifying with his father, who is distinguished by having both a penis and a woman (the mother). Thus the boy creates the strongest possible needs in himself to be his father. These needs are permanently structured in his psyche in the form of the superego. In Freud's words,

the real danger . . . that the child is afraid of as a result of being in love with his mother . . . is the punishment of being castrated, of losing his genital organ. . . . Above all, it is not a question of whether castration is really carried out; what is decisive is that the danger is one that threatens from the outside and that the child believes in it. He has some ground for this, for people threaten him often enough with cutting off his penis during the phallic phase, at the time of his early masturbation, and hints at that punishment must regularly find a phylogenetic reinforcement in him. It is our suspicion that during the human family's primaeval period castration used actually to be carried out by a jealous and cruel father upon growing boys, and that circumcision which so frequently plays a part in puberty rites among primitive peoples, is a clearly recognizable relic of it.[31]

Several aspects of this quotation need to be noted. First, there is a "real danger." The Oedipus complex does not take place at some purely internal, "intra-psychic" level; it is part of the interactions, the social structure, of the family. There is no ambivalence, no hesitation in Freud about this. Every time he describes the Oedipus complex he refers to a castration threat from "outside." The question remains, however: Did Freud adequately conceptualize this "real danger," did he adequately delimit the structural conditions in which this danger will occur? Second, the danger or threat is not general. It refers specifically to the penis and to "castration" (interestingly, misusing the word). To argue that all children experience threats of one sort or another and therefore undergo the Oedipus complex is inadequate. Freud's argument is quite consistent. Only a threat to the penis (or the fantasized penis for girls) will serve the purpose, because the love of the mother is associated with it. Now one must ask: Does the child have this association or is it the parents' association? In the context of the families that Freud investigated, the fact that the child's masturbation elicited adult sexual relations in the minds of the parents seems probable. The child is participating in sexual experience which is prohibited in bourgeois families. In the parent's anxiety over the child's sexual behavior, the child might well pick up unconsciously the association penis-mother. It could also be the case that the association penis-mother does not exist at all for the child until it begins to identify with the father. At any rate, masturbation and its emotionally violent repression are essential conditions to Freud for the development of the Oedipus complex. In situations where childhood masturbation is not proscribed (undoubtedly most human history), where parents do not have a great deal of anxiety about overt sexual behavior in children, the complex is called into question.

One often finds the argument that Oedipus is everywhere because there are always parents and children, parents are always stronger, and parents always threaten children. But the case can never be made from these empty generalities to the rich specificity of the particular complex Freud analyzed. This position is on the same level as the argument that since human beings always produce and consume, capitalism is universal. The effect of this argument is to obscure the *difference* between psycho-social structures, to prevent comprehension of the limits of the present structure and thus to undercut hopes for changing it. Finally, the argument projects ideologically the bourgeois, patriarchal, nuclear form onto all other experience, a tendency of which Freud himself is guilty.

In addition to masturbation, the Oedipus complex also hinges upon the existence and force of the super-ego. As the residue of the Oedipus complex, the super-ego provides proof after the fact for its existence. In Freud's words,

> . . . the super-ego appears as the heir of that emotional attachment which is of such importance in childhood. With his abandonment of the Oedipus complex a child must . . . renounce the intense object-cathexes which he has deposited with his parents and it is as a compensation for this loss of objects that there is such a strong intensification of the identifications with his parents which have probably long been present in his ego.[32]

Freud is certain that the super-ego is not with us from birth and that its development depends upon a set of family interactions:

> Young children are amoral. . . . The part which is later taken on by the super-ego is played to begin with by an external power, by parental authority. Parental influence governs the child by offering proofs of love and by threatening punishments which are signs to the child of loss of love and are bound to be feared on their own account. This realistic anxiety is the precursor of later moral anxiety. . . . It is only subsequently that the secondary situation develops (which we are all too ready to regard as the normal one), where the external restraint is internalized and the super-ego takes the place of the parental agency . . .[33]

The proof of the Oedipus complex is thus bound up with the existence of an *internal authority*. The initial anxiety of the child confronted by a threat is now replaced by an internal anxiety (guilt) that the child experiences whenever it has an impulse that is rejected or invalidated by the super-ego. Freud implies that when human beings are governed by internal morality, when they exercise their own restraints, when moral restrictions need not be reinforced methodically by external sanctions, then there is proof of the existence of the Oedipus complex.

But Freud himself notes instances (in addition to pre-Oedipal children) where the super-ego does not operate. In pre-industrial, small-scale agricultural communities, individuals do not appear to be self-governed, self-repressed, autonomous moral agents. Many external mechanisms govern the behavior of adults, and shame, not guilt, is the predominant moral feeling when a custom has been transgressed. Freud observers, "It is remarkable how differently a primitive man behaves. If he has met with a misfortune he does not throw blame on himself but on his fetish, which has obviously not done its duty, and he gives it a thrashing instead of punishing himself."[34] Since a basic effect of the super-ego is to produce a feeling of worthlessness in individuals when they have failed to attain a goal or when they have committed a moral violation or have desired instinctively to do so, it follows that in most societies the super-ego was not a major aspect of psychic structure or of social control. And hence, no Oedipus complex. Thus one must conclude that Freud has not given us the true criteria or specified the main conditions for Oedipus.

If Freud's analysis of the Oedipus complex is probed further it becomes clear that the privatized nuclear family is the major structural condition. He tells us revealingly that for the child to undergo the extraordinary experience of internalizing the father there must be a certain intensity to the relationship between the child and the parent. In fact, he claims that the reason girls do not develop strong super-egos is because they are already castrated and hence cannot experience deep fear at the threat of the loss. He points to the importance of the degree of aggression the child must experience before it will internalize the father:

A considerable amount of aggressiveness must be developed in the child against the authority which prevents him from having his first, but none the less his most important satisfactions, whatever the kind of instinctual deprivation that is demanded of him may be. . . . By means of identification he takes the unattackable authority into himself. The authority now turns into his super-ego . . .[35]

In this formulation, the castration threat is less important than the intensity of the interaction. Freud admits here that what counts is less a matter of the sexual triangle than the degree of emotional involvement, a degree that would seem to apply only to the isolated micro-world of the bourgeois family in the nineteenth and twentieth centuries (and possibly to the working-class family of advanced capitalism in the mid-twentieth century). In these cases relations are so imploded that the parents alone are emotionally significant figures for the child during the early years. One's suspicion is confirmed when Freud further qualifies the conditions for the development of the super-ego:

A severe conscience arises from the joint operation of two factors: the frustration of instinct, which unleashes aggressiveness, and the experience of being loved, which turns the aggressiveness inwards and hands it over to the super-ego.[36]

The secret of Oedipus is located here: not in the beautiful myths of ancient Greece but in the prosaic bourgeois home. For the combination of an intense love and a severe repressiveness attached to the same people, a combination that began in the bourgeois family, conditions the development of the super-ego. Severe repression, which is probably found in many family situations, is not enough. In the bourgeois family there was both the exercise of total control over children by their parents and an extreme domination and shaping of the child's behavior. In addition, there was an extreme degree of tenderness.

The important consideration for us is that the intense ambivalent feelings that are at the heart of the Oedipal period require that the child have but a narrow range of people to relate to emotionally. The ambivalent feelings of aggression due to repression and of love seem perfectly accounted for in the specific situation of the bourgeois family. With so few sources of identification, with so few adult objects to love, with such severe sexual repression, with the privacy of the parent-child relations, with the removal of the family from the wider community, with the emotional poverty of commodity relations in the business world creating a further need for emotional satisfaction in the family, with the hierarchy of power and needs in the family, it seems indisputable that Oedipus is there in the bourgeois family. The entire structure of this family seems geared to elicit this emotional complex, though Oedipus may be unrecognized and unintended by the parents.

The most elementary social theory would require one to expect just this result. For one precondition of the nuclear monogamous family is that *it reproduce itself.* The family must somehow instill in the child a deep and inexorable need to find a single, life-long mate with whom alone to share emotional and sexual experience. And this, of course, is what Oedipus does. Only Freud's blindness to social theory keeps him from recognizing this.

Oedipus also reproduces the other main conditions of the bourgeois family. It reproduces the social insecurity of the bourgeoisie, since it creates a deep emotional need to become like the father, to be "successful," and it marshals the child's emotional energy through the guardian super-ego toward achievement in work, toward deferred gratification. Oedipus instills a sexual displacement, an economics of the libido that can only find satisfaction in the economics of capital accumulation, at the direct expense of bodily gratification.[37] After all, far from being natural man, *homo economicus* is a rare and strange species.

Unable to theorize the social conditions of Oedipus, Freud displaces its conditions into mythological heavens. Social structures and family structures are wiped away by him in a grand universalizing gesture of misrecognition. Hence social life *in general* becomes the sole condition of Oedipus:

The sense of guilt is an expression of the conflict due to ambivalence, of the eternal struggle between Eros and the instinct of destruction or death. This conflict is set going as soon as men are faced with the task of living together. So long as the community assumes no other form than that of the family, the conflict is bound to express itself in the Oedipus complex, to establish the conscience and to create the first sense of guilt.[38]

But the family has never "assumed the form of the community" except for children in nuclear families. Obscuring the difference between social structure and family structure, between different social structures and between different family structures, Freud also obscures the difference between psychic structures and their interdependence with social and family structure. The consequence of his theory is to present the bourgeois psyche as the human psyche, bourgeois complexes as human complexes, to mask the determinate social practices that maintain this psyche, even while penetrating the structure and mechanisms of this psyche as no one before. Freud is, then, the Adam Smith of the family.

The theoretical consequences of Oedipus go further than this. Not only do they mask the bourgeois psyche but Freud then uses Oedipus to invent a fanciful explanation for modern society. Freud's theory of the primal horde argues that the Oedipus complex is the foundation of the basic institutions of civilization: law, religion, art, morality, etc.[39] By making this claim Freud is acknowledging that there is a social dimension to the Oedipus complex and to psychoanalysis in general which cannot be avoided.[40] But he misconstrues the locus of the social implication, displacing it from the specific context of the bourgeois family and modern society onto some vague universal law of social organization.

In this displacement the crucial question concerns what it is that the Oedipal theory tries to explain. Does it explain a general transformation which all human beings undergo from childhood fantasy (primary processes) to adult "reality" (secondary processes)? The preceding analysis demonstrated that the Oedipal complex explains but one version of a universal

shift from childhood to adulthood. When Freud expands the
explanatory power of Oedipus he obscures the specific configuration of the bourgeois psyche and he withdraws it from its
concrete social dimension. His effort to give a historical and
social ground to Oedipus ironically leads him away from so-
cial-historical analysis.

Freud's treatment of the Oedipus myth in *Totem and Taboo*
can be clarified by comparison with the concept of the incest
prohibition in Claude Lévi-Strauss. The anthropologist views
the ban on incest as the prototype of all social law. The taboo
on incest institutes human society, since it prevents the conjugal family from isolating itself from other families. Man moves
from nature to culture by inhibiting sexual impulses in favor
of social organization. The incest taboo establishes the circulation of women between families and thus society takes shape
as the organization of kinship. Society is an extension of the
family, or better, the family is completely enmeshed in social
organization. One may therefore conclude from Lévi-Strauss
that when society is organized by kinship structure it is precisely Oedipus that is *missing*.

The ban on incest in Lévi-Strauss leads precisely to conclusions opposite from Freud's. Instead of *imploding* and fixating
the emotions of the child on its two parents, the prohibition
of mother-son sexuality *explodes* family life into the larger society. Instead of centering and enclosing the unconscious in the
dyad Mama/Papa, the incest taboo decenters and displaces the
unconscious onto the whole tribe. Kinship subordinates family to society, placing the individual firmly in the collective,
demanding that the individual involve himself in the collective
mythology, the collective totem. Law, authority and custom
come to the individual not from Mama/Papa but from the
tribe.

Just the opposite happens with Freud. Oedipus reduces and
shrinks the individual to the family. The internalization of the
father as super-ego prevents the individual from participating
in collective myth. Oedipus privatizes myth, emotion, fantasy
and the unconscious, centering the psyche forever on Mama/

Papa. By attempting to expand the Oedipus complex to kinship structures Freud destroys its specificity, precisely the
specificity that allowed him to probe the unconscious of the
Victorian bourgeois. Far from a general law, Oedipus is the
special law of the modern psyche. It is bound up with the
nuclear family, not with kinship, and it goes far in revealing
the psychic dynamics of modern families. The neuroses
analyzed by Freud are private myths, individual religions;
they are the fetishism, the magic of the nuclear family, the
myth of people without collective fetishes to relieve guilt. As
long as Freud maintains the universality of Oedipus there can
be no real history of the family since this requires above all an
account of the change from kinship to private families.

There is also a political dimension to Oedipus. Civilization
is established, in Freud, through an act of rebellion by the sons
against the father. Freud ties the emotional aspect of rebellion
to an anti-paternal act, to a bid for sexual liberation and political and economic equality. When he describes the establishment of the super-ego in modern circumstances he employs
the same image of rebellion: "The institution of the super-ego
which takes over the dangerous aggressive impulses, introduces a garrison, as it were, into regions that are inclined
to rebellion . . ."[41] Surely it can be acknowledged that there is
an element of generational conflict in every revolution without reducing revolution, as Freud does, to displaced family
strife.

An important implication of Freud's position, however, is
the conservative nature of the super-ego and the revolutionary
nature of primary processes. In the essay "On Narcissism"
Freud characterizes psychosis as a "revolt" by the libido (desire) against this "censorial institution."[42] An argument can be
made that the family mediates the conservative forces of the
larger society by dampening assertive and revolutionary impulses through the internalization of parental authority in the
super-ego. Without affirming that every unrestrained instinct
is revolutionary, one can say that libido is the subjective level
of revolution and to this degree the liberation of libido is part

of the path to revolutionary social change. Freud's ideological formulation is worth quoting at length:

> Thus a child's super-ego is in fact constructed on the model not of its parents but of its parents' super-ego; the contents which fill it are the same and it becomes the vehicle of tradition and of all the time-resisting judgments of value which have propagated themselves in this manner from generation to generation. You may easily guess what important assistance taking the super-ego into account will give us in our understanding of the social behavior of mankind—in the problem of delinquency, for instance—and perhaps, even what practical hints on education. It seems likely that what are known as materialistic views of history sin in underestimating this factor. They brush it aside with the remark that human "ideologies" are nothing other than the product and superstructure of their contemporary economic conditions. That is true, but very probably not the whole truth. Mankind never lives entirely in the present. The past, the traditions of the race and of the people, lives on in the ideologies of the super-ego and yields only slowly to the influences of the present and to new changes; and so long as it operates through the super-ego it plays a powerful part in human life, independently of economic conditions.[43]

If we move beyond the family and look now at Freud's studies of society his theoretical weaknesses become even more disturbing. For without a social theory, psychoanalysis slips into reductionism: "For sociology too, dealing as it does with the behavior of people in society, cannot be anything but applied psychology. Strictly speaking there are only two sciences: psychology, pure and applied, and natural science."[44] This overestimation of the domain of psychology has serious consequences. The basic questions of social existence are to Freud purely psychological: ". . . our own psychical constitution . . . [is] a piece of unconquerable nature" and is responsible for "the social source of suffering."[45] The meaning and evolution of society is nothing more than "the struggle between Eros and Death."[46] Thus social structures and practices are nothing but a background for the play of psychological forces and mechanisms. Changes in social structures have no meaning in themselves; they affect the conditions of human beings only insofar as they provide outlets for psychic needs. Freud was so consistent on these questions that he recognized one crucial exception to his reductionism: the family. Even though he denied that the family had any history (since its essence, Oedipus, was eternal) he did express concern at the possibility of eliminating the family as an institution. In the important passage below, the consequences of Freud's reductionism emerge:

> The psychological premises on which [communism] is based are an untenable illusion. In abolishing private property we deprive the human love of aggression of one of its instruments. . . . Aggressiveness was not created by property. . . . If we do away with personal rights over material wealth, there still remains prerogative in the field of sexual relationships, which is bound to become the source of the strongest dislike and the most violent hostility among men who in other respects are on an equal footing. If we were to remove this factor too, by allowing complete freedom of sexual life and thus *abolishing the family, the germ-cell of civilization, we cannot,* it is true, *easily foresee what new paths the development of civilization could take;* but one thing we can expect, and that is that this indestructible feature of human nature will follow it there.[47]

Here it seems that Freud introduces the notion of aggression because he cannot defend private property on any positive grounds. If the problem were truly only that of aggression, mankind would have destroyed itself long before private property was introduced. If this argument does not convince, one could point to the remarkable creativity of man in inventing sources for the release of hostile impulses to save us after the comforts of property have vanished.

Much more interesting than the question of private property is the anxiety Freud manifests in this passage over the abolition of the family. Perhaps Freud has guessed that the basic components of his model of the psyche are bound up with exclusive monogamy. Aggression is not the problem: psychoanalysis is. With the abolition of the family, Oedipus, the super-ego, the anal character, the traits of masculinity and femininity, the extreme form of sex-role differentiation in the nuclear family, might also depart. Freud had protected himself against this eventuality with an arsenal of theoretical defenses: the family is eternal since it is rooted biologically in infant dependency and it is part of the racial unconscious that goes back to the beginning of time. When he wrote this passage in *Civilization and Its Discontents* he must have been led along by the logic of historical inquiry, led beyond his tightly secured ideological masks to pose the question of the historical nature of the family for the first time in all his writings. For one moment he entertains the possibility that the major concepts of psychoanalysis are bound to particular social structures, and he is left disarmed. What is this "civilization" that has its "germ-cell" in the family? Is "civilization" that well-known potpourri of values that go back to ancient Judaea and Greece? But surely there has been no single family pattern since that time, and surely no one would want to attribute the notoriously ideological "values" of this civilization—justice, democracy, freedom, equality, God, law, etc.—to the family!

In addition to psychological reductionism, Freud's concept of civilization (*Kultur*) contains many unexamined liberal assumptions. He defines civilization as would any liberal progressist: it is science, technology, art, order and cleanliness. He repeats Lockean postulates as if they were absolutes: the individual and society constitute a basic duality,[48] and people live together in society for reasons of utility.[49] Also, he presents liberal, utilitarian moral principles as unquestionable general truths. Human beings "strive after happiness . . . at an absence of pain and unpleasure and, on the other hand, at the experiencing of strong feelings of pleasure."[50] Furthermore, he says that "strife and competition" in human activity are "undoubtedly indispensable."[51] Throughout Freud's social writings, the milieu of the discourse is that of the cosmopolitan bourgeois. Cultural activities are assumed to be man's highest attainments; work is regarded as sublimation, and so on.

Although there are many of these liberal assumptions in Freud which limit his positions, he is by no means a liberal apologist of capitalism. In fact, the great advances of his psychoanalytic theory emerge as counter-arguments against liberal positions. For example, to Freud the progressive advances of civilization do not lead to happiness, or freedom, or human fulfillment. The utilitarian individual is not a monadic unity, a captain of his soul. Freud uses psychoanalysis to challenge and refute the Enlightenment tradition, but, as we shall see, this challenge is incomplete and he retreats instead to a pessimistic liberalism that leaves liberal institutions unchallenged and legitimates them negatively by discounting any alternative.

In *Group Psychology and the Analysis of the Ego* the inadequacy of Freud's social theory again becomes apparent. He begins properly enough by announcing the field of psychoanalysis as a social one. There can be, he notes, no sharp separation of the individual from social reality: "Individual psychology is simultaneously social psychology."[52] He recognizes explicitly that psychoanalytic study concerns social and more particularly family relationships.

The relations of an individual to his parents and to his brothers and sisters, to the object of his love, and to his physician—in fact all the relations which have hitherto been the chief subject of psychoanalytic research—may claim to be considered as social phenomena . . .[53]

Armed with these basic assumptions Freud is well prepared to develop a theory of group psychology. One finds quickly, however, that such is not the case, that the whole subject of group psychology is distorted by two ideological principles: (1) a liberal one that an individual can be separate from groups, and can be rational only when he is outside the group, and (2) a psychoanalytic one that all human relationships can be reduced to the pattern of the nuclear family and that they never get beyond that pattern.

To establish his own position Freud draws upon Gustave LeBon, Gabriel Tarde and the tradition which sought to dis-

credit revolutionary action by psychologizing it as the out-
burst of an irrational mob. In the twentieth century, liberals
were able to draw upon this anti-revolutionary theory to bolster their critique of mass culture. Threatened by the conform-
ism and the tight interdependence of advanced capitalist society, some liberals defended themselves by reasserting the
Enlightenment claim for independence and autonomy as a
prerequisite of rationality. The mob psychology of LeBon and
Tarde was well suited to defend elitist liberals against the flood
of workers demanding a share of political power, and, at the
time Freud wrote *Group Psychology* in 1920, against radical socialist movements. Recently, historians like George Rudé have
disputed the conservative image of revolutionary action as the
wild, irrational upsurge of impoverished hordes.[54] It is now
understood that such action has been carried out often by
quite respectable artisans, shopkeepers and workers with de-
liberate, clear goals in mind.

For Freud, on the contrary, the group represents a loss of
independence, rationality and discipline for the individual. He
counterposes the group to the individual as a fall into unrestrained emotionality and lack of creative, intellectual ability.
The individual who joins a group undergoes "a profound mental alteration" in which "those inhibitions upon his instincts
which are peculiar to each individual" are removed.[55] This
opposition of individual-group, deriving in social theory from
John Locke, is a misrepresentation of the social system. It
incorrectly presupposes that there are some activities which
are outside social reality and are the ground for private, asocial
property. In fact, Freud cannot imagine a group psychology
which does not aim to reform groups on the basis of the norm
of individual rationality:

The problem [of group psychology] consists in how to procure for the
group precisely those features which were characteristic of the individual and which are extinguished in him by the formation of the
group. For the individual, outside the primitive group, possessed his
own continuity, his self-consciousness, his traditions and customs, his

own particular functions and positions, and he kept apart from his rivals. Owing to his entry into an "unorganized" group he had lost his distinctiveness for a time.[56]

Thus the whole of Freud's *Group Psychology* is flawed by an antithesis of individual and society. Ironically, Freud's image of the individual as a rational, self-restrained and distinctive being goes against his own insights into the unconscious. Normally for Freud the individual is not this *petite bourgeois* utilitarian but a disunified (decentered) set of fragments of family experience. The fact that Freud retreats from his own advances when he is confronted by the problem of the group is a warning that his psychological theory is not properly constituted as an element of social theory. Indeed, more recent efforts at a psychoanalytic theory of groups, like those of Bion, have been forced to recognize Freud's failure to comprehend emotional patterns specific to organized group activity.[57]

Freud's failure is only partially understood through his liberal social theory. The main reason for his failure comes in his effort to analyze the emotional patterns of the group by reducing them to those of the nuclear family. Freud attempts to show that participation in any social organization—church or army, authoritarian or democratic group, bureaucratized or primitive group, involuntary or voluntary group, a group with or without leaders, a group that is homogeneous (racially, sexually or by class) or not—is little more than an extension of the patriarchal nuclear family. This reduction of all social relations to the nuclear family contains the key to much of the difficulty with his theory in general.

The "essence of the group mind," Freud contends, is the nature of the libidinal (emotional) bond that keeps the group together. Groups are composed of individuals who have specific types of love relationships with each other. Psychoanalytic theory allows Freud to reveal the precise characteristics of this bond. The love which group members have for each other is first of all of the aim-inhibited type; it is similar to friendship or affection. Direct sexual

love, on the other hand, is incompatible with group formation since it leads to exclusive, private bonds. Next, the
aim-inhibited bonds are of two types: (1) each group member has a relationship of identification with each other
member which is grounded in the far more profound feeling they have for a common leader; and (2) each member
has substituted the leader for his ego ideal. The first bond,
Freud says, is at the level of the ego: a person consciously
feels friendly toward other people who are in his group.
The second bond is probably unconscious since it is cathected at the level of the ego-ideal, for which one can substitute the term "super-ego" which Freud had not yet begun
to use in 1920.[58] This bond with the leader is the determining factor in group consciousness for Freud. Because the
leader is a "substitute father" the psychic behavior of individuals in the group tends to regress to unresolved childhood fixations. Even the degree to which group behavior is
regressive is determined by the leader, not the members. A
"primitive" leader (like Hitler) will cast such a spell over
the group that its actions will resemble those of "children"
or "primitives," while a more subdued and rational leader
(like Roosevelt) will induce milder forms of emotional excess, unfreedom, loss of intellect and creative incapacity.
These nuances aside, Freud's central postulate is that all
group action reproduces, at the emotional level, the life of
the family. Thus severe forms of psychological reductionism become possible, such as the treatment of the new left
as a generational problem by Lewis Feuer and Raymond
Aron.[59] Freud, of course, would apply his analysis to all
politics, even liberal politics, whereas some of his followers
use the theory only against their enemies.

But Freud is not content to leave his analysis at this
point. In *Group Psychology* he fleshes out his position with
historical and social supports. Historically, he reiterates the
argument from *Totem and Taboo* about the origins of the
Oedipus complex and the evolution of groups. Originally,
at some mythic moment in the past, the primal horde was

characterized by the libininal bonds of the group. Tribal
members identified with each other through their internalization of the father-leader, which presupposed the substitu-
tion of the leader for the ego-ideal or super-ego. At this
point, before the rebellion against the father, the Oedipal
trauma and the erection of the super-ego, it is, of course,
difficult to see how the members could *substitute* the leader
for the super-ego, since they had not yet formed one. Freud
does not clarify this contradiction. His concern instead is
with the formation of "individual psychology" as opposed
to "group psychology," that is, with the leader, not the followers.[60] He is puzzled by the mechanism through which
the "individual psychology" of the leader can be reproduced in the next leader. His conclusion is that after the
rebellion against the father and after the brief interregnum
of matriarchy which ensued, the youngest son of the leader,
who was favored by his mother, became individuated
through writing poetry. Following his student, Otto Rank,
Freud says that in this son "who aspires to the father's
place, the poet now created the first ego ideal."[61] He continues:

The myth, then, is the step by which the individual emerges from
group psychology. The first myth was certainly the psychological,
the hero myth. . . . The poet who had taken this step and had in this
way set himself from the group in his imagination, is nevertheless
able . . . to find his way back to reality. . . . At bottom this hero is no
one but himself . . . the hearers [of the myth] understand the poet, and
. . . they can identify themselves with the hero . . .[62]

Through this argument Freud believes he has solved the historical problem of individuation when in fact he has done no
more than create another myth to legitimize his theory. The
import of Freud's construction is crucial, however, to the
whole edifice of psychoanalytic theory, for it seeks to preserve
psychoanalysis as a theory of the individual.

The hero is able to attain to "individual psychology" only
because he internalizes his father at a deep enough level; he
creates an "ego-ideal" in himself. Hence the mechanism for

reproducing individuals—those who are free, who can think, who can restrain their emotions, who can be distinctive—is the key to history. But the mechanism for this degree of individualization is the patriarchal nuclear family, not the heroic poet. For in the nuclear family alone the intense emotional interaction between parents and children creates the conditions for internalizing one parent as a super-ego. The story of the hero proves to Freud's satisfaction that individuals as he has theorized them are historically possible and are positive alternatives to people who can only participate in "group psychology."

The Oedipus myth fits into Freud's group psychology in a second way: to explain the incest taboo. After the death of the father, the new leader banned the desire for which the rebellion was carried out, the love for the women. Hence, no incest: "A wedge was driven in between a man's affectionate and sensual feelings, one still firmly fixed in his erotic life today. As a result of this exogamy the sensual needs of men had to be satisfied with strange and unloved women."[63] The incest taboo, forcing the males to find women outside the clan, helped preserve the life of the group, since it removed all love bonds that were not aim-inhibited from relations between members. Direct satisfaction of sexual needs was banished from social relations to become established only in a peripheral world of relations with non-members. Society was constituted (and with it group psychology) on the basis of the fundamental repression of the unity between affectionate love and sexual love. This is the first step in Freud's justification of the nuclear family as the only source for the gratification of sex and love.

The next step is crucial. After grounding "individual psychology" in the Oedipus complex and after arguing that sex and society are incompatible, Freud tries to demonstrate that the nuclear family is the best possible family structure:

Directly sexual impulses are unfavorable to the formation of groups. In the history of the development of the family there have also, it is true, been group relations of sexual love (group marriages); but the more important sexual love became for the ego, and the more it developed the characteristics of being in love, the more urgently it required to be limited to two people . . . as is prescribed by the nature of the genital aim. Polygamous inclinations had to be content to find satisfaction in a succession of changing objects.[64]

Thus the nuclear family is the only legitimate form of sexual relations because (1) direct sex is incompatible with groups, (2) the genital aim is "naturally" limited to the couple, and (3) only in the nuclear family are "individuals" formed. Freud has "proven" the incompatibility of groups and sex only on the basis of his view of the nuclear family. If love and sex are limited to the nuclear family, then the group, society at large, cannot include sexual expressions. For if sex is already defined as exclusive and leading to privatization, quite naturally it will tend to disrupt group activities. And if social relations are dominated by capitalist, utilitarian, purely cognitive relations, sex has already been excluded in all its forms, finding its only refuge in the private family. The problem, however, is to study how sex and love become sequestered in the private family in connection with the development of capitalism and urbanization. Then too, if "individual psychology" is the secret goal of history and if it embodies all the bourgeois virtues (independence, rationality, emotional restraint, freedom, etc.) it is then necessary that the group be regressive. The only locus for regression, the only place to go back to emotionally, is the nuclear family as it is sedimented in the unconscious. There, of course, we find Papa. Hence, the group must be in Freud's view a psychic fixation on Papa and nothing more because *all other types of psychic life have been excluded from it:* love to the family and sublimation to individuality.

In one passing comment in *Group Psychology* Freud does recognize the historicity of the bourgeois family, although he does not probe the meaning of this for his group psychology. He noticed that "there are abundant indications that being in love only made its appearance late on in the sexual relations between men and women; so that the opposition between sexual love and group ties is also a late development."[65] If sexual love and group ties are only a recent contradiction, what kind of group psychology existed before they were in opposition? Freud does not probe this important question. At stake here is the possibility of psychic structures that are different from those dominated by the Oedipus complex and the formation of the super-ego. In fact, before the formation of the connection between romantic love and monogamy, before the nuclear family, extended families and kinship structures were dominant and these were integrated into larger social structures. A true psychological history of the family would concern itself with the nature of these differences and hence with the limits of the Freudian model based on the Oedipus complex. Freud himself does everything he can to conceal the import of these historic changes. He limits the psychology of groups to regressive and non-intellectual behavior, thereby preserving the bourgeois concept of the individual, and he extends the nuclear family, with its privatization of love and sex, as the norm of all family structures.

It is only when the affectionate, that is, personal, factor of a love relation gives place entirely to the sensual one, that it is possible for two people to have sexual intercourse in the presence of others or for there to be simultaneous sexual acts in a group, as occurs at an orgy. But at that point a regression has taken place to an early stage in sexual relations, at which being in love as yet played no part, and all sexual objects were judged to be of equal value . . .[66]

But why must an equality of sexual objects be defined as regressive? For Freud a "personal," "affectionate" sexual encounter must be "private," as it is in the nuclear family. This privatization of sexual love, which was not the case in peasant and aristocratic families before the eighteenth century or in working-class families in the early nineteenth century, is connected historically with the rise of possessive love relations among the bourgeoisie, which might be characterized by anal regression as much as by mature, "natural" genital love. The condition of privacy for personalized sexuality derives from the wife's status as property and from psychic needs typical of the bourgeois family. Ironically, Freud in 1908 criticized the privacy of bourgeois sexuality by naming it a source of neurosis.[67]

   Unwittingly Freud reveals the political aspect of the family in *Group Psychology*. The privatization of love and sex are an integral part of modern, capitalist society. All radical threats to the established system cannot, if Freud is correct, challenge the family system. But if they fail to challenge the family system, they cannot challenge the general social system, at least not in its psychological dimension. The economy can never be *socialized* (removed from private ownership and control) because the psychological strength required for such a movement cannot be marshaled. *Collective action will always be nothing more than regressive, childlike action* which cannot *create*, with intelligence and self-restraint, any new social system. Freud states this explicitly: "Social feeling [for justice and equality] is based upon the reversal of what was first [in sibling rivalry] a hostile feeling into a positively-toned tie in the nature of an identification."[68] The demand for equality on the part of group members amounts to a reaction-formation against each member's desire to be given special privileges by the father-leader. Equality for him is a desire to avoid conflicts over Papa's love and nothing more than that. The desire for equal participation and control over social resources cannot be realized because it is simply the denial and reversal of a deep-seated fantasy for the father's love.

   One can see the ambiguity of Freud's liberalism and the way it affects his concept of the family by discussing briefly his concept of therapy. In addition to the medical purpose of eliminating pain, psychoanalysis has a liberal, Enlightenment-inspired concern for making the analysand more in control of himself and hence more rational. Freud maintains that

the therapeutic efforts of psychoanalysis [are intended to] strengthen the ego, to make it more independent of the super-ego, to widen its field of perception and enlarge its organization, so that it can appropriate fresh portions of the id. Where id was, there ego shall be. It is a work of culture—not unlike the draining of the Zuider Zee.[69]

By limiting therapy to the individual Freud gives up any attempt to challenge the system of interactions through which the individual developed and in which he continues to repeat harmful patterns. And more than this, the effort to cure the individual as a praxis leads back to shape the theory. His science must develop an analysis of the structure and mechanisms of the individual divorced from social reality. The practice of individual therapy has a feedback effect on theory, directing the explanatory power of the concepts at intrapsychic phenomena alone. There is no way to gauge the degree of this effect but it is so profound that when Freud addresses himself to the problem of civilization he can deal with it only on the analogy to the individual.

Freud presents the psychological dimension of the history of civilization as the story of the increasing, linear, continuous growth of the psychic structure of the individual. Psychologically, civilization means an increasing repression of the instincts, an increasing strengthening of the character traits of anality, an increasing severity of the super-ego and of the feeling of guilt, an increasing resort to sublimation as the only form of instinctual cathexis, and, finally, an increasing feeling of anxiety deriving from the enormous overall level of repression. Stated in this way, Freud's psychohistory is a myth which projects current structures back through time. Civilization is nothing more than Freud's model of the individual psyche writ large. Civilization to him is in essence a struggle between Eros and Thanatos; the individual is driven by the same duality of instincts. Civilization causes aggression to be internalized resulting in guilt; the individual's psycho-sexual development requires the same process during the Oedipal stage. One could go on with this parallelism. At every point of the individual psychic structure, Freud elaborates an exact homology for the level of society. In philosophical language ontogeny recapitulates phylogeny; plainly stated, the argument is circular, never leaving the individual.

In *Civilization and Its Discontents* Freud explores this position to explain why advanced society leads to nothing but misery. Of course, Freud is concerned only with the middle and upper

classes: the discontents of his "individuals" are not those of
workers struggling to survive materially. But even so, his explanation is inadequate. His conclusion is that the discontents
of civilization are unavoidable, deep though they are. Hence
Freud can be elevated to the lofty heights of the tragic vision,
or so it is often said. In fact his vision is not tragic at all since
there is no alternative.

Yet Freud did analyze and describe the psyche of the bourgeoisie, and if he is read from the perspective of critical social
theory, the psychological dimension of industrial capitalism
becomes available to psychohistory. This reading of Freud can
only be done, however, after his theory of the psyche has been
reconceptualized through a social theory of the family which
would specify the conditions for the development of the Oedipus complex, the anal character, and so forth. Such an analysis
would proceed by looking at the relationship of the family to
society: economically, to see the specific ways in which the
family functions as a work unit and a consumption unit; politically, to see the way in which dominant roles in the family
correspond or do not correspond to dominant political roles;
socially, to see the way in which the family is immersed in the
wider community or separated out and privatized. Next it
would have to look at the specific interactional structures of
the family: at the child-rearing practices; at the number and
variety of sources for identification for the children; at the
sexual patterns of the adults; at the roles and activities of the
adults in the family; at the attitudes of family members about
the family or their expectations and images of other members.
At the same time these questions must be explored at the
psychological level to look for the emotional content, the fantasy content and the unconscious content of the interactional
forms. The psychic structures and mechanisms uncovered by
Freud could then be studied empirically and relativized: to
what degree is a super-ego developed or are emotional restrictions imposed communally; to what degree is sexuality repressed; what is the form of ego-identity and what are the
typical defense mechanisms of different groups; what are the

typical character traits as they develop out of the psycho-sexual stages; to what degree is fantasy supported or contradicted by "rationality"; how are the insane defined, what form does insanity take and what social practices are instituted to deal with it.

Properly reconstructed, Freud's theory would render intelligible the emotional structures of the family mediated by and mediating in specific ways the larger social apparatuses. Its limits would be specified historically and by class. The critical possibilities of the theory, its role in the theoretical and practical movement of emancipation, would then become clear. The last two chapters of this book will attempt to develop such a theory. But before turning to the construction of a critical theory of the family, it is necessary first to review the concept of the family in other intellectual traditions.

Chapter 2

THE RADICALIZATION
OF EROS

> *The bourgeois family becomes the most important ideo-*
> *logical workshop of capitalism through the sexual re-*
> *pression it carries out.*
>
> WILHELM REICH

TWENTIETH-CENTURY Marxists who sought to develop a critical concept of the family could find little help from the founders of socialism. Marx himself wrote almost nothing on the family. In the *1844 Manuscripts,* and again a few years later in the *Communist Manifesto,* Marx, like Fourier before him, denounced bourgeois marriage as a form of prostitution. With financial considerations uppermost in their minds, middle-class men degraded affairs of sentiment by mixing them with motives of economic gain. Bourgeois writers, for their part, considered Marx and Engels, along with other contemporary communists, as wild men who wanted to abolish the family and substitute for it perversions and promiscuity. In the *Communist Manifesto* Marx and Engels answered their critics:

Abolition of the family! Even the most radical flare up at this infamous proposal of the Communists. On what foundation is the present family, the bourgeois family, based? On capital, on private gain. In its completely developed form this family exists only among the bourgeoisie. But this state of things finds its complement in the practical absence of the family among the proletarians, and in public prostitution. The bourgeois family will vanish as a matter of course when its complement vanishes, and both will vanish with the vanishing of capital.[1]

The important conclusion reached by Marx and Engels in this passage was that the family is epiphenomenal compared to the mode of production. In general their writings relegated the family to the backwaters of the superstructure.[2]

Engels took off from this preconception and wrote in 1884 his well-known *Origin of the Family, Private Property and the State*. Based on Lewis Henry Morgan's evolutionary anthropology, Johann Bachofen's interpretation of matriarchy through myths, and Engels' own speculations, *The Origin of the Family* tied family history to economic history in a linear, causal relation. Since Engels' book serves as the primer for Marxists on family theory we must explore its positions.

Bachofen's study of mythology, along with the work of Morgan on American Indians and the writings of other anthropologists, led Engels to conclude that the current form of the family was not, as most social commentators presumed, eternal and natural. Instead, Engels contended, the family had a long and important history which had to be studied, a history which proved that patriarchy and monogamy were limited, relative social forms connected with fateful developments in the mode of production. At stake in this history, according to Engels, was the subjugation of women at a specific stage in the evolutionary process and the connection of patriarchy with the origins of private property. Whatever the defects of *The Origin of the Family*, Engels' application of the method of historical materialism to the family resulted in one of the earliest attempts to comprehend the family historically, removing the moral and ideological shrouds in which it had been hidden from serious investigation.

The important stages in family history took place, Engels wrote, well before the keeping of written records. In the age of "savagery" group marriage predominated; then during "barbarism" a form of pairing became common. The pivotal change occurred with the onset of "civilization": changes in property relations led to modern monogamy or "individual sex-love," which Engels, in agreement with liberal attitudes, viewed as the "greatest moral advance." Presupposing the primacy of the mode of production, Engels argued that at one point in the long evolution of material progress women began to feel uncomfortable with group marriage, desiring monogamy for the same moral motives that obtained among Victorian bourgeois women. This original "longing for chastity," a longing for which there is no evidence, led to women's one great historical act: a movement toward monogamy.

The reason Engels proposed why women and not men initiated the change to monogamy was simple: men, always more lustful than women to the Victorian Marxist, would never, even if their economic interests dictated it, give up group marriage. In Engels' words, the "advance" to monogamy "could not in any case have originated with the men, if only because it has never occurred to them, even to this day, to renounce the pleasures of actual group marriage. Only when the women had brought about the transition to pairing marriage were the men able to introduce strict monogamy— though indeed only for women."[3] Just as in Victorian ideology, women appear, in Engels' discourse, dominated and suppressed but acting toward the moral uplift of civilization, while the aggressive sexuality of the male appears as a constant in history.

In Engels' speculations "pairing" turned out to be a two-edged sword: in one direction, it cut toward moral advance; in the other, however, it opened the way for men to pursue their nefarious property interests and subjugate women even more deeply. Up to this point, society, Engels' implausibly asserts, was matriarchal. The turn to patriarchy began when men, now paired with women, decided to protect their property by insuring the line of inheritance. Thus men overthrew matriarchy for economic reasons to achieve undisputed paternity. Consequently Engels reduces the most profound change in family structure to the mode of production.

From this legendary point in the past up to some future date when socialism would arrive, nothing much happened in Engels' account of family history. The patriarchal family continued to suppress women for economic reasons, yielding men a secondary benefit through the double standard of sexual conduct. History would stagnate forever in this degrading morass except for the onset of industrialization. In his haste to analyze modern capitalism, Engels failed to note the important role women played in the old regime. He wrote, "Not until the coming of modern large-scale industry was the road to social production opened to her again—and then only to the proletarian wife."[4] The full emancipation of women, Engels predicted, will be achieved with the construction of socialism because then women will be allowed to work. "The first condition for the liberation of the wife is to bring the whole female sex back into industry, and . . . this in turn demands the abolition of the monogamous family as the economic unit of society."[5] With women working, the evils of male supremacy —prostitution, the double standard, and so forth—will automatically disappear. Under socialism what will emerge to replace the old exploitative relations will be nothing other than "mutual affection." Socialism will realize for the first time what the middle classes always wanted: monogamy without economic compulsion.

The Origin of the Family, although sensitive to the issue of male supremacy, applies Marx's model of base and superstructure in a crude and speculative manner. Engels has not provided an adequate concept of family structure, nor anything like an accurate outline of the history of the family. Changes in family pattern are encompassed totally within and explained by changes in the mode of production. Anything that does not fit this pattern is overlooked and omitted. We must grant, however, that Engels was working with an undeveloped science of anthropology and almost no historical research on family history. Even so, he suppresses the major issues that might flow from an adequate theory of family structure and a developed family history. For instance, we know now that a socialist revolution does not lead directly to the emancipation of women. Hence changes in family structure are not always the direct result of changes in ownership of the means of production. Research has also shown that the middle-class nuclear family arose *before* industrialization[6] and that the early

stages of industrialization did *not* witness a nuclear family
pattern among the proletariat.[7] Engels' test of the materialist
hypothesis of base and superstructure on the history of the
family proves by its limitations that Marxists need to develop
a critical theory of family structure to account for the disjunc-
ture between family and economy. Among European Marxists
in the twentieth century interesting efforts in the direction of
a theory of the family took the form of trying to synthesize the
positions of Marx and Freud.[8]

Wilhelm Reich, at one time both a psychoanalyst and a
communist, was the first to attempt seriously a synthesis of
Freud and Marx, and on this basis to sketch a new theory of
the family. Within the psychoanalytic movement, Reich's
most important book, *Character Analysis*, reconceptualized the
ego as a product of defenses or armoring against instinctual
impulses. The individual's character structure, his typical
modes of emotional behavior, were not to be understood as the
negative product of sexual repression. Even the "normal" ego
was to Reich a crippling and destructive agent of repression.
Neurotic symptoms were only an extreme form of a general
incapacity for healthy sexuality. "The character consists in a
chronic alteration of the ego which one might describe as a
rigidity . . ."[9] According to Reich, character armor was determined by the family. In a family typified by a negative sexual
morality, the child handled sexual repression by erecting an
ego or personality which was designed to prevent full gratification of the instincts.

As a Marxist, Reich sought to relate his theory of character
structure and sexual economy to social conditions. In *Dialectical Materialism and Psychoanalysis* (1929), the most important
early effort to synthesize Marx and Freud,[10] Reich argued that
psychoanalysis, a fully "dialectical" science, could make important contributions to Marxism. Freud's radical credentials
were won for Reich by his critique of religion and morality,
his destruction of the illusion of individual autonomy, his
theory of the sexual instincts which supplemented Marx's theory of the nutritive instincts, and his ability to explain regressive ideology and politics. In sum, psychoanalytic theory was

able to show concretely how ideas (the superstructure) were not the direct expression of material conditions but were transformed in and mediated by the family.[11] In the 1930s Reich believed in the importance of politicizing sexual and family life. He wanted to show how they are the indirect result of class society and how as structures they act in relative autonomy to bolster capitalism. He did not believe that sexual liberation and the abolition of the nuclear family could precede the economic revolution. By the 1940s, however, he had reversed himself and then maintained that in the timetable of revolution sexual liberation had to come before socialism or the consequence would be repressive, bureaucratic Bolshevism.

Dialectical Materialism and Psychoanalysis fostered the hope that Marxism would find in Freud's writings a valuable theory of sexual repression. Freud's notion of the Oedipus complex, Reich contended, needed only to be "translated into the language of sociology" in order to become a critical theory of the family. Freud had merely neglected to see that the parents who structured the child's experience were agents of society and were themselves determined by their social class. Reich adjusted psychoanalysis to Marxism as follows:

For the child, the family—which is saturated with the ideologies of society, and which, indeed, is the ideological nucleus of society—is temporarily, before he becomes engaged in the production process, the representative of society as a whole. The Oedipus relationship not only comprises instinctual attitudes: the manner in which a child experiences and overcomes his Oedipus complex is indirectly conditioned both by the general social ideology and by the parents' position in the production process; furthermore, the Oedipus complex itself, like everything else, depends ultimately on the economic structure of society. More, the fact itself that an Oedipus complex occurs at all must be ascribed to the socially determined structure of the family.[12]

Freudo-Marxism thus began by historicizing the conceptual framework of psychoanalysis.

If, in Reich's reading, psychoanalysis benefited from Marxism, which specified the social context of psychic phenomena, so Marxism would benefit from the use of Freud. For example, when working-class women, Reich conjectured, voted for fascists and could not be dissuaded by rational argument that their politics contradicted their economic interests, then there was a case for psychoanalytic interpretation, that of authoritarian ideology determined by psychic resistance. The key to such "irrational" behavior lay in an unconscious fear of authority that was related to sexual repression during childhood. The connection Reich drew between authority in the family, sexual repression and ideological conservatism was the most seminal fruit of his Freudo-Marxism. Before we can see how this nexus of ideas was used by Reich and by the Frankfurt School in the analysis of fascism, we must turn to Reich's general theory of the family as elaborated in *The Imposition of Sexual Morality* (1932).

In this essay Reich formulated a psychoanalytic supplement to Engels' *Origin of the Family* by tracing the evolution of family structures in relation to changing economic systems. According to Reich it was not enough to postulate that the family was determined by the economy; it was necessary also to account for sexual repression itself. In addition to the anthropological theories of Morgan and Bachofen, Reich, writing in the 1930s, could avail himself of the writings of Bronislaw Malinowski, perhaps the leading ethnologist of his day. The study of the Trobriand Islanders convinced Malinowski that a matriarchal, sexually unrestricted society had preceded patriarchal capitalism. Like Engels, Reich located the key to human evolution in the change from matriarchal communism to patriarchal capitalism. Malinowski's Trobrianders provided crucial evidence indicating that alterations in the circulation of the dowry by which the chief could accumulate vast amounts of property was the decisive step in the change to patriarchy. Once dowries flowed to the chief it became of absolute significance to him to insure his line of inheritance. Needing to be certain of his male heirs, the chief instituted a strict control of women and hence monogamous, patriarchal marriage began.[13] Reich's evolutionary theory was confirmed by the fact that the Trobrianders only restricted the sexual life of those adolescents who were involved in the inheritance of the chief's property. Other children remained in the matriarchal system of sexual affirmation and freedom.

With capitalism and sexual repression so neatly tied together, Reich was able to develop a Marxist family theory that was superior to that of Engels. While Engels called for socialism to liberate monogamy from patriarchy, Reich saw monogamy itself as a source of sexual repression. Instituted to insure the male's economic dominance, monogamy and the negative sexual morality connected with it were themselves agents of sexual repression. Originally economic in its motive, monogamy developed, claimed Reich, into an independent source of repression. Thus the Freudo-Marxist reading of history led to the call for the abolition of the monogamous family as the key to the liberation of women, children and sexuality in general. Reich proclaimed: "It is only the private enterprise form of society which has an interest in sexual repression, and which requires it for the maintenance of two of its basic institutions, the permanent monogamous marriage and the patriarchal family."[14]

Reich was unclear about the precise mechanisms of family structure which generated sexual repression. At times he put the fault with parental negative *attitudes* to sex;[15] at other times with the *institution* of "marriage and the family."[16] Such ambivalence on his part leads one to suspect that he had not adequately conceptualized family structure. Additionally, he restricted the scope of the question far too much by limiting the discussion to sexual freedom. For if sexual freedom denotes unrestricted instinctual expression, it is clear that such an ideal is impossible. Every society shapes bodily energies from the start of life and hence "represses sexuality." Reich postulated a false naturalism of instincts, assuming that they were complete before social existence begins. Instead of providing clear criteria to analyze the family structures of different classes at different times, Reich, like Engels, gave only a simplified sketch of the alteration from matriarchy to patriarchy, a shift that is much too broad to be of value. The decisive change in his schema occurred in prehistory, was based on the scantiest evidence, and did not ask the important questions about family structure and patriarchy in modern times. These weaknesses in Reich's arguments became manifest in his effort to explain fascism psychologically.

Reich's analysis of fascism will have to demonstrate that there is an important difference between the working class and the bourgeoisie regarding sexual repression. Only by doing so can the historian differentiate by social class the sources of support and opposition to fascism. Working-class sexuality, according to Reich's theory, must be less repressive, since property is not at stake. In order to examine degrees of repression, one must have a clear notion of family structure. And here Reich's argument stops. Although attractive at first reading, Reich's *Mass Psychology of Fascism* fails ultimately to explain why fascism should arise and become successful in one time and place and not another.

The problem begins with Reich's definition of fascism. He related it to an authoritarian family structure, claiming that severe parental repression of infantile sexuality leads to a character armoring which in turn prepares the child for later appeals from authoritarian politicians. The authoritarian father in the patriarchal family deforms the child's emotional needs in such a way that the person, once grown up, has deep feelings of helplessness which can be played upon by authoritarian propaganda. Sexually repressed individuals believe in duty and obedience and are open to, for instance, Hitler's appeals. In this way, Reich defines fascism as "the organized political expression of the structure of the average man's character. . . . Fascist mentality is the mentality of the 'little man', who is enslaved and craves authority and is at the same time rebellious . . ."[17]

In the mid-1930s many Marxists were at pains to explain the rise of fascism. Apparently capitalism was moving backwards, from the formal democracy of liberalism to the police states of Mussolini and Hitler. Marx's formula for analyzing history implied that Germany, the most advanced European capitalist society with the most class-conscious and organized proletariat, should, with the onset of the depression in 1929, be ripe for socialist revolution. Instead Germany was fleeing from freedom. How could the dialectic fail to move forward? Reich's analysis of voting patterns in the early 1930s indicated that some workers were open to the appeals of reaction. Many Marxists evaded the question by blaming the leadership of German social democracy for the rise of Hitler. Reich at least was more rigorous, calling for an explanation of how a revolutionary situation could result in the political success of a reactionary ideology. Either Marx was wrong that the mode of production determined class relations or something had intervened between the depression and the rise of the proletariat. The intervening variables to Reich were sexual repression and the authoritarian family.

Fascism was made possible, in Reich's perspective, by the lag of ideology behind the economic structure. Ideology, in turn, was retarded by the persistence of old family patterns and therefore of old psychic structures. Specifically, the middle-class patriarchal family had remained unaltered for "thousands of years." In this family structure, everyone worked in the retail store or on the farm. The father therefore had an economic base and also the authority for subjecting his wife and children to extreme forms of repression.[18] In addition, the precarious financial situation of the *petite bourgeois* family led it to differentiate itself from social inferiors precisely by its "sexual modes of life." The bourgeois wanted to appear "morally superior" to the worker. This combination of sexual repression and authoritarianism produced among the children a subservient attitude to authority in general. "The compulsion to control one's sexuality, to maintain sexual repression, leads to the development of pathologic, emotionally tinged notions of honor and duty, bravery and self-control."[19]

If all of this was true of the middle class, one would still have to explain how the working class was different. Were not working-class fathers also repressive and authoritarian? At this point Reich's argument faltered. He gave several explanations for an alleged difference in working-class family structure, none of which is convincing. First, he claimed that workers identify with their skills, while middle-class men identify with their superiors. Workers are thus less ready to respect authority.[20] Next, he acknowledged that workers repress their children. But unlike workers, the middle-class father, he wrote, "only represses sexuality," surely a fanciful claim. At other points, however, Reich asserted the opposite position, that is, that workers in the twentieth century, with higher living standards, have adopted bourgeois views and hence have family structures similar to the bourgeoisie.[21] But if the latter claim is correct, it is no longer possible to differentiate psychologically the bourgeoisie and the proletariat. In sum, Reich was not able to explain class differences in psychological terms because he did not properly define the structural categories of the family. His account of family history on the basis of sexual repression and patriarchal authority is not developed in enough detail.

Reich's proposed synthesis of Marx and Freud met with approval neither from orthodox Marxists nor orthodox Freudians. The Freudians were disturbed by his explicit sexual radicalism; the Marxist parties had rejected Freud as an example of bourgeois degeneracy.[22] The Marxists were perhaps bothered less by Reich's theory than by the Sexpol movement he established to promote the sexual and mental health of workers and young people. For Reich took his Marxist psychology seriously and sought a solution in practice to the problem of the class consciousness of the proletariat. "We persist in believing that the fundamental problem of a correct psychological doctrine is not why a hungry man steals but the exact opposite: Why doesn't he steal?"[23] For an answer Reich brought the insights of Freud directly to the working class, hoping thereby to liberate their sexuality and hence to extricate them from subservient attitudes to authority. Such a direct attack on family life was unacceptable to Social Democrats and Communists. Tampering with "respectable" family life was henceforth banished from Marxist "revolutionary" movements.

Three years after the appearance of *Mass Psychology of Fascism*, the Frankfurt School Marxists published *Studien über Autorität und Familie* (1936), a massive collective work which also sought to explain the rise of fascism. In general the intellectual work of the Frankfurt School, stemming from the experience of European fascism, was devoted to the comprehension of contemporary culture. Marxism as presented by the German Social Democrats and the Russian communists relied too heavily, they thought, on the concept of the mode of production.[24] Twentieth-century capitalism required new conceptual tools, ones that could account for the failure of the Western European proletariat to revolt. Marxists would have to show, they asserted, how ideological, cultural and psychological factors intervened to deflect workers' class consciousness from the goal of socialism.[25]

The rise of authoritarianism in Europe was best explained, the Frankfurt School thought, by turning to Freud's theory of psychoanalysis. *Studies on Authority and the Family* relied throughout on Freudian concepts to account for the psychological needs which authoritarian politics apparently fulfilled for the masses. Erich Fromm, a psychoanalyst and a member of the Frankfurt School in the late 1920s and the 1930s, directed the empirical research of the project and contributed a long theoretical section which sought to synthesize Freud and Marx much in the manner of Wilhelm Reich.[26] Although Fromm's contribution deserves attention since it was informed by a sophisticated use of Freudian theory, I will limit my analysis to Horkheimer's essay in *Studies* because it more clearly manifests the strengths and weaknesses of the Frankfurt School's concept of the family.[27]

Max Horkheimer, the director of the Frankfurt School, explained how the concept of the family fit into Marx's theory of society. To begin with, "cultural spheres could not be explained solely by economic events."[28] One must look instead to the family to understand why men behave as they do. The family for Horkheimer was the all-important mediator between the individual and society. This way of conceptualizing the family was, for the Frankfurt School, the key to unlock Marxism from the prisonhouse of economic determinism. As we shall see, such a solution of the theoretical difficulties of Marxism does not provide an adequate basis for a theory of the family. In fact, Horkheimer's strategy resembles closely that of Talcott Parsons. In Frankfurt School writings the family tends to appear as little more than a conservative socializing agency. As Horkheimer contends, "The family has a very special place among the relationships which through conscious and unconscious mechanisms influence the psychic character of the vast majority of men. . . . The family . . . sees to it that the kind of human character emerges which social life requires . . ."[29]

Unlike Parsons, Horkheimer and the Frankfurt School were critical of the element of domination in the family. As a theory of human emancipation, Frankfurt School Marxism sought to unearth the root of psychic oppression in the family. In Horkheimer's lament, "the despair of women and children, the deprivation of any happiness in life, the material and psychic exploitation consequent upon the economically based hegemony of the father have weighed mankind down no less in recent centuries than in antiquity . . ."[30] The family for him was a center of domination which brutalized children in preparation for their submissive acceptance of class society. "The child's self-will is to be broken, and the innate desire for free development of his drives and potentialities is to be replaced by an internalized compulsion toward the unconscious fulfillment of duty. Submission to the categorical imperative of duty has been from the beginning a conscious goal of the bourgeois family."[31] Horkheimer postulated a natural freedom which was then destroyed in the family.

The central mechanism in the family which crushes freedom is the authority of the father over his sons. Of all family relationships, that of father to son is the only one taken seriously by Horkheimer and the Frankfurt School. In this respect they perpetuate a certain masculine blindness which was characteristic of Freud.[32] Like Reich, Horkheimer adds an economic dimension to Freud's view of parent-child relations: "Sons and daughters of bourgeois families learned that the fulfillment of all wishes depends in reality on money and position."[33] Horkheimer's general critique of patriarchal authority hardly accounts for the specific authority and psychic structure of the bourgeoisie. Like Reich again, his attempt to correlate class structure and psychic structure was not successful.

In trying to account for the class nature of psychic structure Horkheimer only found the same repressive authority everywhere. Working-class psychology was as authoritarian as that of the bourgeoisie. Yet he insisted that authoritarianism stemmed exclusively from the bourgeois family: "The impulse to submission, however, is not a timeless drive, but a phenomenon emerging essentially from the limited bourgeois family."[34] After showing how the bourgeois family in particular was so perfectly geared to the suppression of sexuality, he reported lamely that in times of prosperity the working class had simply adopted the bourgeois family model. Even if this were so, it could not be maintained that working-class families, untainted by bourgeois models, were less rife with authoritarianism. And surely aristocratic families were as patriarchal as any other. Horkheimer and the Marxists were right to turn to class in order to provide the social basis of Freudian theory, but it is necessary to specify the precise interactional structures and conditions which account for the psychic structure of each class.

Horkheimer did not adequately conceptualize the conditions for the development of submissive personality types. At one point he explained them through the dominance and repressiveness of the father; at another point he stated that the degree of permissiveness is not the real issue. Instead what matters is the unconscious structure of the family: "The decisive thing here is not whether coercion or kindness marked the child's education, since the child's character is formed far

more by the very structure of the family than by the conscious
intentions and methods of the father."[35] Yet we had earlier
quoted Horkheimer's claim, in the same essay, that bourgeois
fathers were totally conscious of their tactic of repression. In
attempting to account for the precise family mechanism of
personality formation, he ends up with a bundle of contradictory statements. The father is conscious and unconscious, repressive and permissive; working-class families are like bourgeois families and they are different.

Horkheimer's difficulties in conceptualizing the family—
difficulties which characterize the Frankfurt School in general
—derive in part from an improper concept of freedom or
emancipation which is defined as the *autonomy* of the individual. Because Horkheimer relied on a notion of individual autonomy, he could not define properly the nature of the social
interactions in the family through which the psyche is formed,
and he could not define clearly the nature of the authoritarianism that he wanted to criticize and overcome.

To begin with, Horkheimer assumed in 1936 that patriarchal
authority could not be eliminated and that the problem centered on the degree to which the larger society reinforced that
authority: "It makes a difference whether this coercion is the
spontaneous reflection in the father-son relationship of the
prevailing social contradictions or proves rather to be a provi-
sional relationship which is eliminated as the individual grows
and moves out into the larger society."[36] At this point Horkheimer has given up an argument for the significance of the
family in the problem of mass psychology. In democratic society presumably the "bad" experience of authority in the family can be overcome during adulthood. The hub of the seeming
contradiction lies in Horkheimer's reliance on traditional rationalism. In adulthood reason for him works against the submissive instincts formed in children, and the individual can
assume full autonomy. In the 1936 essay, Horkheimer's individualism appeared in his definition of authority. He states:
"Authority is the ground for a blind and slavish submission
which originates subjectively in psychic inertia and inability

to make one's own decisions . . ."[37] With this individualist-
rationalist norm of autonomy, Frankfurt School theories of
the family were unable to revise Freud's concept of the family
in the direction of critical social theory.

By the 1950s Horkheimer's essays on the family revealed a
limitation in Frankfurt School social theory. In the later period the critique of culture became a tirade against mass society with strong elitist implications. The paean of individual
autonomy became more strident and the proletariat no longer
appeared as the historical agent of emancipation. Looking
back to classical capitalism of the nineteenth century, Horkheimer no longer saw the bourgeois family as the source of
authoritarianism. Quite the reverse: the bourgeois patriarchal
father has now become the bastion of freedom and individual
autonomy:

> In that earlier day the father was in large measure a free man. . . . He
> became for his child an example of autonomy, resoluteness, self-
> command, and breadth of mind. *For his own sake* he required of his
> child truthfulness and diligence, reliability and intellectual alertness,
> love of freedom and discretion, until these attitudes having been
> internally assimilated by the child, became the normative voice of the
> latter's own conscience and eventually, in the conflicts of puberty, set
> him at odds with his father. Today the child is much more directly
> thrown upon society . . . and the result is a human being cast in a
> different mold. As interiority has withered away, the joy of making
> personal decisions, of cultural development and of the free exercise
> of imagination has gone with it.[38]

Paradoxically, Horkheimer had not changed that much: for
the punitive super-ego he now substitutes the benevolent ego-
ideal. In both cases the fault with the analysis lies with the
notion of individual autonomy. In the 1930s this was threatened by fascism; in the 1960s the danger lay in "mass society."
In fact, family structure was never really conceptualized at all:
the family played a role for Horkheimer, shifting with the
exigencies of his argument, in defending his perfectly un-
Marxist and un-Freudian concept of individual autonomy. In
one place the father appeared as the source of authoritarian-

ism, in another as the basis of freedom—in either case it is a question of the father and that is the problem.

The other major figure in the Frankfurt School to develop a Freudo-Marxist concept of the family is Herbert Marcuse. Marcuse's contribution to *Studies on Authority and the Family* was an intellectual history of the idea of authority.[39] It was not until the mid-1950s, with *Eros and Civilization*, that Marcuse dealt systematically with the problem of Freud. In this book, Marcuse was consistent with the earlier positions of Hork- heimer and Fromm in *Studies*.

The claim of *Eros and Civilization* is that Freud's theory already contains the elements for a Marxist theory of the psy- che. Marcuse argued that Freud's original instinct theory is genuinely materialist, while those who sociologize Freud, like Erikson and the ego psychologists, disavow the instinct theory and, intentionally or not, transform psychoanalysis into a con- servative doctrine.[40] To find a radical Freud one need only study dialectically the ways in which civilization comes into conflict with eros. To Marcuse, Wilhelm Reich had not accom- plished this task because he saw sexual liberation as a total cure for social ills and because he neglected the "historical dynamic of the sex instincts and of their fusion with the destructive impulses."[41]

Marcuse uncovered the radical core in Freud first by making some important distinctions. He relativized Freud's reality principle, through which the ego finds limits in the world to which it must adjust both the demands of the id and the stric- tures of the super-ego, by specifying its current capitalist configuration as a "performance principle."[42] The limits im- posed on the ego by society now are defined by the Prome- thean imperative to achieve and produce. The notion of the performance principle leads to a second distinction, one be- tween the level of instinctual repression necessary to any so- cial system and the extra degree of repression required by authoritarian institutions. Social relations characterized by domination, Marcuse contends, call forth a "surplus-repres- sion," a degree of repression which is not determined by the requirements of psychic development itself. Fromm argues[43] that Marcuse here confused social oppression with intra-psychic repression. Yet surely there is some relation between, for example, the strictness of toilet training and the separate but related defenses in the child against instinctual enjoyment of the anus. Social forms of repression may be distinct in kind from psychic repression, but the two are interrelated. Freud agreed with Marcuse's position, since he attributed a "high water mark of repression" to the demands of contemporary civilization.

In the argument for instinctual liberation Marcuse went beyond Reich in specifying certain aspects of instinctual life as the source of revolt, of the negative dialectic. Marcuse discovered the realm of fantasy, of childhood memories as expressions of the instincts that return inexorably to haunt the stability of adult psychic armoring. In activities of playful fantasy, the individual regresses to early memories. The importance of fantasy to Marcuse was that it alone is beyond the governance of the reality principle. The problem is not simply as Reich thought that instincts were curbed and needed to be unshackled; this "naturalism" of the instincts does not reach Freud's critical insight. Instead, for Marcuse, imagination and fantasy are restored by Freud to an independent status, one of eternal opposition to social repressions. Regressive fantasies have, he asserted, a progressive side. They enable the individual to imagine a utopia, a world beyond contemporary psychic discontents. Marcuse writes, "Against a society which employs sexuality as means for a useful end, the perversions uphold sexuality as an end in itself; they thus place themselves outside the domination of the performance principle and challenge its very foundation."[44] Paradoxically, the path to progressive liberation is strewn with oral and anal perversions. In fantasy, the gates are unlocked that lead down and back toward the wonderful cellar, polymorphous perversion. Marcuse's peculiar strategy is to find sources of revolution in the most unlikely places. In Freudian terms, however, it is not true that the "perversions uphold sexuality as an end in itself." Rather they are unconscious repetitions of component instincts and childhood traumas. The way to affirmative sexuality, according to Freud, can only be through genital sexuality.

Marcuse's second path to freedom is by way of the death instinct. While Reich denied the primacy of the death instinct, reducing it to a mere secondary phenomenon, unworthy of Freud's theory, Marcuse found in it a revolutionary potential. The death instinct was not to be understood in its usual meaning as an urge to destruction or aggression which turned outward, against one's fellow man, preventing forever a rosy image of human association. On the contrary, the death instinct was at bottom an urge to let things be, a refusal to perform. The secret of the death instinct according to Marcuse was located in narcissism, where eros and thanatos were combined in a pre-differentiated unity. Freud chose the cultural image of Narcissus to denote a capacity for joyous, unhurried self-indulgence, and Marcuse found here a source for a new reality principle, for an instinctual need beyond the work ethic of capitalism.

The death instinct and polymorphous perversity were the two *instinctual* sources of social progress. They suggested a new structure of consciousness, a new psyche that threatened the bourgeois, civilized image of Promethean man. Hence Marcuse used Freud to demonstrate the force of what Freud himself did not think possible: a psychic structure beyond civilization. The argument was won for Marcuse by references to the heroes of ancient mythology, Orpheus and Narcissus. Here in fantasy were represented possibilities of human liberation. As a Marxist, Marcuse recognized the need to demonstrate the social conditions under which these fantasies might become new reality principles. The material conditions for Orphic self-indulgent joy were provided by the success of capitalism in overcoming scarcity: "Now it is precisely such a reactivation of polymorphous eroticism which appeared as the consequence of the conquest of scarcity and alienation. The altered societal conditions would therefore create an instinctual basis for the transformation of work into

play."[45] Given today's affluence, a "great refusal" becomes
possible in which deep unconscious fantasies may arise again,
auguring a new revolution in the form of an orgasmic return
of the repressed.

It can be argued against Marcuse[46] that play, fantasy and
imagination are not at all beyond the reality principle; that
they too are subject to the fate of repression and represent not
freedom but only another level of domination. The game of
the child who made his toy appear and disappear was to Freud
a compulsive repeating in fantasy of his separation from his
mother, not a "free" play in any sense. It is debatable whether
the instinctual manifestations of children at play are really
examples of polymorphous perversity or rather imitations of
adult repressed patterns. It can also be argued against Marcuse
that regression cannot be a source of progression, that the
component instincts of the oral and anal stages cannot provide
a form of sexuality that is somehow more liberated than the
genital sexuality described by Freud. Finally, it can be shown
that the reliance on instincts leads to a pre-social, individualist
definition of human nature. The child is in this view already
a locus of energy "before" it enters into social relationships.
As a Marxist Marcuse should not want to be burdened by the
individualism inherent in his reliance on instinct theory.
Whatever the force of these counter-arguments, the astonishing failure of Marcuse for us pertains to his lack of a concept
of the family.

In attempting to avoid the conservative pitfalls of ego psychology, Marcuse erected an exceedingly weak link between
psychic structure and social structure. Instead of relating instinctual structures directly to social relations he introduced
the cosmic cop-out of Narcissus and Orpheus. The concrete
totality is lost in a haze of fanciful images, and the reader is
urged to move from the simple fact of affluence to mythic
self-transformation. The family, the crucial mediation between psyche and society, gets lost amid aesthetic fantasies of
pure rapture.

Marcuse conceived of the family in the manner of Horkheimer in *Studies on Authority and the Family*. Horkheimer's nostalgia for patriarchy was repeated by Marcuse in his argument that "organized capitalism" coordinates the psyche at a hitherto unreached depth. Like Reisman in *The Lonely Crowd*, the Marxist points out that individuals are no longer socialized in the family, and the price that is paid is widespread conformity. Marcuse writes: "With his consciousness co-ordinated, his privacy abolished, his emotions integrated into conformity, the individual has no longer enough 'mental space' for developing himself *against* his sense of guilt, for living with a conscience of his own."[47] The society without the father means individuals without autonomy. The reader is asked to believe that only in the patriarchal family could he become a real person. In the fascinating passage below Marcuse outlined precisely why the patriarchal family was a humanizing agency:

The technological abolition of the individual is reflected in the decline of the social function of the family. It was formerly the family which, for good or bad, reared and educated the individual, and the dominant rules and values were transmitted personally and transformed through personal fate. . . . In the passing and inheritance of the Oedipus conflict they became individuals, and the conflict continued into an individual life history. Through the struggle with father and mother as personal targets of love and aggression, the younger generation entered societal life with impulses, ideas, and needs which were largely *their own*. Consequently, the formation of their super-egos . . . were very personal experiences . . . and life . . . still retained a sphere of private non-conformity.[48]

Like Horkheimer, Marcuse celebrated the very individual autonomy which he so sharply rejects elsewhere in the text as a liberal illusion bound to the performance principle. The utopian Marxist who heralds the new age of Narcissus, who applauds the revolutionary needs represented by the youth culture, still finds it necessary to paint rosy pictures from the time of his own childhood in a patriarchal family.

The first generation of Frankfurt theorists set the stage for the inability of critical theory to conceptualize the family.

More recent books by Reimut Reiche and Michael Schneider[49] continue in the footsteps of their intellectual fathers. Schneider, for example, argues for a synthesis of Freud and Marx through a critique of work and consumption. The family becomes even less significant than it was for the earlier theorists as Schneider finds contemporary psychic structure to be a product of secondary socialization outside family networks. His interesting and important insights into the mental damage of work activity and consumption patterns still lack an adequate account of family structure not only regarding socialization, but also as a sphere of life itself.

In sum, the Marxists' concept of the family, relying generally on a theory of instinctual liberation, is most helpful in probing the interaction between the family and the economy. They point to a problem that cannot be overlooked: the family must be studied in relation to the mode of production, and particularly one must be aware of class differences in family structure. Furthermore, they remind us of the importance of the sex needs, which also must be conceptualized in relation to family structure, even though they base sexuality on a suspect notion of the instincts. Beyond this, existing Marxist theory[50] on the family is surprisingly weak. One of the major purposes of this study is to develop a critical theory of the family and thereby enrich the capacities of radical social theory to make intelligible important issues in the history of modern society.

Chapter 3

EGO PSYCHOLOGY, MODERNIZATION AND THE FAMILY

"Families are factories which produce human personalities."

TALCOTT PARSONS

IN THE UNITED STATES, the Freudian concept of the family was influenced by a shift within the psychoanalytic movement toward ego psychology. At the end of World War II a new journal, *The Psychoanalytic Study of the Child*, was a main organ of the new direction. Led by Heinz Hartmann, Ernst Kris and Rudolf Loewenstein, the journal advocated a new emphasis on studying the strengths of the ego in comparison with the id and the ego's capacity for adaptation to reality.[1] Much like the "culturalist school" of Harry S. Sullivan, Erich Fromm and Karen Horney, the ego psychologists were concerned with problems of psychic health and the adjustment of the psyche to the demands of society. Where Freud saw the predominance of unconscious instincts in mental life, Hartmann spoke of an independent "ego energy"[2] which was not bound up in narcissism or dependence on the id.

Hartmann, Kris and Loewenstein, exiles from Nazi Germany, seemed bent on adapting psychoanalysis to the dominant American culture. Their notion of health through adjustment to society fit well into the ethos of liberal capitalism. They removed all the strange, threatening aspects of Freud's theory, such as the unconscious, sexuality and instinct theory. Ego psychologists remodeled Freud to the American ideal of individual autonomy through social adaptation. For support from sociology Hartmann turned to Talcott Parsons, the leading social theorist of American middle-class values.[3] Underlying ego psychology was a concern to foster personality development and to bolster democracy against the dangers of "totalitarianism."

Among the ego psychologists, Erik Erikson went furthest in the direction of a theory of the family. His concept of the life cycle established a developmental theory of the ego which was rooted in social experience. For the early stages of ego growth the family, therefore, was a structured and formative condition. Erikson attempted to supplement Freud's theory of psycho-sexual stages with a theory of ego stages and a theory of social institutions. The dialectic of biology was now enhanced by the dialectics of ego and society. Here surely was a promising program for psychoanalytic theory, a program that would enable it to account for the embeddedness of the psyche in a social world. Yet, as we shall see, Erikson's theory, although widely accepted in many sectors of the psychological, educational and historical disciplines, fails to provide a satisfactory psychoanalytic model of the family.

Erikson's clinical practice in child psychology, in studying American Indians and in treating the neuroses of war all led him to a concept of the ego as the center of "a sense of coherent individuation and identity; of being one's self, of being all right, and of being on the way to becoming what other people, at their kindest, take one to be."[4] Against Freud, Erikson restored to the ego its relative autonomy from the instincts and provided it with the role of active organizer of experience. No longer subordinated to the more powerful influences of the super-ego and the id, the ego was again the center of the self, the place where the individual maintained a sense of meaning and coherence.

The revaluation of the ego was only the first step. Erikson's major achievement was a theory of the stages and crises through which the ego passed at each point in the life cycle. In each phase of life, the ego has to organize its experience, both internal and external, in order for the self to establish its continuity. Freud's first instinctual stage, the oral, was now also and equally a period when the ego established an attitude of trust or mistrust toward the world. If successful in this period, the individual would have for the rest of his life, and as a sort of possession, an unconscious sense of faith and optimism, a sense that the world was basically a good place. Similarly, for Freud's second, anal stage, Erikson added one of autonomy vs. doubt; for Freud's Oedipal stage, one of initiative vs. guilt; for the period of latency, one of industry vs. inferiority.

Whereas Freud viewed the third or genital stage, with its Oedipal crisis, as most crucial for instinctual and indeed all psychic organization, Erikson placed the fifth stage of identity, during adolescence, as the pivotal phase of ego development. At each stage, success or failure influenced the ego for the entire cycle of life, but the identity crisis, by now part of our everyday vocabulary, was most influential to an individual's sense of coherence. Erikson suggested that this shift of emphasis within psychoanalysis might be due to changing historical circumstances. Technological capitalism, delaying the individual's entry into society and undercutting the value of the older generation's experience for the younger generation, accentuated the problem of finding a place in the world for adolescents.[5] We can let pass for now the middle-class bias in Erikson's explanation. More than this resort to history, Erikson's stress on identity derived from his special concerns with the ego rather than with the instincts. The unconscious might well be organized around the fifth year, while the ego becomes structured during the period of youth.

In Freud's theory, the crucial phases of development end with the Oedipus complex. The focus on the ego led Erikson to extend his theory throughout the life cycle. After the identity crisis came one of intimacy vs. isolation, followed by one of generativity vs. stagnation and concluding with one of integrity vs. despair. While many Freudians, like Melanie Klein, were studying childhood more intensively than Freud had and concluding that the pre-Oedipal phases were more significant than Freud thought, Erikson went in the opposite direction and expanded psychoanalytic theory to account for the entire life cycle, adulthood as well as childhood.[6]

Erikson's theory of ego development is very well known, so I need not summarize it more extensively than I already have. Its implications for a theory of the family, however, have been virtually unexplored so it is here that I will concentrate my analysis.

The major theoretical implication for psychoanalysis of Erikson's concept of ego stages is a decided shift toward society as a determinant of psychic structure. Erikson is explicit in pointing out the failure of Freud's psychoanalytic theory to account conceptually for social structure: "The traditional psychoanalytic method . . . cannot quite grasp identity because it has not developed terms to conceptualize the environment. Certain habits of psychoanalytic theorizing, habits designating the environment as 'outer world' or 'object world,' cannot take account of the environment as a pervasive actuality."[7] From Erikson's perspective, Freud was not able to specify the social field in which psychic structure is formed.

Erikson goes on to question some of the fundamental assumptions of psychoanalysis about the biological, natural quality of childhood experience. "A stubborn tendency persists [in psychoanalysis] to treat the 'mother-child relationship' as a 'biological' entity more or less isolated from its cultural surroundings."[8] For a Freudian, Erikson is moving far toward bringing psychic experience into focus as part of the social world. Finally, Erikson goes to the heart of the problem: "Instead of accepting such instinctual 'givens' as the Oedipus trinity as an irreducible schema for man's irrational conduct, we are exploring the way in which social forms codetermine the structure of the family . . ."[9] From now on family structure and psychic structure must be conceptualized as interdependent.

Erikson had discovered that the ego, the center of individuality, could not be understood in isolation from the others and the wider world around it.[10] The study of the ego led directly to the study of "the interdependence of inner and social organization . . ."[11] The ego was nothing but a precipitate of its relations with others. Identity depended directly on the ability of the individual to integrate these residues of identifications with others into a coherent whole. Certainly Freud recognized the ego as the internalization of the immediate community. His concept of the ego-ideal was precisely this. But Erikson, unlike Freud, announced that the relation of ego and world was a major theoretical problem which was not resolved by the idea of a "reality principle." In Erikson's words, "We are in need, then, of concepts which throw light on the *mutual complementation* of ego synthesis and social organization."[12]

Erikson approached the problem by focusing on child-rearing methods. A notion of biological inevitability was insufficient to comprehend the oral stage. The particular social customs surrounding feeding were important determinants in regulating the mutual relations of mother, father and child in these activities. Not only was the child developing an erotic attachment to its mouth along with organizing its libido in relation to the mother, but the mother's capacity for giving, the society's customs concerning how the baby was to be fed, how much it should be fed, how often, even by whom (only the biological mother, the father, any lactating female, certain lactating females)—all these were integral parts in the child's developing a trusting ego. Erikson has thus enabled us to comprehend the oral stage as a social experience; we are able to see not simply an intra-psychic phenomenon, but a complex social interaction. In the comprehension of psychic levels, the social world emerges as a structured and intelligible reality, not merely as an opaque "reality principle." Above all, the false individualism of Freud's theory is replaced by a notion of the primacy of the social nature of psychic reality.

Unfortunately these apparent advances are flawed seriously on many levels. Perhaps the most obvious difficulty with Erikson's theory of the life cycle is its claim of universality. For example, can generativity (defined as the adult's need to guide the next generation) be the central problem for adults in all societies? Could this be true in a monastery? More seriously, David Hunt, in his book on seventeenth-century French families,[13] found it impossible to apply Erikson's category of generativity to the French aristocracy. Family structure among the aristocracy called for a minimum of child care and nurturing by parents, and parents received no special social recognition for providing these functions. In fact, aristocrats felt that a noble mother who spent much of her time with her children, especially during the first years (today regarded as an absolute demand on the mother), was unworthy of her high social station. Clearly there is a problem with Erikson's category when applied to a very different social situation. It seems, however, that his categories can be tested, as Hunt does, and rejected when inapplicable. Because Erikson's theory, unlike Freud's, is so flexible, the claim of universality does not lead necessarily to an ideological justification of categories that apply only to the present. Since the general notion of a life cycle applies to all societies and classes, research can establish the appropriate categories for any situation. Thus Erikson has sensitized us to the problem of the life cycle itself and to the importance of child-rearing methods as areas for research.

The difficulties emerge when we ask precisely what the significance of the life cycle is. To Erikson, the concept of the life cycle provides the key to understanding the way the individual and society form a unity, the way in which the society provides for a pattern of reciprocal functioning between the generations, in short, the way in which the *values* of the society become internalized in the individual as he passes through the set of psychological growth crises. Erikson is not interested in the character structure of the individual, as Wilhelm Reich was; he is not interested in the way the instincts are shaped and repressed. Nor does his concept of the life cycle provide an explanation of how the society shapes individuals. In using the theory of the life cycle, Hunt, for example, refused to argue that certain child-rearing techniques result in certain psychological patterns in the child. But Erikson does not really argue for such a mechanistic causality. He simply assumes that the patterns the adults use in raising children have a built-in social wisdom, an implicit unity with the expectations of the adult world. This assumption contains some difficulties, as we shall see. But for now it is imperative that we emphasize Erikson's own position: his concept of the life cycle is designed to show how the individual finds meaning in the world, how the individual attains positive ego strengths, and, finally, how the individual achieves the spiritual values which enable him to cope with living in his world.[14]

The shortcomings of Erikson's position for a critical theory of the family may now be apparent. We have moved from the tough-minded, almost materialist dialectic of Freud to a theory that points from its beginning essentially to idealist questions. In Freud, religion was mankind's collective neurosis; in Erikson the entire psychology turns back to an affirmation of religious values and experience. The impact of the life cycle upon the individual is a set of values; each stage of life, if successfully achieved, implants in the individual a spiritual resource. Erikson enumerates them in his "schedule of virtues,"[15] in the order of the seven stages, as follows: hope, will, purpose, competence, fidelity, love, care and wisdom. Thus, the concept of the life cycle leads not to a comprehension of family structure, but to a set of religious virtues. Erikson's lofty spiritual quest ends in an affirmation of all social orders as providing adequate chances for each individual to attain these values.

From the vantage point of this study, the danger of Erikson's grand, humane intent is that it skews his theory of the life cycle away from a critical analysis of family structure toward a search for the organic unity of individual and world. In his own words,

we are speaking of goals and values and of the energy put at their disposal by child-training systems. Such values persist because the cultural ethos continues to consider them 'natural' and does not admit of alternatives. They persist because they have become an essential part of an individual's sense of identity, which he must preserve as a core of sanity and efficiency. But values do not persist unless they work, economically, psychologically and spiritually; and I argue that to this end they must continue to be anchored, generation after generation, in early child-training; while child training, to remain consistent, must be embedded in a system of continued economic and cultural synthesis.[16]

The main difficulty for a theory of the family with this focus on synthesis is that it shifts the field away from conflicts, from discontinuities, from antagonisms, and allows one only to see society as a harmonious unity, as a self-regulating mechanism, always readjusting itself, never needing to be challenged fundamentally or to be overturned, never really oppressive. All family structures are adequate, to Erikson, as long as they provide for values that will fit the individual into society armed with his "schedule of virtues."

If the theory of the life cycle is slanted toward synthesis and unity and if it leads primarily to a comprehension of values, it also is inadequate because it reintroduces individualism. The theory brings the social field to light *through the individual* and his quest. The life cycle is something *the individual* goes through. The psychological categories—trust, identity, etc.— are those of the individual. Although these are developed in mutual interaction with the social system, there are no concepts for comprehending psychologically the wider world, institutional patterns or interpersonal relations. One still does not grasp directly what goes on *between* people, but only what happens *to* them. Thus for each stage in the life cycle, society somehow provides an appropriate institution: religion for the stage of trust, law and order for the stage of autonomy, the economy for the stage of industry, and so forth. But the economic system, for example, is important for the first stage as well as the second: impoverished peasant families cannot provide sustenance for their babies, so they die of malnutrition or become deformed or are destroyed by their parents. The economy might be more significant for the first stage of life than religion. Yet Erikson offers no concepts to analyze this problem. Erikson assumes that we live in the best of all possible worlds and that everyone else lives there as well. Social institutions for him simply are not a problem. They will manage to adjust themselves. He states, and even repeats the statement word for word later:

Each successive stage and crisis has a special relation to one of the basic elements of society, and this for the simple reason that the human life cycle and man's institutions have evolved together.[17]

Furthermore, the focus on the individual's development leads conceptually to a wholesale legitimation of the society. For the individual to achieve "wholeness" and spiritual fulfillment social arrangements which are very suspect become advantageous. Requirements of the identity crisis, for instance, supercede theoretically requirements of social justice. Since adolescents require a social order led by virtuous and able adults, Erikson states that these adults must be presented as capable even if they are not. In his own words, "In order not to become cynically or apathetically lost, young people must somehow be able to convince themselves that those who succeed in their anticipated adult world thereby shoulder the obligation of being the best."[18] This is close to endorsing indoctrination of youth in loving and respecting any given political leader since it is crucial to mental health. The import of Erikson's individualism is that his theory allows one to see problems arising in the psychological development of the individual, but not in the social system—so that even though he calls repeatedly for an understanding of the mutuality of the individual and the social, his theory leads back ultimately to the same intra-psychism one meets in Freud. The fault for Erikson lies not in the social relations or family structure, but in the individual. The exception is with great leaders who alter the society to fit their own psychic needs and hence automatically readjust the social mechanism for all.

The focus on the individual is also detrimental to a family

theory in that it regresses from Freud's advances in comprehending the libido and the unconscious. Although Erikson wants to synthesize these with his understanding of the ego, he loses, as a follower of Hartmann, the sharp edge of the Freudian concepts. In the last instance Erikson's individual is overcentered in his ego, fully conscious of his quest for values. Therefore no connection can be made between the individual's unconscious and the family and social structures, which are also unconscious.

The primary weakness of Erikson's theory is his failure to develop his concept of child-rearing patterns in relation to a concept of family structure. Here is where all the previously enunciated criticisms come to a head. Spiritualism, organicism, and individualism all lead away from the necessity to conceptualize family structure. Instead, child rearing is important to Erikson only for its role in his fundamentally idealist concern.

We believe that we are dealing here, not with simple causality, but with a mutual assimilation of somatic, mental, and social patterns which amplify one another and make the cultural design for living economical and effective. Only such integration provides a sense of being at home in this world.[19]

But if one wants to understand what families are, how they work, how they transform individuals into the not always comfortable model of their class and society and thus feel "at home in this world," how they change in history and what their optimum structures are, one needs to focus not on the quest for a spiritual home but on the relation between child-rearing patterns, psychic development and family patterns.

When one examines in detail some of the early stages of the life cycle, the residual individualism of Erikson's position emerges clearly. In place of Freud's anal stage, Erikson substitutes the following categories: (1) the psycho-sexual aspect in which the body's libido becomes attached to the anus around the functions of retention and elimination; (2) the ego-strength quality of autonomy vs. shame and doubt; (3) the psycho-social modality of holding on or letting go; (4) the social institution of law and order; and finally (5) the radius of significant relations as "parental persons."[20] Unlike Freud's, Erikson's set of concepts appears to go far in accounting for the social nature of psychic structure and specifically for the family. Yet the relations between the five categories are not well developed and family structure is overlooked.

Erikson's general argument about stage two is that as toilet training becomes the central drama of the child's life, the ego develops a capacity for autonomy or self-doubt. In conjunction with anal eroticism and with the parents' ability to relate their generativity to the child, the child struggles with the task of delimiting the boundaries of its control. The child becomes highly assertive with great shows of will as it discovers its capacity for controlling its bodily pleasure and functions. If the parents respond well to the child's crisis, the child will have the chance to feel good about its efforts at self-control, and will avoid terrible doubts about self-worth. Emotionally, the child has to give up its anal eroticism, its enjoyment of excrement and spontaneous bodily evacuation, in favor of the milder gratification of receiving parental approval for using the toilet. It has to de-eroticize its anus and subject the anus to the regulation of the ego, thereby, Erikson emphasizes, establishing the basis of individualism.

Long ago Freud showed how the anal phase was the basis of the character traits of punctuality, cleanliness, thriftiness— in short, many of the bourgeois virtues. With his wider concern for social issues, Erikson relates these personality traits to the history of capitalism, but in a remarkably inadequate fashion:

A movement in child training began which tended to adjust the human organism from the very start to clock-like punctuality in order to make it a standardized appendix of the industrial world. . . . In pursuit of the adjustment to and mastery over the machine, American mothers (especially of the middle class) found themselves standardizing and overadjusting children who later were expected to personify . . . virile individuality . . .[21]

Confronted with one of the most dramatic transformations of social character in modern history, Erikson can say only that mothers wanted to reduplicate the mastery over machines, a highly dubious claim in any case. First of all, the shift in training methods was not unique to American middle-class mothers, but to bourgeois families everywhere during this phase of capitalist industrialization; it thus has nothing to do with "American" character structure in particular, which is what Erikson is trying to explain. More significantly, there were basic changes in the structure of the family among these groups which Erikson ignores but which are crucial to understanding the new anal character. These toilet-training methods were introduced among families which were increasingly set off against society as private worlds, and in which the child was subject to the authority mainly of its immediate parents, intensifying its emotional attachment to and dependency upon them. These families also demanded a tremendous degree of self-control, of de-eroticization of the body: for males in the activities of the entrepreneur, for females in attaining middle-class respectability or frigidity. They defined themselves by rejecting aristocratic sensuality and lower-class filthiness. They were like the aristocracy in that they did not work with their hands, even though their blood was common. An extraordinary demand for cleanliness thus was prevalent among them. It was in the middle-class family structure that some children were strapped to the potty before the age of one.

Still rooted in individualism, Erikson finds himself imputing motives to mothers because he needs to find an adjusting mechanism between society and personality. Indeed the class which "needed" the anal personality most, the factory workers who were related directly to the schedule of machines, were not, during the early stages of industrialization, organized into privatized nuclear families, and hence did not develop rigid toilet-training methods and anal personalities.

That ego psychology does not come to grips with family structure may be seen also in Erikson's concept of femininity. Instead of Freud's view of women as a negative other, as those who lack a penis, Erikson characteristically emphasizes the positive: feminine psychology is characterized by the presence of inner space. Based on a study of children's play, Erikson concluded that boys' fantasies concerned "outdoor spaces," "free motion of animals, cars and people in open spaces," and "high structures," all symbolic of the penis, while girls' fantasies were represented by the "interior of houses," a symbol of the womb.[22] This data meant, for Erikson, that identities can be divided into masculine and feminine and that these were based on the body. He surmised that the "modalities of a woman's existence reflect the ground plan of the body *among other things* . . ."[23] Aside from a vague "among other things," we are back to Freud's biological determinism. It would appear much more sensible to explain whatever preference for "inner space" might exist in contemporary women by the work they do in the house, since in patriarchal society they are confined there more than men, and by the example of their mothers, who were also confined there and who served as sources of identification. As Erikson describes his notion of "inner space," it is unclear exactly what it explains. Even if, at best, women have body images based on the reproductive organ, it is difficult to see how one can leap from this to a concept of femininity as "inner space." Surely an explanation of girls' playing with interior spaces would be easier if based on family structure rather than body structure. Such a theoretical strategy would permit one to comprehend existing feminine psychology as a consequence of the constituted social world rather than through a fixed biology. In fact, Stoller, in his studies of transsexuals, has argued convincingly that the social world, especially family structure, has far more to do with the psychological determinants of masculinity and femininity than any biological givens.[24] In certain family patterns *biological* males can be *psychological* females and vice versa. Hence society supercedes nature.

The problems in Erikson's theory can be located in his attempts to apply it to history. First, his theory leads him to define the domain of psychohistory not in terms of family history but as the analysis of individuals. Second, the individuals he has selected tend to be religious figures (Luther and Gandhi) who illustrate Erikson's emphasis on the ego's search for spiritual values. Third, Erikson selects periods of great crisis—Reformation Germany, Nazi Germany, de-colonizing India—and presents the resolution of the crisis as a harmonious mediation of individual leaders and their times. Erikson wants to show how the individual's quest for ego strength at each stage of psychic development leads to a resolution for the individual and for the society. Thus Luther and Gandhi struggle for psychic stability in the domain of their personal history. The positive values they attain enable them to present new solutions to the dilemmas that confront their followers.[25] Ego strength and social stability emerge as two sides of the same coin. What Erikson underemphasizes in *Young Man Luther* and *Gandhi's Truth* are the failures and the conflicts. To take one example, Luther's revolt against Rome succeeded only at the cost of suppressing the peasants in the rebellion of 1525. Lutheran religion was established at the cost of reinforcing the oppressive class structure of princely and aristocratic rule. As rich and suggestive as these studies are, they are deeply limited by Erikson's underlying concern with the relation of spiritual values to psychic health.

Erikson's psychohistories also are flawed by failing to illuminate family structure. This failing is most peculiar because scholars who use Erikson's theory focus on the family as a primary subject of investigation. These non-individualist uses of Erikson's theory are often most fruitful. I would like to advert to the work of Lee Rainwater on black ghetto families. Using Erikson's concept of identity, Rainwater suggestively shows how ruling-class images of black inferiority filter down to the black parent, who then projects them onto the children.[26] Rainwater illustrates how ego identity can serve ideological and political purposes in a racist society: how a lower-

class child can have a clear sense of identity, satisfying Erikson's criteria of ego strength, but that this internalized identity can also be self-destructive. Rainwater's study also suggests an explanation for the concern with revising the black
group image in the late sixties. The success of black militant
organizations, and slogans such as "black is beautiful," were
probably associated with an effort to undo psychologically the
negative identities internalized in childhood. Perhaps all protest movements have a psychological dimension such as this.
The example of the consciousness-raising groups of the
women's movement comes quickly to mind: women struggled
to extricate themselves from "feminine" identities which fit
well into patriarchal, sex-role differentiated families. In all of
these cases, we see the rich possibilities of Erikson's theory for
family history.

In the main, however, Erikson's theory flounders by trying
to explain historical changes through the reciprocal interplay
of individual life cycles. The force of structural transformations, such as the industrial revolution, which are by no means
always synchronized between various levels of society, is lost.

I now turn to Parsons and his school, who try precisely to
integrate a version of Freudian theory with their own theory
of the social system. The Parsonians are much like the ego
psychologists in de-emphasizing the role of the instincts and
in viewing the individual's relation to society as an organic,
harmonious, self-adjusting interplay. The Parsonians advance
beyond Erikson, however, in comprehending social reality
through a model of interpersonal relations, rather than depending on a notion of individualism.

The comparison of Erikson and Parsons is striking: a psychologist and a sociologist, both so in tune with the dominant
American culture, both nourished spiritually in Germany
(Erikson by Freud and by a youth spent in Germany, Parsons
by his debt to Max Weber). While Erikson makes liberal hu-
manism into religious values, Parsons transmutes social values
and myths into liberalism. The psychologist strives for the
spiritual wholeness of the individual by studying the life cycle;

the sociologist conceptualizes the spiritual wholeness of society by studying the socialization process. Both theorize about values from their separate disciplinary perspectives and both find an organic harmony between individual and society. In neither case does social experience damage, torment or oppress the individual; in neither case does the domination, conflict, and misery fostered by a particular social order come into relief. Both theories are eminently historical and geneticist, only to end by extracting the core of their positions from the temporal dimension. As Erikson universalizes the life cycle, Parsons eternalizes virtually every major institution of contemporary capitalist society.

After World War II the theories of Talcott Parsons dominated American social science, with strains in this hegemony only beginning to appear in the late 1950s. Parsons philosophized world history as a process of "modernization" in which social functions are increasingly "differentiated" into separate structures. Adam Smith's notion of economic progress through the division of labor was now applied to the total social system. If Smith saw efficiency coming out of capitalism, Parsons saw order and equilibrium crystallizing out of advancing modernity. Parsons is the anti-Marx par excellence: society to him is a system whose parts are delicately balanced in the whole and whose essence is not the mode of production but values and roles. Hence the family, in Parsonian sociology, takes on an importance that it never had for Marx. The family is the agent of socialization, the prime mechanism for imprinting in the new generation the values of the old, and thereby guaranteeing social order.

This notion of the family's function, whatever its difficulties, would appear to support a wide relativism with regard to family structure. Any family structure could, in principle, provide the service of socialization to society at large. Yet here as elsewhere Parsons' general principles of society have a way of reducing themselves to the particular institutions of capitalism. All families are reduced to a few socializing mechanisms which turn out to be those of the "nuclear family." The result of Parsons' theory is that by collapsing abstract principles into concrete capitalist practice he makes our institutions appear as universal and necessary, unchanging and unchangable. Parsons conceives the modern family by picking out certain features of it which he then claims to be the essence of all families.[27] This theoretical sleight of hand is the essence of ideological thinking. Yet while most ideologists proclaim the given order as natural, Parsons first deduces his basic principles of society and then claims that all of history is moving toward them.

Parsons defines the structure of the family in relation to its basic function of socialization, and minimizes the importance of reproduction. He reasons that two structures only are essential to the family: a hierarchy of generations and a differentiation of socializing agents into "instrumental" and "expressive" figures.[28] He postulates that all families contain these features and that the nuclear family manifests them particularly well. Without going any further one can see that Parsons has elevated parental domination of children as well as contemporary sex roles into inviolable principles. The husband, for Parsons, alone can provide the instrumental role model, and only the wife can provide the expressive role model.

Confronted by anomalous anthropological evidence in which either the role models do not conform to the nuclear family or the immediate parents are not the primary socializing agents, Parsons and his followers employ two strategies. Thus in the case of Margaret Mead, who has shown that women can serve as instrumental role models, they deny the validity of her demonstration out of hand.[29] Alternately they argue that such data bespeaks a society at a low level of "differentiation" or "modernization." When, for instance, a Parsonian is faced with a pre-industrial community which is dominated by kinship, he manages to find beneath the primary socializing group which happens not to resemble a nuclear family the family mechanisms of today's middle-class family.[30] In this way, kinship structures become nothing but the nu-

clear family prior to differentiation. Even in these radically
different worlds Parsons is able to find the American middle-
class mother nurturing the boy to manhood and the American
middle-class father providing the instrumental function
which orients the boy toward achievement and skills. Finally,
to Parsons, the incest taboo serves the same function in kinship structures as it does today, guaranteeing the authority of
the parents over the child by securing the father's sexual privileges with his wife.[31] Parsons thinks he has proven that the
nuclear family is universal, when in fact he has denied the
intelligibility of non-industrial society. The family of industrial capitalism is protected ideologically since its structure no
longer appears to be new and historically constituted but only
the result of progressive "differentiation."

Parsons is unhappy with Freud for much the same reasons
as Erikson. He notes Freud's incapacity to understand psychic
structure as mutually dependent on social interactions:
"Freud and his followers, by concentrating on the single personality, have failed to consider adequately the implications of
the individual's interaction with other personalities to form a
system."[32] Again like Erikson, Parsons diminishes the role of
the instincts, inflates the proportions of the ego, and points to
the importance of the internalization of values in the family:
"The central focus of the process of socialization lies in the
internalization of the culture of the society . . . [its] patterns
of value . . ."[33] But more than Erikson, Parsons is unhappy
with Freud for not taking into account the cognitive level of
child development: "The cognitive definition of the object
world does not seem to have been problematical to Freud."[34]

In presenting the cognitive level Parsons denies the instinctual level of the psycho-sexual stages. For him these stages are
nothing but learning experiences. In the oral stage, the mother-child interaction is for the child simply a process of learning
about the meaning of the mother's acts.[35] The personality is
formed not as a process of the modification of the instincts, but
as the differentiation of an internalized object system.[36] Parsons is right to argue that the object, in psychoanalytic theory,

is inert: it simply receives a "charge of cathectic significance" by the subject, while the mutuality of the interaction is overlooked. Yet his model is equally one-sided, for it leaves out the level of unconscious emotional structure as well as the body.

In 1955 Parsons responded to arguments that the nuclear family was collapsing. In its defense he proclaimed that what appeared to be a collapse was in fact only another step in the process of differentiation. He observed in America a reduction in the importance of kinship units other than the nuclear family and a transfer of functions from the nuclear family to other institutions, such as schools, social-service organizations, churches and the state. Parsons interpreted these changes not as a threat but as a deepening significance of the nuclear family. The particular functions that it was best suited to perform were becoming more emphasized, more crucial to the society. In this context he revised his model of the nuclear family. The structure of the nuclear family now consisted of the following: a separate dwelling for grandparents, insuring privacy and isolation of the family; an equal division of inheritance; a separation of "occupational organization from kinship"; a personal world beyond public affairs; a function of socializing children to "stabilize adult personalities"; a small size; a total commitment of parents to supervise scrupulously the child's life.[37] Parsons specified a set of social conditions, incomplete and inaccurate in some cases to be sure, which develop in the child the values of capitalism but, more important, which implant the psychic structure articulated by Freud. In developing my own theory of the family a major problem will be to generalize the social conditions, some of which Parsons names, so as to account for family structures other than the bourgeois one.

Although it appears that Parsons has given us a concept of the family which is far more historical and social than Freud and Erikson,[38] this is only partly true. Parsons deals quite well with the problem of relating the formation of psychic structure to social interactions. He points to internalization and identification as the crucial mechanisms of socialization and the formation of psychic structure. He also comprehends the nature of society as a system, and he cannot be accused of introducing atomistic individualism in his theory of the family. Where Parsons falters, however, is in taking the patriarchal bourgeois family as the norm.

His treatment of women, for example, betrays this flaw quite clearly. In place of the traditional idea that anatomy is destiny, he presents the American social order as destiny. Women alone can provide the expressive function. Boys alone can be oriented to achievement in the adult world because they undergo a more difficult process than girls of shifting identifications from Mama to Papa. Even where Parsons sees the historical source of male dominance he obfuscates the issue. The primacy of the father, he notes, results from the "strong emphasis in the Western world on types of achievement and rules of conduct which transcend the familial situation."[39] But he will say equally that only the male parental figure can provide the instrumental function and the point of change from family to society *in any social system.* In fact, the whole distinction between expressive and instrumental socializing agents must be called into question. At most, it applies to the division of labor between husband and wife in bourgeois families. When used in relation to other family structures it serves only to obfuscate the situation.

Although rejected by many sociologists, Parsons' theory of society and the family has been used extensively by historical sociologists and historians themselves. In each case they have been led by the theory to search for the fit between the family and society—for, in other words, the parallel origins and ultimate congruence of industrial capitalist society with the nuclear family.[40] But the facts do not bear out the theory: the nuclear family began before industrialization, on the one hand, and on the other industrialization did not lead immediately and for all levels of society to the nuclear family. Modernization theory leads to a unitary view of social change. Yet there can be no linear, continuous, homogeneous view of the history of the family, no one-to-one match between the economy and the family, and no privileging of the traits of the nuclear family as the index and standard for all others. To the extent that Parsonian theory leads to such privileging it must be rejected as an inadequate conceptual tool for comprehending the family.

Chapter 4

THE LANGUAGE OF
THE FAMILY

> *This mention of the forms of familial ideology (the*
> *ideology of paternity-maternity-conjugality-infancy*
> *and their interactions) is crucial, for it implies the*
> *following conclusion—that Lacan could not express,*
> *given his theoretical formation—that is, that no the-*
> *ory of psycho-analysis can be produced without basing*
> *it on historical materialism (on which the theory of the*
> *formations of familial ideology depends, in the last*
> *instance).*
>
> LOUIS ALTHUSSER

THE WORK OF the French psychoanalyst Jacques Lacan[1] and his
school in reconstructing Freudian theory in relation to linguistic and anthropological structuralism claims to have enormous significance for the theory of the family. Lacan has indeed accomplished the most extensive rethinking to date of the
basic concepts of psychoanalysis. If his positions are correct,
a critical theory of the family would be impossible. For Lacan
claims to have discovered the primordial psychic experiences
through which an infant passes from the realm of nature to the
realm of culture. Psychoanalysis, according to him, speaks to
a universal process which cannot be historicized and which
has deep implications for fundamental questions of philosophy. In Lacan's reading, Freud is a philosopher concerned
with the question of the nature of truth, not a mere social
scientist. In France, Lacan's writings are debated not only in
the limited context of professional psychoanalysis but among
students of culture in general.

From his earliest writings, Lacan's polemical thrust was to oppose the main directions of psychoanalytic thinking. In particular he rejected American ego psychology with its emphasis on social adjustment and ego strength. Under the sway of the Americans, psychoanalysis had given up, in Lacan's words, "the most living terms of its experience: the unconscious and sexuality."[2] But the call to return to the unconscious and sexuality was not for him, as it was for the Freudo-Marxists, a reemphasis of instinct theory. Lacan rejected the biologism of instinct theory just as did the ego psychologists. Instead, the key to reviving the original genius of Freud was found in the Word. The project of Lacanian psychoanalysis was to explore in depth the notion of the "talking cure." Lacan's famous return to Freud was an elaborate reconceptualization of psychoanalysis from the axiom that it begins and ends with the words spoken between the analyst and the patient.

Very selectively Lacan accepted certain trends in recent psychoanalysis. He applauded the emphasis being placed on counter-transference, on the active role of the analyst in the process of therapy. The analyst represented to him, as we shall see, a certain function of language with which the patient had not adequately come to terms during childhood. Also he accepted the new concept of libidinal object relations, since this allowed psychoanalysis to benefit from the insights of "existential phenomenology." Above all Lacan viewed as helpful to his own effort the work of Melanie Klein and her group in England on the analysis of children and the pre-Oedipal relation of child and mother.[3] Here precisely was an advance in psychoanalysis that could be integrated into Lacan's own understanding of the formation of the psyche through language.

Behind Lacan's use of language theory in psychoanalysis stands the tradition of the structural linguistics of Ferdinand de Saussure and Roman Jakobson. In order to understand Lacan's terminology, only a few basic principles of structural linguistics need be summarized. Saussure and Jakobson analyzed language as a system, not as a tool for individual expression. To Jakobson language is possible only by a combination of elements based on the difference between the elements. Parts of words (phonemes) are combined unconsciously in the language system. The speaker is not aware of language at the level of phonemes, but this level is essential nonetheless. A similar shift away from the conscious individual to the language system was earlier developed by Saussure in his concept of the sign.[4] Nineteenth-century linguistics was concerned with the mental image (the signified) which the speaker sought to represent, and with its relations to the referent (the thing). Saussure placed a new emphasis on the intelligibility of the word itself (the signifier) and how language is composed of relations between signifiers in which the speaker becomes an *object* of the system. Thus the speaker's use of the pronoun "I" refers to the speaker not as a subject but as an object for the implied other object "you." Primacy falls on the difference between the two signifiers. In this way language is understood as a theory of signifiers which are completely relational. Meaning is not a product of the speaking subject using language as a tool of expression: instead meaning is a result of the structure of differences between signifiers. The structuralists shift the level of understanding language away from that of the subject with his intentional meaning to the objective system of signifiers. Hence the signifiers structure the subject and language forms the individual, not the reverse.

Here exactly was the theory that Lacan needed to remove psychoanalysis from its dependence on biologism and on the hydraulic metaphor of the instincts which derived from the physics of Freud's day. Through language theory, that is, through a theory of the constitution of a specifically human nature, psychoanalysis could be established on firm scientific grounds. The way the child enters the system of language, the world of the symbolic, was the key for Lacan to the formation of the psyche. Language would be understood not in the Chomskyan fashion as an innate capacity for learning rules of speech but as the insertion of the subject into a system which was in contradiction with the emotional nexus of the mother-child relation.

The application of structural linguistics to psychoanalysis made by Lacan is extremely complex; indeed one suspects it is almost incomprehensible except to the initiated.[5] Nevertheless some aspects of the project are clear enough and important enough to mention briefly. In the first place, Lacan redefined the unconscious in terms of language: his notorious basic rule is "The unconscious is structured like a language." The principles of dream work uncovered by Freud—displacement and condensation—were to Lacan homologous to the language rules of metaphor and metonymy. Far from a "seething cauldron" of instinctual energies, the unconscious, according to Lacan, was a realm of linguistic mechanisms, a text requiring deciphering. Henceforth therapy sessions became a text as well, in which the unconscious made its appearance and was subject to analysis through linguistic principles. The patient spoke "empty words," words whose absences were indications of the unconscious. The role of therapy was to restore the "full word" to the patient, which meant that the patient would recognize himself in his unconscious without eliminating the unconscious or making it conscious. This was impossible, since the individual was always decentered in the unconscious.

The analyst was to make a "symptomatic reading" of the words or text of the patient, looking for absences, words not there, and analyzing them as repressed metaphors. The unconscious of the patient, working through metaphors and metonymies, was continually deflecting him from his true desires. Lacan interpreted Freud's motto "Where id was there ego shall be" to mean that the result of therapy was not to absorb the id into the ego of the patient, to make the patient fully conscious or fully centered as the ego psychologists claimed, but to bring the patient to an understanding, reconciliation or acceptance of his lack of unity. It is the ego of the analyst which takes the linguistic place of the patient's id, Lacan asserted. The end of therapy is an acceptance by the patient of the discontinuity between his ego and his unconscious desires. In this sense the "empty word" has become the "full word," the word restored to the expression of unconscious desire.

The preceding description of Lacan's position remains incomplete without some consideration of his concept of the symbolic. According to Lacan the subject is simultaneously within three different levels or functions: the symbolic, the imaginary, and the real. He used these terms in so many different ways that I make no pretense to a complete account of them. It is fairly clear, however, that "the symbolic" means the world of language, of culture, of discourse. "The imaginary" is the realm of the ego, of the subject's false self-consciousness, of his biographical unity. What ego psychologists call identity, Lacan calls the imaginary. It is just that illusory sense of the self-centeredness of desire in the ego which he tries to work against at all points. The third notion, that of "the real," is very weakly defined and erratically used.[6] We can say, with some oversimplification, that the real is the world of material objects and relations.

The strong concept in the triad is the symbolic. For Lacan, every human being must enter into the symbolic, the world of language, through a circuitous path which leaves one scarred for life. If men were creatures of the symbolic all along there would be no need for psychoanalysis. But this is impossible to Lacan, not only because of one's individual history, which is always damaging, and not only because of one's incapacity for the symbolic during early, pre-linguistic years as infants, but finally because even language itself posits the individual and shapes the individual in unconscious ways. The subject does not form the symbolic, Lacan warns, but the reverse, the symbolic structures the subject. In order to comprehend how the subject enters the symbolic, we must turn to Lacan's notion of the mirror stage.[7]

At birth the individual is not a complete human being. Physiologically the nervous system is not fully formed and socially language has not yet been acquired. Above all, Lacan asserts with Freud that the psyche has not yet been structured. In the early months and years of life, the individual lives in a symbiotic relationship with the mother. Even after the sever-

ing of the umbilical cord, the child has not yet separated itself
from the mother psychologically: it is not yet able to differentiate itself consciously from its maternal environment. Yet right
from the start language has begun to work.[8] The child is
spoken to and named, and therefore it has a place in the discourse of the other, the words of its mother. As the child
begins to become aware of itself as separate from its mother,
as a distinct psychic entity, it does so only by taking itself to
be its mother. There is a mirror effect, Lacan argues, in which
the image the child has of itself is in fact the image of its
mother. Hence the child's early ego, or pre-ego—Lacan calls
it the ideal ego—takes shape as a misrecognition: the child
understands itself not as itself but as the other, as its mother.
From the beginning the ego is constituted as an illusory incor-
poration of the other; when it names itself it is only naming
the other, or, in linguistic terms, its place is defined by the
discourse of the other.

Lacan also conceptualized the mirror stage in relation to
Hegel's concept of recognition and desire.[9] The infant has a
sensuous relation with its mother. Its needs are fulfilled by her
and she is in tactile relation with it. In addition to needs, and
quite distinct from them, the child has desires (libido) and, as
Hegel says, the prime desire is to be recognized by the other's
desire. The desire of the mother and the desire of the child
thus enter into a complex, confused relation. The mother's
desire concerning the child has formed even before it was
born. When the child arrives it is incorporated by the mother's
desire for it before its own desire is really distinct. The child's
desire is thus structured by the mother's desire for it. The
mirror image that is incorporated by the child as itself is the
mother's desire for it. The realm through which the unconscious desire of the child becomes structured is what Lacan
terms the imaginary.[10]

The significance of the mirror stage is profound. It means,
in the first place, that there is a necessary, an inherent condition of human maturation, in which the child's ego will be set
in an illusory misrecognition of itself. There is an inherent

alienation, one could say, in the structure of human life. In addition to this, Lacan shows that the structuring of desire in the mirror stage also points beyond itself to the symbolic. The path out of the imaginary is provided by the symbolic. In the fullness of the mother-infant relation something is missing, something profoundly important to the psychic formation of the child—and this is the phallus, the symbol of the absent "law of the father." Both mother and child are sexual beings. Sexuality for Lacan as for Freud is crucial to the libido of the child, whose desire must take shape either as male or female. In the mother's discourse the child is labelled sexually, and hence the mother's sexuality determines in important ways the formation of the child. But the mother is the one who does not have a phallus. Hence an *absence* is inserted into the mother-child relation. This absence is the essence of the symbolic to Lacan.[11]

In order for the child to attain the function of the symbolic it must be able to deal with absence. What is not there causes the child to discover and handle a new sort of phenomenon. In this way the phallus which is absent is above all a symbolic, not a real phallus. It is the mother, according to Lacan, who names the father in her discourse as the one with the phallus. The name of the father is equated with the phallus in the child's experience. The absence of these signs compels the child to integrate them into his experience in a way not required by his relation with his mother, that is, through the symbolic. The name of the father is the first symbol the child learns which is not associated with sensuality and which is beyond the structure of the mirror stage.

Lacan explains, however, that the name of the father involves something else which is crucial for the symbolic, that is, castration. In Lacanian psychoanalysis castration plays a role quite different from that in Freud. As we have seen, Freud spoke of castration in terms of a ubiquitous threat that middle-class parents carried out against their children during the genital phase of libidinal formation. Lacan, on the contrary, views castration in relation to language. Castration is not so much a physical or emotional threat to the sexual organ as it is a confirmation that something is not there. He uses castration in an extremely metaphorical sense to mean that any inhibition of the child's desire is like the absence of the phallus in the mother.

The mother as a being without a phallus or as a speaker who names the father introduces an absence which "castrates" the desire of the child. In order to cope with this situation the child must restructure its desire to account for absence and this can be done only through the symbolic order. The child then is able to speak language in a full sense. But there is another twist. The loss, so to speak, for the child is that its desire will always be a desire for something absent, or, in Lacan's term, the child's desire will always be a lack. Desire itself can never be fulfilled, since desire is structured primordially around an absence. The initiation of the child into the human world of language has thus required two forms of alienation: first, that the ego is fixed in the imaginary, forever naming itself but actually referring to another; second, that desire is structured in a continuous but futile effort to satisfy a lack, and hence it goes from one object to another without ever being capable of satisfaction.

The importance for family theory of Lacan's use of linguistics is that it appears to shift the center of psychoanalysis away from the study of intra-psychic instincts toward the spoken patterns of interaction between family members.[12] Since Lacanian psychoanalysis views the unconscious as constituted by the linguistic play between parents and child, the individualistic character of Freud's categories has perhaps been transcended. The failure of Lacan to provide case studies compels one to turn to his followers to examine this question.

Françoise Dolto and Maud Mannoni, both child psychologists of the Lacan school, provide lucid examples of Lacan's theory which we can use to test its value for family theory. Studying children who have been labelled mentally retarded and institutionalized accordingly, Mannoni demonstrates how the child must be understood through the linguistic operations of the entire family. In cases of retardedness she writes: "What misleads us is the influence of the family that is also determined to preserve the place which it has assigned to the child. This is why the study of the retarded, like that of the psychotic, is not confined to the subject but begins with the family."[13] The desire of the mother, her unconscious attitude toward the child, operates as a signifier which the child's desire incorporates. This dialectic establishes a family pattern in which the child takes a place that it cannot alter. As Mannoni explains, "The Oedipus complex (the introduction of a Symbolic Order) is above all the expression of an unsolved problem of the parents in regard to their own parents, of which the child, by his symptom, has become the representative signifier."[14] In *Dominique,* a masterfully presented case study, Dolto analyzes a boy's unconscious through the reciprocal structure of the family's desire. She writes, "Children are cancelled out as individuals to become part of the carefully balanced system of unconscious libidinal dynamics in the family group, whose love requires the child to respect authority and submit to it."[15]

The developing child requires spoken words from its mother in order to allow it to express and communicate its own desires. Mannoni shows how the desire of the child depends on the relation with the mother:

When the child cannot gain recognition by the Other in his status as a subject who desires, he becomes alienated in a part of his body. The child's relationship with his mother remains in a field from which he has no outlet but the perpetual renewal of demands, without ever acquiring the right to assume desire. In effect, he enters his mother's dialectics as a partial object.[16]

In one particularly clear case, a mother was disturbed by any movement in the house, by a change in any object or person. Accordingly, the child became passive and immobile, and was diagnosed as mentally retarded. As Lacanians, Dolto and Mannoni regard the development of the symbolic function in the child as the crucial step in the formation of its desire. The way the child appropriates the symbolic function determines its psychic fate. Within the mother's discourse with the child, the father is introduced as a castrating figure. The burden is placed on the mother, according to them, to present the child with the castrating name of the father, and by dealing with castration the child will enter the symbolic realm, in their words, become "humanized." In the case of Dominique, Dolto concludes, "What traumatized Dominique as the result of the birth of his little sister was not the frustration of tenderness, it was the fact that he was put back to the breast and deprived of the fatherly educative demands that would have preserved and supported his human identity."[17] Similarly, Mannoni, speaking of a case of feeblemindedness, writes:

The feebleminded or psychotic child responds to the threat of the Other with his body. His body is inhabited by panic; he lacks the Symbolic dimension that would enable him to confront the desire of the Other without being in danger of being ensnared by him. . . . Because the paternal signifier has never come into confrontation with the maternal unconscious, the subject finds himself deprived of the meaning of his own life, and in danger of not feeling himself to be the master of his own impulses.[18]

In this way, Lacanian psychoanalysis leads to the comprehension of the language of the family. Whatever the therapeutic value of Lacan's theory—and reading the works of Dolto and Mannoni convince one of its efficacy—certain limitations appear in its conceptualization of the family.

In the first place, Lacan only reinforces Freud's masculine bias, albeit at the level of language and not that of anatomy. Luce Irigaray, a critic of Lacan, asks if the Freudian reliance on the phallus as a symbolic law is not the result of patriarchal culture rather than an inherent necessity of language or biology. She questions why the phallus alone is a "guarantor of meaning," why there cannot be "vagina envy."[19] If the devaluation of the female sexual organ is simply the result of its relative invisibility in comparison with the male, Irigaray suggests that this may be the consequence of the long Western metaphysical tradition, which is trapped in the valuation of the visible. It is more likely, she contends, that the culture blinds us to the value of the female organ. In another criticism along these lines, Catherine Baliteau complains that the Lacanians are always blaming the mother for the child's problems, even to the point of insisting that it is the mother's task to introduce the father and the principle of the symbolic phallus. But where is the father while the mother tends the child, seducing it to her desire at the level of the imaginary? Is it a biological or a linguistic necessity that the father not speak to the child or care for it during the first years of life? Or is he busy somewhere else, in the business world? Against the Freud-Lacan phallocentrism, Baliteau asks, "How is it that the woman really lacks a penis, while the man does not really lack a clitoris? Is it true that the clitoris presents, in relation to the penis, a 'real morphological inferiority' (Dolto)? But since when is the Symbolic evaluated in centimeters?"[20] Irigaray also questions Lacan's phallocentric law. Is it really the universal law of mankind that the phallus alone can represent the symbolic, or is this the law merely of men? She continues:

If under the cover of the Law current practice resolves the seduction, it would appear just as urgent to investigate *the seductive function of the law itself*, and its role in the production of fantasies. The law, by suspending the realization of a seductive desire, organizes, arranges the imaginary universe as much as it prescribes it, interprets it, symbolizes it.[21]

The point of these feminist criticisms is not to deny the reality and current force of the law of the phallus; it is to question its universal and inevitable theoretical status and power.

The feminist critique of Lacan calls in question, beyond the specific charge of phallocentrism, the entire conceptualization of the symbolic. Lacan's use of the symbolic is opaque and riddled with difficulties. At some points, he seems to define it as simply the realm of discursive language, while at other points he uses it in a more Freudian way (perhaps even Jungian) as the organization of the unconscious. In the latter case, certain symbols become privileged over others: the phallus, the name of the father, the law—all these become key terms with significance well beyond the mundane world of communication. There does not seem to be any convincing reason why these signifiers in particular should play such a large role in defining and organizing the human psyche.

Furthermore, in Lacan's effort to point to the importance of language, his theory takes on the cast of idealism. In a totally undialectical manner, Lacan introduces surreptitiously a metaphysics of the Word. He proclaims, "It is the world of words which creates the world of things—things originally confused in the *hic et nunc* of the all-in-the-process-of-becoming —by giving its concrete being to their essence, and its ubiquity to what has been from everlasting."[22] Lacan's axiom—words create things—is fundamental to his thought, since it gives primacy to language over social structure. While language certainly has a determining as well as mediating role in the formation of consciousness of the world, the social system also determines and limits linguistic possibility. To speak to a child as if one lives in a matriarchal society is probably impossible, for example. Language is not totally malleable but shaped by a social and natural system which in good measure precedes it. Lacan's metaphysic of language becomes damaging from our perspective in that it precludes an analysis of family structure. It would be difficult to use Lacanian psychoanalysis to register the criteria for differentiating family patterns and their relation to social systems, except in the weakest manner through variations in language.

These inadequacies in Lacan's thought become especially prominent when one analyzes his reliance on the incest taboo in relation to the Oedipus complex, which is for him the point of entry into the symbolic order. Since the prohibition of incest, a form of castration, is found in numerous societies, Lacan employs it as an argument for the universality of the Oedipus complex. In doing so he relies heavily on the concept of the prohibition of incest developed by Lévi-Strauss in *Elementary Structures of Kinship*. Lacan writes:

This is precisely where the Oedipus complex—insofar as we continue to recognize it as covering the whole field of our experience with its signification—may be said, in this connection, to mark the limits that our discipline assigns to subjectivity: that is to say, what the subject can know of his unconscious participation in the movement of the complex structures of marriage ties, by verifying the symbolic effects in his individual existence of the tangential movement towards incest which has manifested itself ever since the coming of a universal community. The primordial Law is therefore that which in regulating marriage ties superimposes the kingdom of culture on that of nature abandoned to the law of copulation.[23]

The entire structure of Lacan's argument depends upon his claim that his use of the concept of incest prohibition is the same as that found in Lévi-Strauss. I want to argue in what follows that this claim cannot be sustained.

It is true that the general problematic of the two thinkers is parallel: both want to apply the insights of structural linguistics to their respective fields of psychoanalysis and anthropology. In other words, they search for the structural universals in the formation of the psyche and society and they understand this formation as parallel with or analogous to the universal of learning language in childhood. Lévi-Strauss has redefined the field of anthropology as the study of the systems of exchange which constitute society. He claims that exchanges of goods and women must be analyzed like exchanges of language in communications.[24] Society is constituted and held together, according to him, precisely by its system of reciprocal exchanges. The essence of society is the flow of signs, back and forth between sections of the community, creating a continuous sense of mutual obligation among the members and reinforcing the bonds of solidarity. Anthropology, in the vision of Lévi-Strauss, should not be concerned primarily with institutions understood as functions satisfying needs in the tradition of Malinowski, but with the unconscious structure of exchange. Lévi-Strauss writes,

The primitive and irreducible character of the basic unit of kinship, as we have defined it, is actually a direct result of the universal presence of an incest taboo. This is really saying that in human society a man must obtain a woman from another man who gives him a daughter or a sister. Thus we do not need to explain how the maternal uncle emerged in the kinship structure: He does not emerge —he is present initially. Indeed, the presence of the maternal uncle is a necessary precondition for the structure to exist. The error of traditional anthropology, like that of traditional linguistics, was to consider the terms, and not the relations between the terms.[25]

Just as an infant has the capacity to utter every phoneme but loses this facility in the process of learning a specific language with a limited repertoire of phonemes, so each society develops a specific system of exchange of women and a specific system of myths. The anthropologist can study these particular structures with the goal of accumulating the entire repertoire and thereby having at his disposal the universal structures of mankind. With his project of deriving anthropology from linguistics, Lévi-Strauss adopts the same weak premise that we saw earlier in Lacan; namely, that "symbols are more real than that which they symbolize; the signifier precedes and determines the signified."[26]

In the prohibition of incest Lévi-Strauss believes he has found the primordial rule which transforms a group of biological creatures into a human society. The incest taboo can reveal the essence of society since it is responsible for constituting society. The mystery of the incest taboo that has for so long puzzled anthropologists is unravelled when it is seen as establishing a structure of exchanges between separate groups. Since it is virtually universal—some restriction on marriage is found in every society—the incest taboo has the spontaneity of a natural impulse. But since it is not a biological necessity (and Lévi-Strauss demonstrates this very convincingly through the case of cross-cousin marriage, which is desired, whereas parallel-cousin marriage, no closer biologically, is often proscribed) it partakes of a rule, of a cultural imposition. Part nature and part culture, the incest taboo serves as the transition to human society. In the words of Lévi-Strauss, the prohibition of incest is in origin neither purely cultural nor purely natural, nor is it a composite mixture of elements from both nature and culture. It is the fundamental step because of which, by which, but above all in which, the transition from nature to culture is accomplished. . . . The prohibition of incest is where nature transcends itself. It sparks the formation of a new and more complex type of structure and is superimposed upon the simpler structures of physical life through integration. . . . It brings about and is in itself the advent of a new order.[27]

The incest taboo is not so much a *negative restriction* on the pool of marriage partners as a guarantee that one group will send its daughters to another, providing that the other group does likewise. For Lévi-Strauss—and this is most important for family theory—the incest taboo prevents the conjugal family from closing in on itself and insures that the wider society will take precedence over the family by marrying outward to non-family groups. The direction of impact of the incest taboo in primitive society is not inward toward relations between the immediate family, but outward to the larger society. It refers not to the sexual interests of the individual but to the requirements of the society at large. The restriction of sexual activity and marriage partners establishes society at large as the prime field of sexual objects and undercuts the autonomy and the authority of the immediate family. For Lacan and for psychoanalysis in general, on the contrary, the incest taboo sets the emotional relationships *within* the family in their final structure.

One could argue that the result of the castration threat and the denial of the parents as sexual objects for the children is to direct the children beyond the family for sexual partners. The little boy gives up his mother but comes to understand that some day he will be a man like his father and be able to possess a woman of his own. In this way, the passing of the Oedipus complex appears to function like the incest taboo in Lévi-Strauss. Such an interpretation, which is that of Jacques Lacan, would effectively prevent an historical understanding of family structure and personality, engulfing all family structures under the same universal law with the same psychological consequences. We must therefore analyze carefully the alleged identity of the incest taboo and Oedipus.

The first major difference which calls the identity of the concepts into question is the locus of authority for the prohibition. In the case of Lévi-Strauss it is clear that the social system in general institutes the prohibition of incest; it is an agreement, conscious or unconscious, between families or clans. For Lacan and Freud, on the contrary, the place of authority is the immediate parents, real or symbolic. Their action in relation to their children institutes the law. This difference is crucial because it is the key to the wide disparity, covered up by Lacan, between the two situations. The Oedipus complex, which begins with the prohibition of the child's sexual activity, falls within the emotionally charged context of parent-child relations in the privatized, nuclear family. Isolated in the nuclear family, the child's entire emotional life is centered on its parents, on their affection and hostility, on their autonomous power to set the rules for the child, on the depth of the identifications the child makes with them. In such a context, the inhibition of the child's new-found genital play only serves to intensify its emotional ties with its parents. Castration, a highly traumatic event arousing deep anger in the child which it can only internalize, sets in motion a deep and permanent alteration of personality structure: the child internalizes the authority of the parents in the form of a super-ego. The super-ego, in turn, assures that the child will *forever be a member of the family*, will forever carry within the dictates and emotional representations of the father. It assures that even when the child goes outside the family to seek a mate the emotional meaning of the choice will echo heavily the parent of the opposite sex. It makes certain that the bourgeoisie, a group without strong kinship ties, will be able to transmit property through generations. One could say that the nuclear family insures that the psychic meaning of marriage is only to repeat, to reduplicate the original family relations: the boy finds only his mother in his wife.

Things proceed quite the opposite in the context of the
incest taboo in Lévi-Strauss; there the weight of the prohibition falls not on imploding the experience within the conjugal
family. If this were true the whole purpose of the prohibition
would be lost. In Lévi-Strauss' primitive societies it is crucial
that the prohibition of incest lead to an alliance between separate groups, that it extend the family outside itself, destroying
its social and emotional autonomy. The exchange of women in
primitive society establishes the priority of the society over
the family. Any suggestion that the daughter is doing no more
than seeking a substitute father would vitiate the whole game.
The rules of exchange and reciprocity would become a sham
and the groups would dissolve into conflicting factions. Societies can be instituted for Lévi-Strauss only by destroying the
conjugal family.

This argument is reinforced by understanding the differences between primitive and modern societies and their family
structures, differences which Lévi-Strauss minimizes because
of his concern with discovering universal laws. The anthropologist wants to argue that the kinship system of primitive society, exchanging women between sub-groups, constitutes the bonds of solidarity which congeal diverse individuals
into a society. Hence the individual takes his social position
through the system of exchange. But in modern society, capitalist and socialist alike, social position is not established automatically through kinship. With the destruction of the European
aristocracy, kinship no longer was the primary means of establishing the social status and relative positions of individuals.
Property took the place of blood ties. Bonds of solidarity were
shifted from kinship to relations of labor and capital or to
national identity. Marriage rules no longer served the heavy
purpose of instituting reciprocal obligations between sub-
groups of society. Lévi-Strauss recognizes the difference:

In our opinion, the source of all the uncertainties surrounding the
problem of incest and the study of marriage prohibitions is none
other than our tendency to think of marriage in terms of our own

institutions, as a unilateral act of transfer and as an asymmetrical institution, when in fact (and even among ourselves) it is a bilateral act and a symmetrical institution. The only difference is that preponderantly in primitive societies the symmetrical structure of the institution involves two groups, while in modern societies the symmetrical elements are on the one hand a class tending to be reduced solely to the individual, and on the other a class which extends so far as to be confused with the social group as a whole.[28]

In other words, while the prohibition of incest is common to primitive and modern societies, the kinship structure of the latter tends to confront the individual with the entire society of the opposite sex, who are not married, as possible mates. Now it can surely be said that the incest prohibition is universal and that is the end of it, as Lacan would like. But one can also study the enormous difference in family structure and, by implication, emotional structure, between the two social formations.

If this argument has sown seeds of doubt about the wisdom of equating the incest prohibition in primitive society with the Oedipus complex uncovered by Freud in the context of late nineteenth-century Europe, efforts by Lacan's followers to find the same Oedipus in Africa, contrary to their intentions, only reinforce the doubt. Echoing the debate between Ernest Jones and Bronislaw Malinowski of the 1920s, and later between Géza Roheim and Erich Fromm, Marie-Cecile and Edmond Ortigues, Lacanian psychoanalysts, claim (in *Oedipe Africain*) to have discovered in Senegal the universal complex of Oedipus. Four years of therapeutic practice there converted the Ortigues to the notion of the universality of Oedipus. The problem of the father, they contend, is present with the same urgency and force in Africa as in Europe. "The child enters inevitably into a game of seduction and defense against this seduction which, in different forms, lasts throughout his life."[29] The ground for the universality of the Oedipus complex, in their view, is fashioned through a synthesis of Lévi-Strauss and Lacan: the transition from nature to society through the prohibition of incest works its effects on the struc-

ture of desire. Operating through language, the law against
incest locates the name of the father as the mediator which
displaces fantasy life toward an absent other. The Ortigues
reason that

the prohibition of incest is a corollary of the logic of alterations
imposed by the rule of language; in a system of names it is necessary
that the choice of certain combinations prohibits that of others . . .[30]

The Oedipus complex is universal, say the Ortigues, because
there is always a mediator inserted between the mother and
the child: socially, the girl child must be given away to form
an alliance with another group; psychologically, the rule of
filiation imposes a symbolic phallus, whether of the father, the
maternal uncle or the ancestors, between the child and the
mother. There is always someone who is desired by the child
(mother, sister, etc.) but who cannot be enjoyed. The sanction
and authority for this repression can be equated with the
phallus.

At this extremely general level of argument, the Ortigues
can show that Malinowski was wrong to proclaim the absence
of Oedipus where the maternal uncle substitutes for the father
as the authority figure. Malinowski states: "In the Oedipus
complex, there is the repressed desire of killing the father and
marrying the mother, whereas in the matrilinear society of the
Trobriands, the desire is to marry the sister and kill the maternal uncle."[31] Malinowski's alleged mistake was to deny the
function of the Oedipus complex simply because the personages had changed. Thus the maternal uncle can take the place
of the father as the symbolic phallus. Without arguing in favor
of Malinowski, it can still be claimed that the position of the
Ortigues, while containing an element of truth, prevents analysis of important differences in psychic structure and family
structure.

The Ortigues themselves provide the evidence for this argument. They show that in Senegal the father is often not even
known by his children, that rivalry is displaced from the fa-

ther onto the child's peer group or brothers, and that the authority figures who insure the maintenance of customs are the deceased male ancestors. Faced with these differences in the structural positioning of the father, the Ortigues still argue in favor of the existence of the Oedipus complex. They argue that the image of the dead

has been the guarantee for thousands of years of laws, institutions and social rules. But, the Oedipus complex is achieved by an identification with the lost object, that is, by a mechanism analogous with mourning. Through mourning a normative instance is formed in us which we call moral conscience. Far from depending on a particular institution, the nuclear complex of childhood must be placed parallel with the mythic manner by which the authority of institutions is justified, the ground of law.[32]

Based on their therapeutic practice in Senegal, however, the Ortigues are unable to find evidence of just this mourning or melancholia which would confirm the existence of the Oedipus complex.[33] The crucial absence of neurotic forms of mourning indicates, as they themselves write, that the formation of the super-ego or moral conscience is either very weak or takes entirely different forms from those of Europe. The collective rituals surrounding the cult of the ancestors replaces the personal super-ego and its concomitant guilt feelings. Similarly, anal eroticism also is elaborated in collective rituals, losing its importance for purely individual psychodynamics which is proved by the virtual absence of "obsessional delusions."[34]

The conclusion reached by the Ortigues is that the Oedipus complex is "unavailable" to therapy in Africa and that "the conditions of its repression are not present in the same way as in Europe."[35] They should have gone one step further and admitted that the Oedipus complex, defined by Freud as the severe internalization of the father due to highly ambivalent emotional patterns, is also absent in Senegal. While it is true that there is an incest prohibition and that the ancestors play a "phallic" role, these are not grounds for equating the psychic and family structures of Europe and Africa. There may be indeed universal principles of prohibition and language formation, but an adequate theory of the family must be able to account for the concrete differences these universal forms take. Marx showed the universality of the mode of production, but his theory would remain empty and ideological unless he provided the means to account for differences in varying modes of production and how one mode of production is transformed into another. Just this historical quality of social structures is foreclosed by Lacan and Ortigues.[36]

In opposition to Lacan, Gilles Deleuze (a philosopher) and Félix Guattari (a psychoanalyst) have written their controversial book *L'Anti-oedipe: capitalisme et schizophrénie*. Against Lacan's concept of the unconscious as a language, *Anti-Oedipus* views it as a place of libidinal production *(la production désirante)*.[37] The unconscious, to Deleuze and Guattari, neither expresses nor represents, but produces a flux of desire. Far from a lack, as desire is for Lacan, in *Anti-Oedipus* desire is full and complete. Deleuze and Guattari go back to the notion of pre-Oedipal, partial objects to locate the pure pulse of desire, whose nature, they assert, can never be represented in the personages of the family. Instead of being familial, the unconscious production of desire is at bottom social. Deleuze and Guattari view desire as part of the Marxist infra-structure, since it is always social, since its impulses are always "territorialized" or cathected onto a thing.

In their effort to delineate a radical psychology (schizo-analysis), Deleuze and Guattari oppose the "Oedipanization" of the unconscious by Freud and Lacan. They turn the Oedipus complex inside out and throw it back at Freud, insisting on its reactionary function. Since desires are immediately social, the Oedipus complex, which in Freud's thought structures the psyche at the level of individual fantasy, becomes the way in which capitalism represses desire. Capitalism for them is an abstract system of production which does not allow desire to become territorialized; it is totally impersonal and not subject to libidinal cathexis at any point in its structure. In fact it encourages schizophrenia—pure individual flux of desire with no social connection—to emerge among the workers. Hence the family is utilized by the capitalist system as the only place where desire can become coded and territorialized.

When the Oedipus complex is viewed from this perspective Freud's categories are turned upside down. Oedipus is not a law, as Lacan thought, imposed on the unconscious to prevent the realization of incestuous wishes. Instead those wishes themselves, Deleuze and Guattari argue convincingly, are elicited by the law. The parents attempt to repress a desire that was never there in the child in order to code the child's libidinal production:

> For it happens that the law interdicts something perfectly fictional in the order of desire or "instincts," so that it can persuade its subjects that they had the intention corresponding to this fiction. This is the only way for the law to bite at the intention and to render the unconscious culpable.[38]

Far from a necessary stage in psycho-sexual maturation, the law of Oedipus ensnares the unconscious into the trap of personified desires. The Oedipus complex is not a simple repression of an existing desire, but a double operation of first structuring a desire and then interdicting it. Without the Oedipus complex and before its appearance, "father and mother exist only in pieces and are never organized into a figure nor into a structure capable at once of representing the unconscious and of representing in it the various agents of the collectivity, but always break into fragments . . ."[39] The Oedipus complex "triangulates" the unconscious into Papa, Mama and child, who, far from natural or universal figures, are the specific products of capitalism.

Nor should it be thought, Deleuze and Guattari argue, that the parents are independent agents in the play of Oedipus; that is only another aspect of the familism of psychoanalysis. Instead they view Papa-Mama (the emotional configuration that is given to parents and elicited by them in the nuclear family) more as products of capitalism than as autonomous agents. Starting from society as a whole, they see the family and its psychic drama only as a segment of the whole and in relation to the whole. In pre-capitalist societies Oedipus exists only as a potentiality, as a space not filled. After capitalism has deterritorialized or reduced the libidinal value of kinship structures, of relations of alliance and descent, Oedipus emerges as a repressing and potent form:

> In order that Oedipus be occupied, a certain number of conditions are indispensable: it is necessary that the field of social production and reproduction be made independent of familial reproduction, that is, from the territorial machine which declines alliances and filiations; it is necessary that, for the aid of this independence, fragments of detachable chains are converted into a detached transcendent object which crushes their polyvocity; it is necessary that the detached object (phallus) operates a sort of folding, application or flattening, a flattening of the defined social field as a collection of discriminations on the familial field, now defined as an accomplished collection, and institutes a network of bi-univocal relations between the two. . . . It is necessary that [a limit] migrate to the heart of the system, and that it come itself to occupy the place of the representative of desire.[40]

This difficult passage means that the family is constituted under capitalism as the place where the production of desire will be blocked and misshapen, will be coded and marked through the castrations of the Oedipus complex. Since, according to Deleuze and Guattari, desire is revolutionary, every society must limit it somehow. The Oedipus complex is universal only in the sense that all societies must repress "their most profound negation, that is, the decoded flux of desire."[41]

Psychoanalysis takes the perspective of the individual and his symptom, working back to the family. It presents the Oedipus complex as the eternal order of the law of desire, whereas, Deleuze and Guattari show, Oedipus is a socially imposed repression against the free flux of the unconscious. Freud had discovered the realm of libidinal desire, but he went on to mask it by the "idealism" of Oedipus. Reich had gone further toward preserving Freud's discovery, but he failed to conceive of desire as fundamental to social existence, limiting it to the realm of ideology. By viewing desire as a social production, Deleuze and Guattari are able to demonstrate just how the family nexus and the Oedipus complex are social solutions to the threat of the unconscious. They indicate how Freud again and again misconceived his discoveries by reducing them to individual fantasy. They insist rather upon always viewing the fate that desire undergoes in a society as the means by which it is integrated into group life.[42] Such a perspective they call schizo-analysis as distinct from psycho-analysis.

If the argument of *Anti-Oedipus* is sustained, the study of the family takes an entirely secondary place in social analysis. In their haste to criticize the Oedipus complex, Deleuze and Guattari reject even a mediating role for the family. Even the nuclear family, they assert, is not an autonomous world or a microcosm:

> The family is by nature ex-centered, decentered. One tells us about fused, divided, tubular, repressing families. But from where come the breaks and their distribution which prevent precisely the family from being an "interior"? There is always an uncle in America, a brother gone astray, an aunt who took off with an officer . . .[43]

Always open to the world and always structured by it, the family is no more than the locus of desire during a certain period of life. When the family is the central object of study, they think, the true processes of encoding desire will be lost. The family will appear more autonomous than it actually is. In the history of libidinal structures provided in *Anti-Oedipus*, there are only three periods: savagery, barbarism and civilization. Hence even if one agrees with Deleuze and Guattari that desire is always social, that it is a flux which becomes encoded, that it is revolutionary in the sense that it demands an indeterminate social field of objects implying the end of private property and private love objects, their analysis, at least at the present stage, remains too abstract for concrete historical study, study which can pose and answer the important questions, among which are the meaning of the nuclear family and the meaning of how the working class was integrated into this family form. It is not possible to view the family as determined by the social system and at the same time to preserve a relative autonomy for it that would allow for the analysis of discontinuities between the family and society.

In sum, the French reading of Freud is important for the light it throws on the unconscious as a structure, whether viewed by Lacan in linguistic terms or by Deleuze and Guattari in libidinal terms. Cast by Lacan in structural terms, the theory of the family will not get lost in individualism, nor in a notion of an illusory autonomy of the ego.

Chapter 5

FAMILY THERAPY AND COMMUNICATION THEORY

One member of a family to another: "Be spontaneous!"

ONE REASON for the lack of theorizing about the family among psychoanalysts was their practice of individual therapy. Developed in the context of treating single patients, Freud's theory tended to follow from his practice, illuminating the intrapsychic dynamics of the individual.[1] After World War II, however, therapeutic practices began to change dramatically. During the war, psychiatrists were confronted with the task of treating large numbers of soldiers, and doing so quickly and cheaply. The psychological problems of these soldiers, furthermore, could hardly be considered private, personal or unique. All of them had similar traumatic experiences.[2] As a result, the Freudian view of the psyche as a dark, hidden realm within the recesses of the individual lost some of its verisimilitude. Working with soldiers, Bion and others began to treat patients in groups and began to uncover emotional dynamics specific to people in groups.[3] It became clear to these therapists that earlier theories were deficient in articulating the social nature of psychic life.

Parallel with but distinct from the origins of group therapy was the practice of treating an individual by including the entire family in the therapeutic sessions. The practice of family therapy, which did not begin until the late 1950s evoked the need to reconceptualize the nature of mental disorder on the basis not of individual fantasy but of interactional patterns. The therapist was compelled to see the family as a "system," avoiding at all costs the labelling of one member as "sick" since this was a tactic, in many cases, of the family itself. The practice of family therapy, which has become remarkably widespread since the early 1960s, is seemingly of great value for the development of a critical theory of the family.

The first important center of family therapy was at the Palo Alto Mental Research Institute. Gregory Bateson, along with Don Jackson, Jay Haley, John Weakland and others, began to treat schizophrenia, theoretically and practically, as a problem of the family system.[4] Rejecting Freudian preconceptions, Bateson, by training an anthropologist, found theoretical support for family therapy in systems theory, cybernetics, information theory, ecology, communications theory—in short, in those postwar epistemologies that stressed the priority of the relationship over the individual.[5] These theories, which were connected with the war, with the development of computers and with advanced capitalist society, led Bateson to emphasize communication patterns over private fantasies. The analysis of the message and the circuit required a set of concepts which made the individual intelligible only in the social matrix. All behavior could be viewed as communication, according to Bateson, but not in terms of the intentions of the individual. Communication was a question above all of interaction and rules for interaction; meaningful words and gestures implied both a sender and a receiver. In sum, communication was intelligible not from the point of view of the individual but only in the context of a relation.

To Bateson and the Palo Alto group, communication theory provided a new scientific basis for psychotherapy. Freud's theory, based on nineteenth-century physics and biology, had to be modernized.[6] While Lacan, with the same general orientation of founding psychology on a new scientific basis, turned to Saussure, family therapy in the United States borrowed heavily from the latest technological and scientific advances. As early as 1951, Bateson redefined psychology in terms of

communication jams, faulty processing of signals and infor-
mational deficiencies,[7] and rejected completely Freud's energy
model. Confronted by patients who were troubled not by hysterical symptoms but by a perplexing array of bizarre behaviors and profound withdrawals that were habitually labelled
schizophrenia, Bateson replaced Freud's vertical theory,
which probed genetically into the depths of the individual, by
a horizontal theory that illuminated the surface expanse of the
patient's family life. In applying communication theory to
mental disorder, Bateson's great advance was to suggest that
the fault lay not with the individual patient but with the logic
of interactions in the family network. The question to face as
we explore the theories of Bateson and other family therapists
is whether they provide an adequate theory of the nature of
family systems or whether they elaborate merely a dichotomy
of normal/pathological family systems that does not take into
account the structure of the nuclear family itself.

Bateson's application of communication theory to psychotherapy deals exclusively with problems of schizophrenia. Although as a diagnostic category schizophrenia goes back to
Emil Kraepelin and Eugene Bleuler in the early twentieth
century, it was used with increasing frequency only after
World War II. Just as with Erikson's theory of the identity
crisis, schizophrenia is a new form of pathology which suggests a new type of social crisis. The symptoms of schizophrenia are defined in extremely vague ways by the mental-health
industry, but the following traits are normally mentioned:
fragmentation of experience that splits feelings from ideas and
acts from thoughts, and results in "bizarre" behavior; confusion of fantasy and reality, so that words become things and
the person generates a private mental world; poor ego bound-
ary, so that the person cannot discriminate between his own
action or thoughts and those of others; reified perception of
the self, so that the person feels dead or empty or manipulated
by others; feelings of terror and isolation so that trust in others
is impossible.[8]

Two kinds of criticisms have been made of the category of

schizophrenia: (1) that it is an empty label applied arbitrarily and which leads, as a consequence of treatment, to worse problems than it pretends to cure (this is the viewpoint of Laing and anti-psychiatry and will be dealt with below); (2) that these symptoms are specific to capitalist society and are found in the "normal" experience of all oppressed groups today (the Marxist position).

The Marxists[9] argue that advanced capitalism leads to a general reification of experience, in which people are treated (by bosses, by advertisers, by the government) as objects to be manipulated. The market system has reached its logical conclusion separating concrete, intrinsic values completely from exchange values. Commodities are reinvested with the qualities of persons, while people are shorn of their human traits. Hence "schizophrenics" are only troubled a bit more deeply by what affects everyone. In the Marxist critique, the focus shifts from the family to the economy and the general culture. Whatever one thinks of the Marxist position, it does at least attempt to explain the sudden rise of schizophrenic symptoms in the contemporary period.

Schizophrenia to Bateson is the result of distorted communication in the family. Starting with Bertrand Russell's theory of logical types, in which a class cannot itself be a member of the class, Bateson goes on to show how certain communications embody logical errors which prevent a message from being perceived correctly. Bateson postulates that

in the psychology of real communications [the discontinuity between a class and its members] is continually and inevitably breached, and that a priori we must expect a pathology to occur in the human organism when certain formal patterns of the breaching occur in the communication between mother and child.[10]

These pathogenic "breaches" are called "double binds." A double bind is a message in which the receiver cannot distinguish the logical type or order of the message regardless of the interpretation he chooses to place on it. Bateson distinguishes three traits of the double-bind situation: (1) an intense, vitally important relationship exists; (2) the sender of the message expresses two orders of message in which one order denies the other; and (3) the receiver of the message cannot comment about it to correct the confusion or even point it out.[11] The definition of the double bind becomes clear in an example Bateson gives. A schizophrenic patient, well on the way to recovery, was visited in the hospital by his mother. He greeted her with enthusiasm, putting his arms around her in an embrace. She stiffened in response and he withdrew his arms. Then she asked, "Don't you love me any more?" The patient blushed, and the mother responded: "Dear, you must not be so easily embarrassed and afraid of your feelings." The patient then relapsed into another schizophrenic episode.[12]

In the example, the patient, if he interprets his mother's messages correctly, must conclude that to keep his mother's love he must not show that he loves her (by embracing her) but if he does not show that he loves her (withdrawing arms, blushing) he will lose her love. Either way he loses. Bateson claims that schizophrenia will develop in double-bind situations when the person has a "weak ego function" to begin with and therefore begins to lose the capacity to discriminate and interpret messages correctly. The schizophrenic will fail to assign the right communicational mode (1) to messages from others, (2) to his own messages to others, or (3) to his own thoughts or feelings. In such messages as the command "Be spontaneous!" the message content is simply to act with spontaneity, without foresight. But since the message is a command, the second level of the message requires that the receiver follow an order, initiated by someone else, or, in short, act with foresight and at another's behest. If the receiver of the message is also not in a position to ask about the confusion, any response he makes will be incorrect. In the example of the patient and his mother, for instance, there are numerous instances of the double bind. Bateson argues that when a person is confronted habitually by communications of this type his responses will be labelled "schizophrenic." The only way out of the double bind is to destroy completely ordinary rules of communication, and this is what the schizophrenic does.

If Bateson is correct, traditional Freudian psychology would at the very least require enormous revisions. The theory of the double bind assumes that pathological symptoms must be understood not as a return of repressed instincts as in Freudian theory, not on an energy model, but on a communicational model as the consequence of habitual confrontation with distorted messages. In other words, Bateson's theory leads to an examination of the structure of social interactions of the patient and it provides a means of comprehending a communicational system. Freudian theory is designed to interpret intra-psychic fantasies; Bateson's theory is designed to interpret social interactions. Freud's theory leads to individual therapy aimed at the patient's unconscious fantasy; Bateson's theory leads to family therapy aimed at the communicational patterns of the group.

As one might expect, Bateson has elaborated not only the communicational conditions of schizophrenia (the double bind) but also the family pattern in which schizophrenia is likely to occur. He distinguishes three common traits of the schizophrenic family system:

1) there must be a child whose mother becomes anxious and withdraws if the child responds to her as a loving mother;
2) there must be a mother who cannot accept her own feelings of anxiety and hostility toward her child and who denies them by overtly expressing love to persuade the child to respond to her as a loving mother;
3) there must be an absence of anyone (father, sibling) in the family who can intervene between the mother and the child.[13]

In a later article, Bateson adds other characteristics to his list. He takes Jackson's concept of family homeostasis into account by noting that all families tend to develop patterns of interaction which become very stable and fixed. Any effort to disrupt the family system, especially in pathological families, will be met with great resistance by all members.[14] If a schizophrenic's condition improves during hospitalization, his return to the family will often cause a crisis of the family system. Either the patient will resume his schizophrenia or some other member of the family will become ill. The stability of the family system, Bateson and the Palo Alto group contend, comes from its communicational structure which is based on the feedback loop. The family cannot be seen as a composite of discrete individuals, but as a set of relations. The ties between members are deeply rooted because these relations are composed of patterns of mutual expectation. Batseon notes, "We have to consider, not only A's reactions to B's behavior, but we must go on to consider how these affect B's later behavior and the effect of this on A."[15] In the feedback loop such as this, the system is maintained not at discrete points of individual action, but through the resonating actions of all members. Thus if a father makes a dominance gesture about family finances most often this must be responded to by the mother and children with messages of submission and acceptance, and only then is the loop complete. Both sides of the communication must be considered in order to understand how the family works. In this sense, schizophrenia is not "caused" by the mother, nor is it a "deficiency" "contained within" the schizophrenic child; rather it is part of the family system as a whole. Feedback loops are vicious circles in which the husband blames the wife for nagging, while she blames him for withdrawing affection, each thinking the other is the cause of the family's problems. In fact they are both involved in a mutually confirming pattern.

Bateson gives a fifth criteria of the schizophrenic family: each member is continually undergoing the experience of "negation of self."[16] In the double-bind situation, the receiver of the message tends to have his perception, interpretation or thought rejected and cancelled. In the example given above, the patient's expression of love for his mother was negated by her. Bateson does not develop this trait of schizophrenic families in great detail. In fact, it appears to have more of an existential quality than a communicational quality. As we shall see, the characteristic of negation of self is developed at great length by Laing and his associates.

One frequent criticism of Bateson pertains just to this lack of an existential dimension to his position. Why, it is asked, should problems of communication lead to mental disturbance? Unlike Freud, Bateson does not seem to be able to explain the relation between miscommunication as a technical error and emotional disturbance. Why should the form of messages lead to emotional pain? Bateson's only response to this charge is again not at the communicational or behavioral level but at the existential:

> Human beings have a commitment to the solutions which they discover, and it is this psychological commitment that makes it possible for them to be hurt in the way members of schizophrenic families are hurt.[17]

Interestingly enough, Bateson was unable to explain mental pathology purely through a systems approach to language. (His communication model also contains weaknesses as a theory of therapy, but we are not directly concerned with this.)

In large part due to his reliance on communication theory, Bateson's five indices of schizophrenic families tend to individualize and dehistoricize the understanding of the family. His criteria tend to discriminate between family systems without saying anything about contemporary family structure. For example, could a schizophrenic pattern develop in an aristocratic family in rural France in the fifteenth century? Bateson's criteria do not offer us a theory of what the contemporary family is or what its prospects are. His index that relations must be of vital importance to the schizophrenic pertains to all families and does not distinguish the peculiar emotional closeness of the nuclear family. Furthermore, unlike Marxist psychologists, he does not relate patterns of schizophrenia to the social structure, or even to the language patterns outside the family. Because of that there is no way of judging the extent to which schizophrenic families are autonomous in their communicational pattern or dependent upon circumstances in the wider society. Bateson's position has the serious flaw—one which tends to characterize all of family therapy—of isolating the understanding of the family from history and from society. Nevertheless, the value of Bateson's theory must not be overlooked: he has begun to develop a method to comprehend the family as an interactional system, to make intelligible the emotional life of the family without individualizing the problem. Family therapy begins with Bateson for just that reason. His argument that one must understand the individual only within his social context has enormous import for family theory in general. After Bateson, family therapy spread very rapidly, because aspects of individual pathology which had until then seemed unintelligible suddenly took on meaning when viewed in a family context.

In the well-known book *Pragmatics of Human Communication*, Paul Watzlawick and his associates attempted to formalize more carefully Bateson's double-bind theory. They tried to expand the double-bind theory into a general theory of "pragmatic paradoxes." They begin with a fundamental distinction between symmetrical and complementary relationships, arguing that paradoxes may exist in numerous forms as confusions between the two. With great elegance and logical rigor they argue for the same general position as Bateson: that pathologies are products of distorted communication. They go on to develop a clever tactic for purposes of therapy. Since the patient is caught in a network of paradoxes which he cannot escape, the therapist should move one level up and make a paradox of the pathological paradoxes by ordering the person not to change at all.[18] The patient can do nothing in this situation unless he steps outside the whole dilemma. While "paradoxical" therapy is certainly interesting and has achieved some acceptance professionally, the theory of Watzlawick points up a danger that was not particularly pronounced in Bateson's writing, the danger of behaviorism. Unlike Lacan, the double-bind theorists base themselves on a behavioral understanding of reality. There are no gaps or breaches in family communications to them, no unconscious level of fantasy. Instead, the family group forms a neat system of interactional patterns, all of which exist on the surface level of perceptual reality. Hence, as Lacanians have complained,[19] there is no symbolic level in the analyses of the Palo Alto group, hence no tension, no depth to their theory. In the final analysis, the Palo Alto group's theory of *un*distorted communication cannot account for the problem of domination and freedom. From the viewpoint of the Lacanians, systems theory cannot save behaviorism from its determinist error.[20]

Bateson and the Palo Alto group influenced family therapy in general by sensitizing practitioners to communication patterns and to the nature of the family as a system. But family therapy arose at about the same time in several centers without a single theoretical leader.[21] The theory of family therapy thus reflects the broad continuum of diverse psychotherapies, from psychoanalysis to behaviorism, from gestalt to transactional analysis, including a good portion of plain eclecticism.[22] Within this diversity, however, there seem to be some common themes shared by most, if not all, theories of family therapy.[23]

Theorists of family therapy begin by defining their field through a critique of Freud's individualism: in order to comprehend the pattern of a family one must look at what goes on between individuals, not simply within them.[24] They go on to argue that the pattern in each family is unique, that each family develops myths, rituals, a shared view of the outside world, mutual definitions of each other, and so forth, elements which effectively individualize the family. In this way the family defines itself as a coherent whole with more or less clear boundaries. In the words of one family therapist team,

However its life spreads into the wider community, there is a sense in which a family is a bounded universe. The members of a family —parents and their young children—inhabit a world of their own making, a community of feeling and fantasy, action and precept.[25]

The effort throughout the literature is to focus on the individual family as a world unto itself. Theorists omit for the most part a historical understanding of the privatization of the family, and omit as well a sociological understanding of the structural requirements (such as sex roles) imposed on the family by the wider society. Instead their efforts are directed at the psychological level exclusively in an attempt to arrive at a concept of how families operate emotionally. Perhaps family therapy is unwilling to go further, since it is likely that when they call into question the normality and well-being of the family, family therapists will meet the resistance of society. To claim that families, even some of them, are disturbed goes against the general belief in the sanctity of the family. In a kind of reaction formation, family therapists may unconsciously be suppressing the important connections between family structure and family psychology. If this is correct, it would also explain their effort to separate disturbed families from "normal" ones. At least in this regard, Freud was more aware of what he was doing and of the resistance or opposition he faced than are family therapists.

A good example of the current state of family therapy is the work of Lyman Wynne at the National Institute of Mental Health. In a widely read article,[26] Wynne and his associates define three types of families based on three types of relatedness: mutuality, non-mutuality and pseudo-mutuality. Each type is a different combination of two universal needs, that of personal identity and that of relationships with others. Families with pseudo-mutuality, which tend to develop a schizophrenic member, are defined by a pattern of emotional investment directed toward not perceiving accurately the changing needs and expectations of the family members but instead maintaining a sense of reciprocal stability,[27] a rigid structure of relationships or a fixed family role structure. In families with schizophrenics, there is a great effort to maintain a fairly rigid pattern of attitudes against the inevitable changes undergone by family members. The theoretical pattern of Wynne's work is important to notice: the family therapist sets up an ideal of family functioning (mutuality) which is presented without much theoretical defense. The theory then tries to separate out sick families from healthy ones in order to isolate the group mechanisms which have elicited the disease. Hence the actual structure of "normal" families will not be called in question. Wynne enumerates, for example, several features of families based on pseudo-mutuality: they tend to suppress or reinterpret delusionally all deviations from the established family role structure; the schizophrenic perceives the structure as all-encompassing; an attitude of catastrophe surrounds the possibility of changes in the role structure; parents give indiscriminate approval to children; there is much secrecy in the family; the family often relies on outside intermediaries; changes in family structure are met with scapegoating; the family role structures, not just the parental authorities, are internalized; and so forth.[28] When these mechanisms operate, Wynne contends, the family is in danger of producing a schizophrenic. These families have over-emphasized the human need for relations against the need for individual identity.

Implicit in family therapies such as Wynne's is the assumption that the general structure of the nuclear family is optimal and that deviations from it are (1) caused solely within the family and (2) need to be eliminated to bring the family back to the norm. As a whole, the family therapy industry, including not just individual therapists but private groups (like the Family Association of America), child guidance centers, community mental-health centers, hospitals, institutes, asylums, and numerous other therapeutic agencies, is devoted to the preservation of the current family form, as well as to the preservation of the general institutions of society (capitalism, representative democracy, etc.) which are seen as dependent upon healthy families but in no way damaging to them. In the past ten or fifteen years the United States has witnessed the birth and rapid expansion of this new form of social control and regulation.

The styles of therapy practiced on families varies to a considerable extent. In general, however, the therapist tries, after diagnosing the troublesome family pattern, to alter the family system in some way. In a film called "A Modern Little Hans," from the Philadelphia Child Guidance Center, for example, a young boy's phobia of dogs was treated by the therapist by trying to change the authority pattern over the boy, which until then had been only the mother's responsibility, to include the father. Once the boy learned that his father, a postman, knew a great deal about fending off dogs which he could teach his son, the therapist was satisfied that a "normal" pattern of parental authority had been achieved or at least begun. He presumed that faulty authority patterns were the cause of the boy's fear. He then shifted the focus of conversation to the interaction between the parents, hoping to dissolve the barriers to their coalition of power. In "A Modern Little Hans," the boy's intra-psychic fantasies were ignored, and there was a strong presumption that family normality depended on a good working alliance between the parents to exercise authority over the children.

Among psychoanalysts, the same pattern of treating families is prevalent, although they do focus more on a genetic model of illness, concerning themselves with the transmission of super-ego problems through the generations. When there are "lacunae" in the super-egos of the parents, blind spots in their ethical codes, the children internalize them and act them out as symptoms. What was a problem of conscience in one generation becomes a problem of behavior in the next. Psychoanalysts applied their theory at first to delinquent children, avoiding the obvious social questions raised by this issue. Here again there is an assumption of a "normal" super-ego or "normal" authority structure which the sick family has not achieved.[29]

Among family therapists the tendency is very strong to avoid the assumption of a continuity between "sick" and "healthy" families and therefore to avoid placing the family in a historical and social context. Even though researchers have shown that schizophrenia tends, with a statistically significant correlation, to be diagnosed in poor families as opposed to rich families, where neurosis predominates,[30] the importance of class in differentiating family structure is often overlooked by theorists of family therapy. Moreover, family therapy, with its heavy reliance on communication theory, tends to have a parliamentary vision of reality in which all disagreements and antagonisms can be ironed out. The tendency in family therapy is to assume that there are no irreconcilable differences, no recalcitrant contradictions beyond the capacity of the family to handle. Because each family is seen as a microcosm closed unto itself, structural contradictions of the nuclear family form do not impinge on communications within them. The inequities of sex roles, the dependence of children, the isolation of the family from a broader community in no way influence, in the writings of the family therapists, the ability of the family to attain a "normal," "healthy," "fulfilling" existence.

The work of Theodore Lidz and his associates at Yale on family therapy and schizophrenia is instructive. Lidz relies heavily on ego psychology and the theories of Talcott Parsons in his writing on the family. The normative, conservative role of the nuclear family is most explicit in Lidz: sick families are those quite simply where the "proper" differentiation of sex roles and the proper authority of the older generation over the younger have been violated. He states:

I propose that the essential dynamic structure of the family rests upon the parents' ability to form a coalition, maintain boundaries between the generations, and adhere to their appropriate sex-linked roles. Then I examine how failure to meet these few requisites leads to distortions in the ego structuring of their children.[31]

How is it possible, one might ask, for anyone to defend patriarchal sex roles as crucial to mental health and general well-being? How can such oppressive discrimination be psychically beneficial? Lidz borrows directly from Talcott Parsons the notion that men have instrumental roles and women have expressive roles in the family. When these are not fulfilled, Lidz warns, "weakness" in the man will lead to "coldness" in the woman, with disastrous consequences for the whole family.[32] Lidz apparently wants us to believe that women turn cold when they are not dominated by men.

With his Parsonian theory, Lidz seems more aware of social and historical factors in family structure than most family therapists. But the effects of such awareness are deeply conservative: he uses Parsonian theory to show that the modern nuclear family is inevitable, unchangable and in any case completely desirable. He proposes

the thesis that the isolated nuclear family, despite its paucity of stabilizing forces, is better suited for preparing its children to live in a society that is rapidly changing its adaptive techniques than are families with extended kinship systems.[33]

The marriage between the nuclear family and capitalism is a happy one because the former generates flexible egos which can go where the money is without ever questioning the social alternatives to new "adaptive techniques." Problems within the nuclear family itself call not for restructuring, according to Lidz, but for reinforcement of the norm. Family therapy thus plays a vital role in bolstering the established order:

The instability of the isolated nuclear family can, however, reach such proportions that it provides insufficient structuring, security, and satisfaction for its members. The instability affects not only the stability of individuals raised in these families but also the stability of the society through undermining the family unit and the culture's ethical directives. *As the trend toward isolated families cannot be undone,* the continuity of this culture may well depend upon strengthening this unstable family form by gaining coherent concepts of what essentials to family life must be maintained.[34]

Questioned about new family forms in communist society, Lidz homilized on family love:

Question: What do you suspect would happen if we tried to eliminate the family?

Lidz: I think we'd have tragedy. I considered this recently particularly in regard to the Chinese communes, where parents are kept apart from their children except for visits once a month or every few weeks. My feeling is that for most people, without meaningful family relationships, and the feeling for children whom we must care for and help make life meaningful for, life will not seem worthwhile. A society of such people would, I think, ultimately disintegrate.[35]

The import of Lidz's speculations are that even if society does not provide satisfying experience, the family can instill meanings in the child. Life becomes worthwhile in the family so that the meaninglessness of society cannot be criticized. When work in the community is meaningless, the family steps in to save the day.

When Lidz looks closely at the way the nuclear family instills meanings in the child, the outlook is not so bright. The nuclear family tends to drown children in their parents' emotional bath, providing relations so intimate that any independence for the child is prevented. Lidz describes many families in which "children have difficulty in becoming discrete individuals for they are living their mothers' lives rather than their own . . ."[36] Locked into her sex role as mother, one woman interviewed by Lidz said of her son, "He is not just part of my life he is all of my life,"[37] a pathetic statement that speaks to the woman's confusion but also to the irrationality of the role of mother in the nuclear family. Lidz's theory of the family proposes to cure the family when the craziness originating in the society overwhelms it. His family therapy would teach the family to function smoothly under the burdens of oppressive norms and roles. By means of family therapy he would transmute misery into happiness without touching the basic conditions of the misery.

There is one tradition of family therapy, however, that has attempted to relate family problems to social problems and to define particular family problems in relation to contemporary family structure. This is the work of R. D. Laing and the anti-psychiatry movement in England. Unlike the modest and limited work of most family therapy, Laing has sought to connect family therapy with an attack on mental-health institutions, with new left politics, with Far Eastern mysticism and with a validation of schizophrenic experience as a healing process. Drawing heavily on Sartre's philosophy and on existentialist thought in general, Laing has associated the practice of family therapy with a general radical social theory. For this reason Laing's work will be treated in greater detail than other family therapies.

Laing's work begins not with family therapy but with an effort to uncover the intelligibility of schizophrenic language and behavior. For him Freud's great advance began with his ability to find meaning in the symptoms and utterances of hysterics. Since the late 1950s Laing's own goal has been to find a way to listen to schizophrenics and hear them. His assumption has therefore been that people who are classified as severely psychotic are still human beings with intentions and desires which can be comprehended by other human beings. His purpose is "to make madness, and the process of going mad, comprehensible."[38] He has, in short, attempted to humanize schizophrenia, to bring back into the community those who have been abandoned in the asylums. Laing's project is thus similar to that of Michel Foucault, who has argued that since the eighteenth century, since the victory of modern rationalism, the insane have been labelled "irrational," beyond nature, and have been confined and excluded from society with the complicity of the medical profession.[39] Like Foucault, Laing's attempt to humanize schizophrenia has led him at times to celebrate it romantically as an experience which is superior to that of the normal psyche.

There are two sides to Laing's project. First, he searches for a general philosophy of human experience (existentialism) which can account for schizophrenic as well as normal consciousness. Second, he launches a thorough and sharp critique of psychiatry.

Laing is not a particularly consistent or systematic philosopher.[40] Yet his use of existentialism does make his point clear. Contemporary social experience tends to become reified; people treat others as things, not as persons. Consequently they clutch their identities so tightly that they become masks, hiding their true selves. Laing tries to relate the phenomenon of reification to broad social and political trends but he is not able to analyze reification the way Marxists have by tying it to capitalism. Instead, Laing looks with great sensitivity at the consciousness of those who are treated as things, finding that the terror of the experience leads to "ontological insecurity" and to a "divided self."[41] Laing has a great facility in taking the side of the psychically oppressed and turning the tables on the normal world. He writes sardonically, for example, "A man who says that men are machines may be a great scientist. A man who says he *is* a machine is 'depersonalized' in psychiatric jargon."[42]

While reification and madness reign unchecked in the normal world, the mad world represents to Laing a more authentic experience. The mad are protesting against a bad state of affairs which is not recognized as such by the majority. When examined carefully, through a phenomenological analysis, the mad reveal the reigning insanity. Existentialism allows us, Laing thinks, to treat the insane as persons, to validate their consciousness as human. For this reason he, like Thomas Szasz also writing in the 1950s and 1960s, is outraged at the way people are treated by the mental-health industry. People who are considered "abnormal" for some reason by their relatives or friends are brought, Laing and Szasz contend, to doctors who treat them as things, reproducing the worst features of the general society, categorizing them in the crudest manner and subjecting them, involuntarily in many cases, to what Laing describes as a form of torture (confinement without privileges, electric shock, drugs of all sorts, humiliating treatment, etc.).

The label schizophrenia is Laing's favorite target. A loose category, as we have seen, which includes diverse, contradictory forms of experience and behavior, schizophrenia is used by psychiatrists, social workers and others in a mythical way, as if it had the specificity and diagnostic accuracy of the label "pneumonia." People who are so labelled have been "objectified," Laing argues, by the "medical model." They have not been listened to or understood, and their experience has been invalidated. Many psychiatrists even believe, like the doctors who treated hysteria before Freud, that schizophrenia is "caused" by a physical or chemical abnormality. Laing quotes from Kraepelin, who began to treat schizophrenia (then called *dementia praecox*) around the turn of the century. Kraepelin's reports, stunning examples of the medical model, are worth reproducing at length:

The patient I will show you today has almost to be carried into the rooms, as he walks in a straddling fashion on the outside of his feet. On coming in, he throws off his slippers, sings a hymn loudly, and then cries twice (in English), "My father, my real rather!" He is eighteen years old, and a pupil of the Oberrealschule (higher-grade modern-side school), tall, and rather strongly built, but with a pale complexion, on which there is very often a transient flush. The patient sits with his eyes shut, and pays no attention to his surroundings. He does not look up even when he is spoken to, but he answers beginning in a low voice, and gradually screaming louder and louder. When asked where he is, he says, "You want to know that too? I tell you who is being measured and is measured and shall be measured. I know all that, and could tell you, but I do not want to." When asked his name, he screams, "What is your name? What does he shut? He shuts his eyes, What does he hear? He does not understand; he understands not. How? Who? Where? When? What does he mean? When I tell him to look he does not look properly. You there, just look! What is it? What is the matter? Attend; he attends not. I say, what is it, then? Why do you give me no answer? Are you getting impudent again? How can you be so impudent? I'm coming! I'll show you! You don't whore for me. You musn't be smart either; you're an impudent, lousy fellow, such an impudent, lousy fellow I've never met with. Is he beginning again? You understand nothing at all, nothing at all; nothing at all does he understand. If you follow now, he won't follow, will not follow. Are you getting still more impudent? Are you getting impudent still more? How they attend, they do attend," and so on. At the end, he scolds in quite inarticulate sounds.[44]

It is obvious to anyone reading this passage today that the patient is mocking Kraepelin and the medical profession while also pathetically appealing against the inhumanity of being placed before medical students as a specimen. Kraepelin, however, sees none of the meaning of the insane person's words. He goes on:

> Although he undoubtedly understood all the questions, he has not given us a single piece of useful information. His talk was . . . only a series of disconnected sentences having no relation to the general situation.[45]

As Laing sees it, Kraepelin's general inability to find meaning in the words of someone labelled a psychotic was due to the underlying objectification of the patient in the medical model and is exemplary of most current psychiatric practice.

Freud had gotten beyond the medical model at least partially by assuming significance to the words of neurotics (symptomatic significance), developing a practice of listening to them and a theory of the unconscious which registers the distorted meanings. Laing has tried to develop a parallel method for schizophrenia. What is interesting from the point of view of this study is that Laing has maintained that the only way to render intelligible the words of the schizophrenic is to place them in the context of the patient's family, to go to the family, study its interactions, to see how the patient is labelled and has a fixed place in the family network, to see how the patient responds to this place, internalizing it in distorted ways, struggling to escape from it yet caught in it, and finally to develop strategies to alter these patterns.[46] Laing's success has not been perfect with regard to all of these tasks. He is surely weak on developing a theory and practice of the non-objectifying therapist. But his achievement has been his ability to demonstrate in case studies how the schizophrenic is intelligible when placed in his family context.

It is difficult to convey here how convincingly schizophrenic experience becomes comprehensible when placed in the family context. To this end Laing has written many case studies[47] *(Sanity, Madness and the Family),* reproduced the journals of schizophrenics *(Politics of Experience),* and reported on numerous cases throughout his writings. To give the reader some sense of how madness becomes intelligible when studied in relation to the person's family interactions, the case of David will be described briefly and schematically.[48]

David is a nine-year-old diagnosed by a Child Guidance Clinic as "incipient schizophrenia." The boy has seen a psychiatrist and a social worker, who also interviewed the mother. Laing was called in and insisted on visiting the family at their home. The "trouble" with the boy, according to the mother, was that he was "out of control"; he did what he wanted and went where he wanted. Laing discovered that the boy went habitually to a construction site to watch the workers, preferring this to going to school. It also became apparent that the mother viewed the boy as being just like her father, who, it turned out, would also disappear without notice from his home. To Laing, there was no schizophrenia here, only a boy's acting out the unconscious wishes of his mother; that is, being his grandfather and disobeying his mother by obeying her. But no one had looked at the setting, the social context of the "bizarre" behavior. Without studying the family the boy's actions would be interpreted individualistically, as stemming from unconscious fantasies (Freud) or as "abnormal behavior" requiring treatment such as drugs and confinement (psychiatry).

After deciding that the behavior can best be comprehended in the family context, the therapist must face the question of how to define this context. Laing has offered different definitions, using different theories at different times. Through the 1960s one constant thread in his work was an effort to define the "family nexus" as the heart of the problem.[49] He sought a method to get at the way people in families are defined by their relationships. The family nexus was conceived as the particular pattern of relations specific to one family. Like Bateson, Laing's model was anti-individualist, but unlike Bateson Laing relied on Sartre's existentialism rather than on communications theory. In *The Politics of Experience,* Laing attempted to apply Sartre's categories from the *Critique of Dialec-*

tical Reason[50] to the family. The family was seen as a group in which each member was defined by his relations with other members, by the manner in which each internalized the views of them held by others. These internalizations included an element of "violence," since the family as a group had to maintain its existence against dangers of dissolution. The family nexus, then, was "the 'entity' which has to be preserved in each person"[51] so that the family may continue. Any effort to change the nexus would be treason and would be resisted by other family members. Laing was arguing that for any family to maintain itself a great deal of terror and violence was necessary because members had to deny continually, at a deeply internalized level, their freedom to change or to leave the family.

But nowhere in Laing's account was there an explanation for the terror of family relationships, nowhere was there an analysis of family structure which would indicate why family unity was won at so great a cost. If there is some truth in Laing's account of the family nexus, he would also have to show how it was built up historically in connection with the privatization of family life. The depth of interpersonal experience in the nuclear family, which Laing is describing in all its negative aspects, must be understood as part of a specific family structure which was formed in relation to the formation of a particular society. The profundity of emotional involvements in families is not something found in the same degree at all times and places. Only after the family was reduced to the conjugal unit, after work was removed from the household (not counting housework, of course), after the family severed its ties with the community—only after a wealth of historical change occurred did the level of emotional intensity described by Laing become actual. By viewing the family as a nexus of internalizations under the pressure of the dissolution of the group, Laing is taking Sartre's concept of the group without seeing the family as a special kind of group, requiring special concepts for analysis.

In a later book, *The Politics of the Family*, Laing, in his effort

Critical Theory of the Family

to analyze the family nexus, shifted metaphors from Sartre's phenomenology to one of mapping, to an analysis of positions and locations. It is often overlooked that Laing's new method still was grounded in an attempt to make intelligible the internalized relations of the family; only now he would be more precise in his categories. The general problem with the nuclear family remained the same for him: in the emotionally tight space of the family, each member "attempts to regulate the inner life of the other in order to preserve his own."[52] Laing was still maintaining that the fault with the nuclear family—and by implication, the ground for schizophrenia— was a necessary over-intrusiveness by each member toward the others which is inherent in the structure of this type of family. Ironically, true privacy, the much-vaunted asset of the nuclear family, is not attained there. In nuclear families, parents claimed that they knew what was in their children's minds *better than their children* and children had difficulty forming their own separateness, their identity being locked up psychically with that of their parents. These confusions of intersubjectivity became manifest during the child's efforts to separate himself from the family during adolescence and they tend, as Mitchell says,[53] to be more pronounced among girls because girls are allowed less independence in patriarchal culture than boys. Hence Laing's case studies concerned predominately adolescent girls.

In *The Politics of the Family* Laing began the task of distinguishing the typical experiences of the nuclear family. Most characteristic was the deadly game of "attributions," in which the parent would give an identity to a child: Sally is like her father, or her grandmother. The strategy of attributions is one of mind control: "To get someone to *be* what one wants him to be . . ."[54] Laing regards attributions as

many times more powerful than orders (or other forms of coercion or persuasion). . . . When attributions have the function of instructions or injunctions, this function may be denied, giving rise to one type of *mystification*, akin to, or identical with, hypnotic suggestion.

Hypnosis may be an experimental model of a naturally occurring phenomenon in many families. . . . So, if I hypnotize you, I do not say, "I order you to feel cold." I indicate it is cold. You immediately feel cold. I think many children begin *in* a state like this.[55]

The trouble with attributions is that, coming from people so emotionally close, it is impossible or very difficult for the child to escape internalizing them. The child's own identity, own experience, own individuality becomes denied in favor of living the mask of the parent's attribution.[56] Now as an ongoing, everyday experience, with no space to escape to, with the child's emotional and physical dependence on the parents, a system of interpersonal relations, of patterned dialogues is constructed gradually based on the bizarre projections and attributions of the parents. In some cases the attributions are so difficult for the child, involve so great a denial of self—when for example the child is a "black sheep" or a scapegoat for everything that goes wrong in the family—that he chooses what is called schizophrenia as an escape from the family nexus, although that usually only strengthens the balance of roles in the family. Schizophrenia for Laing is a type of getting stuck between the family nexus and the way out, which only serves, from the point of view of the family, to confirm its pattern.

Three types of criticism must be raised against Laing. First, Laing states that the family nexus is unconscious.[57] The family does not know what the situation or the nexus is. Yet he has no theory to account for this type of unconscious (which is very different from Freud's since it is social and interactional). Laing's work has stopped at the surface level: he has done important work in analyzing the structure of family interactions at the emotional level. But Laing is unable to account for the "absences" in family experience, the unconscious, invisible pattern. How is it possible for the therapist to map the family nexus and the family *not* to see it? Unless Laing can account for the dynamics of the family unconscious, he will not be able to specify the type of knowledge the therapist can attain and the type of intervention the therapist can make in the family. The fault rests with Laing's failure to get beyond the subjective level of interactions and account for the social structure of the family and the interpenetration of family and society.

This may become more clear when the second criticism is raised. In almost every case study he presents, Laing finds the mother to be the intrusive, attributing, projecting agent. But he does not try to explain this astonishing consistency of events. Why is it the mother who is the "covert schizophrenic" (Bateson) or the schizophregenic agent (Laing and others)? Of course, Laing does not want to blame the mother in a personal way, or even to isolate the mother as a unilinear, determining cause of disease. He wants to remain at the level of family structure and see the process as an interaction. But the crucial interaction turns out to be between the mother and her child (usually her daughter). We must ask, since Laing does not, is there anything in the social function, role and experience of the mother in nuclear families that would lead to the tendency to over-intrusiveness? Answers appear immediately and are related to patriarchy.

Motherhood, after all, is defined in the nuclear family in a unique way—as having the mother's identity connected with the well-being of her children. To a degree not found before in European or North American history, motherhood involves the constant supervision of children with a deep concern not simply for their physical growth and social skills but for their psychic health. Quite simply, when women were relegated to the home, one of their primary tasks was explicitly to supervise the minds of their children, to project into them, to attribute to them, to influence them emotionally, and so forth. When it is recalled that women during the early years of their child's growth are restricted to a very queer, as Laing would say, life of total child care in almost complete isolation, it should not be too surprising that they develop deep attachments to their children and sometimes resist, with all their emotional strength, losing the child, losing their total involvment with the child as it matures to independence.

If the implication of Laing's work is that the schizophrenic is not so crazy and that his parents are rather crazy themselves, it must also be pointed out that the nuclear family requires parents, especially mothers, to perform functions that are rather "crazy" as well. None of the above is meant to imply that Laing's method of analyzing the family nexus at the inter-subjective level (which has been sketched only barely) is invalid. Rather it must be supplemented with a historical and social analysis of family structure. And in this way Laing would not be led into the mysticism of schizophrenic experience, toward which he tends, but instead toward critical social theory.

The third criticism of Laing's notion of family nexus concerns his reliance on an absolute subject. The notion of attribution, involving the denial of the subjectivity of others, contains an important element of truth, but in Laing's formulation it tends (1) to assume that the person who is denied is a totally free, unitary presence and (2) to degenerate into an attack on roles. Laing takes over Sartre's concept of the free subject but he uses it in a metaphysical, not an ontological, a substantive and not a structural manner. He assumes that if the subject did not suffer the attribution he would be free, thereby the necessary interdependence of people and their relative subjectivity in mutual recognition is lost. The problem is not to free the subject from the other but so to structure their relations that each can recognize the place and desire of the other. Although at times Laing comes close to this formulation he tends too often to slide into a romantic individualism.

As a consequence, he also tends to attack not simply a particular social form, like attribution, but all social forms. This happens in part through his reliance on Erving Goffman and ethno-methodology, which pretends to see through all social "roles" as crude, secondary masks covering some true reality. The attribution foists a "role" on the child. Its danger, however, lies only in the reified manner in which the role is born. The problem lies not with roles but with their fixity, their inescapability, their class and patriarchal nature, their unitary quality. Laing forgets Sartre's maxim that the self is formed only in a situation, only by dealing with the roles and the meanings thrown at us by others. Bad faith for Sartre concerns not simply having a role, like a waiter, but the *way* the waiter relates to his role. No one can place an attribution on anyone else unless that person is complicitous. The trouble with nuclear families, perhaps, is that their close intimacy tends to encourage the giving and receiving of roles which become fixed in the nexus.

Without relating the theory of the family nexus to family structure, Laing was left with the much-criticized resort of romanticizing the schizophrenic. He takes the side of the schizophrenic against his family and the medical establishment, viewing the "disease" as a heroic pathway to health, as a "natural healing process."[58] It is certainly desirable that people labelled schizophrenic should be seen as human subjects, and that their experience should be treated as valid and perhaps as a necessary process of temporary regression, as something they must go through. But this process of internal flight, of loss of ego, in no way warrants being considered a superior and desirable mental state. Laing often lapses into a celebration of schizophrenics as the spiritual avant-garde of the twentieth century. Such a position undercuts any effort to develop a therapy for psychosis, suggesting instead that the therapist himself take flight into a schizophrenic voyage.

During the 1960s Laing and his colleagues did set up, under the auspices of the Philadelphia Association, a series of therapeutic communities based on the view of the schizophrenic as a spiritual voyager. In Kingsley Hall, the best known Laingian "asylum," the therapists' role was eliminated, and the "inmates" explored their regression without hindrance.[59] Here was a place where the patients were treated as subjects, with no hospital staff to objectify and harass them. If Laing is right, what the schizophrenic needs is an accepting community where he can act in bizarre ways if necessary without suffering the methods of the mental-health industry. But what are the implications of Kingsley Hall for Laing's theory of the family nexus and family therapy? Laing seems to have concluded that troubled families cannot be "cured," that schizophrenics must leave their families for the unstructured therapeutic community.

An associate of Laing, David Cooper, in *The Death of the Family*, carries the concept of the family nexus to its logical political and social conclusions. The book, polemical and often violent in style, argues for the dissolution of nuclear families into communes as part of the revolution against capitalism. Cooper's politics turn out to be more anarchist than Marxist, advocating the emergence of total selves and free subjects against the mystifications of society. He outlines the "factors that operate within the family" as follows: (1) "gluing together of people based on their own incompleteness"; (2) "formation of roles . . . rather than . . . laying down of conditions for the free assumption of identity"; (3) instilling more social controls in children than are needed even in class society; (4) instilling an elaborate system of restrictive taboos in children.[60] These "factors" follow directly from Laing's position. But Cooper goes on to claim that the family, not the economy and not politics, is the fundamental problem of society which must be solved first in the revolutionary process; he thus registers an esteem for the position of the family in society held only by ultra-conservatives. Cooper defines the commune as "a potential alternative form of microsocial organization" through which love can be diffused more widely throughout the community than with the nuclear family. Pairing of lovers might still exist in the Laingian utopia, but relations would not be cemented for life. Children, the main beneficiaries of the new society, would have "free access to adults beyond their biological parental couple."[61] While in many ways attractive, Cooper's Fourierist vision does not relate family problems to wider social structures and does not indicate carefully enough the precise mechanisms of the nuclear family that need to be altered. *The Death of the Family* is a wild book which swings freely at everything the new left of the 1960s found objectionable without illuminating very much about the structural sources of discontent. A sure sign of analytic weakness, Cooper talks much about the horrors of the nuclear family without being able to account for the strength of its appeal. At bottom the theoretical problem in the book is that it assumes too quickly that after eliminating current oppressions a pure subject will emerge in a completely non-repressive society. But the glorification of schizophrenic non-repressiveness in Laing and Cooper bears the difficulties it has in Reich and more recently in Deleuze and Guattari: as I have noted above, human society requires a forming or shaping process which precludes any definition of freedom that relies on a pre-social base. The problem is not that society repressively institutes roles which destroy autonomy or the "free assumption of identity." It is rather that hierarchical authority prevents the collective regulation of life in which the needs and desires of all have an equal right to be recognized.

Despite all of these reservations, the theorists of family therapy offer important contributions to a theory of the family. They define as nowhere before the emotional system of the nuclear family. If they do not relate their analysis to history and society they still provide a basic understanding of the family which may be used in elaborating a more adequate theory.

Chapter 6

ELEMENTS OF A CRITICAL THEORY OF THE FAMILY

> *Progress in work on the history of the family is as much dependent on the formulation of models and hypotheses as it is upon the existence and exploitation of suitable source material.*
>
> E. ANTHONY WRIGLEY

THE CRITICAL THEORY of the family begins with self-reflection, grounding the construction of theory in the context of the contemporary situation of the family. The sense of uncertainty and malaise that surround the family today informs the theoretical project. In advanced capitalist society, the fate of the nuclear (or bourgeois) family is in doubt. Commentators ask if the family is falling apart or merely evolving into a new form. Amitai Etzioni asks if the family is worth saving in any case.[1] Challenged by feminists, child liberationists, advocates of sexual freedom, libertarian socialists, humanistic psychologists and radical therapists, the family is indeed losing its long-standing sanctity. Indicators of family disequilibrium are rising alarmingly: divorces, child abuse, alcoholism, single-parent families, single-person households and mental illness. Many family analysts conclude that the family no longer provides the context of emotional support it once did.

Compelling questions intrude upon the social scientist. How can the family be defined so that the validity of the criticisms and the indicators can be tested and evaluated? Does the family contribute to the oppression of women and children, to sexual repression, to capitalist exploitation and to psychic ailments? Are the values of monogamous love, privacy, individualism, domesticity, maternal child care and emotional fulfillment realized in or corrupted by the family? Are these values themselves in doubt?

The critical theory of the family cannot avoid these issues. Instead, theory must be constructed so that it contributes to research that can clarify them. Theory will need to define the family in a manner that will face squarely the possibility that alternative family structures may be desirable.

Epistemologically, a critical theory of the family must constitute the family as an object for research. It must provide a set of categories that point to the kinds of data needed for the comprehension of the family in a given society. And it must indicate the parameters of meaning of the possible findings. The role of theory is that of midwife for the birth of empirical studies. Theory does not produce a closed set of concepts that exhausts the meaning of its object, but provides a set of categorical guidelines enabling researchers to discover the concrete configurations of the object in question.

The tasks for theory at the level of the development of categories is distinct, at least partially, from what is normally called explanation. There are two levels of theoretical elaboration: the synchronic and the diachronic. At the synchronic level the object is determined structurally by a set of categories which outline how the object operates at a given time. At the diachronic level, changes in the structural form of the object are explained. The example of Marx's concept of the mode of production illustrates this distinction. The concept of the mode of production, consisting of forces and relations of production, defines the structure of the economy at any given time. The notions of contradiction and class struggle explain how one mode of production changes into another. Research on the mode of production often proceeds simultaneously at the synchronic and diachronic levels, indicating both the state of development of a given mode of production and how it is changing. With regard to the study of the family, however, the existing state of research is so sparse and so conceptually un-clear that it is not possible at this time to offer a theory of how one family structure changes into another.

The reasons for the difficulties with a diachronic theory of the family may not relate to the body of research but to the object itself. It may be that the family is so dependent on other levels of society (the state or the economy) that changes in its structure cannot be understood by reference to aspects of the family itself. It may be that the structure of the family is determined almost wholly by the economy or by politics. However, there are important theoretical reasons for doubt-ing this conclusion. Just as political forms do not emerge in lock step with economic forms, so family forms are not per-fectly contemporaneous with other levels of society. Industrial capitalism and representative democracy, for example, do not emerge at the same time as modern family forms. Therefore family forms enjoy at least a partial autonomy from the state and the economy. Since the family enjoys partial autonomy, changes in its structure will ultimately need to be explained separately from explanations of the birth of industrial capital-ism or democracy.

For the present, then, the theoretical task can be restricted to the synchronic level, to the precise determination of family structure by a set of categories. There are, in fact, enough difficulties in defining family structure to keep the theorist busy. Before a theoretical strategy can be developed, the theo-rist must confront a thorny problem: the family is defined by different societies in greatly divergent ways and it is given greatly divergent degrees of importance. In pre-industrial Europe the family denotes either household or lineage and even then is relatively indistinct as a social category. In the modern period the family is defined as a prominent unit of society but it tends increasingly to be limited to the conjugal unit of parents and children. In "primitive" societies kinship seems to dominate family almost completely. Hence different societies do not have comparable definitions of the family. Historians cannot, therefore, trace the history of the family by relying upon the meanings provided by the societies themselves.

The variation in the social definition of the family accentuates the problem for the theorist. The theorist must provide a categorical definition of the family which is broad and loose enough to encompass the varying family configurations of the pre-industrial and industrial periods. The mistake made by Parsonians and Freudians has been to take the modern family configuration as the norm and project it backward or, more precisely, to derive categories that fit neatly with modern family structure but fail to permit important differences in earlier forms to emerge with equal validity. The theorist must avoid stacking the conceptual deck against premodern family structure. The family must be theorized in such a way that a priori premodern forms are neither less intelligible nor less viable than modern forms. In fact, the theory must allow for future forms and avoid any implication that the present family is unchangeable.

If flexibility of categories is one requirement for a theory of the family, so coherence of categories is another. The definition of family structure must be tight enough to render the family intelligible as a defined pattern of human association. There must be clear boundaries designed in the theory delimiting what is and what is not part of the family structure. More significantly, there must be a hierarchy of meanings about the family which define what is central to family structure and what is not. In other words, the theory must provide a strategy which unpacks and orders the levels of family experience in such a way that a final core of coherence defines a given family structure.

Many theories of the family accomplish this end by listing a set of functions specific to the family, such as reproduction, socialization, sexuality, reproduction of labor power and so forth. These functionalist theories of the family, exemplified by Parsons and Marx, tend to reduce the specificity of family experience to the operations of the social totality. They assume that the kind of reality contained in family experience is no different from the kind of reality contained in any other region of society or any other set of social interactions. In the Parsonian case, norms, roles and values enacted in a business transaction are no different from norms, roles and values in the family. As an agent of socialization, the family is only an aspect of the equilibrium of social values. Competition, for instance, in the one case is the same as competition in the other. But this is inadequate. The family is different from the economy not simply in the functions it performs for the society but in the quality of the relations it contains. For this reason, the theory of the family cannot be functionalist. It must develop categories that allow the regional uniqueness of family structure to be defined on its own terms.

In order, therefore, to develop categories of family structure that account for a wide diversity of social definitions and for the coherence and uniqueness of family experience, the theory of the family must turn to the psychological level and develop categories which permit the understanding of vastly divergent family structures in terms of their emotional pattern. The family is thus the place where psychic structure is formed and where experience is characterized in the first instance by emotional patterns. The function of socialization is clearly implied by this definition, but the family is being conceptualized not primarily as an institution with the function of socialization. Instead it is the social location where psychic structure is most decisively prominent.

In addition to being the locus of psychic structure, the family is a distinct social space to the extent that it generates and embodies hierarchies of age and sex. Political institutions are studied in terms of power relations; economic institutions are studied in terms of wealth or class. By the same token, differences of age and sex are specific to the family and most easily made intelligible by studying the family. The family is the social space where generations confront each other directly and where the two sexes define their differences and power relations. Age and sex are, of course, present as social markers in all institutions. Yet the family contains them, generates them and realizes them to an unusually deep degree. In other words, the study of the family provides an excellent place to learn about how society structures the determinations of age and sex.

Historians and social scientists have until recently not placed age and sex hierarchies high on their agenda. The dominant social theories of Tocqueville, Mill, Marx, Weber and Durkheim have focused attention on the great questions of religion, politics and the economy. The study of the family is one place where the neglected areas of age and sex domination can become incorporated into the historical picture. The patterns of age and sex domination have been as brutal as those of the other great historical questions. Generational and sexual conflict must be captured and understood in the same way as conflicts of class, race and religion. There is a rich and important history that has not yet been written of the domination of women and children which can be illuminated to a considerable extent within the history of the family.

The family has often been studied in terms of demography, economics and politics. Family size is fundamental to the problematics of demographic research. Inheritance practices are basic to the comprehension of economic mobility. Marriage patterns of elite families are at times crucial for politics. When the family is studied for these purposes its own coherence tends to be absorbed by concerns for other institutions. The family can be studied as its own center of intelligibility, generating its own problematics, when it is viewed as the place where psychic structure is internalized and becomes a mechanism for instituting hierarchies of age and sex.

Freudian psychology provides the best categories for defining family structure in terms of emotional patterns. Just as Marx, Weber and other great social theorists developed their systems in terms of the problematics of an emerging industrial world, so Freud developed psychoanalysis in close connection with the context of modernization. Even though Freud did not explicitly theorize psychic structure in relation to family structure, his work is rooted in the issues of an emerging modern family form. Although psychoanalysis cannot be adopted without revision for the purpose of a theory of the family, it does provide foundational elements. Freud's theory of psycho-sexual development—the oral, anal and genital stages—can be set in a context of age and sex hierarchies specific to a given family structure. When this is done, the family appears as an emotional configuration which generates personality types in relative autonomy from other social levels.

More concretely, there are patterns of authority and love unique to different family types which can be interpreted in relation to the oral, anal and genital stages, and from which hierarchies of age and sex are both realized and reproduced. The combination of authority and love in relation to the three stages provides a theoretical model for discriminating family types as well as for analyzing their coherence. The oral, anal and genital stages indicate the points of emotional tension between adults and children, although this tension can concern very different matters, not just the specific problems noted by Freud. In the context of this emotional tension, the psyche becomes organized and patterned to reproduce the authority-love configuration of the older generation. At the same time the sexes are distinguished for the first time within the individual and given their social determinations.

Social psychologists, developmental psychologists and related branches of social science have studied numerous aspects of the parent-child relation. The ordinal position of children has been given much attention by Adlerians and others. Stages of moral development have been intensively examined by Piaget and his school. Cognitive development, intelligence and learning in general have been scrutinized by many schools, including behaviorists and linguists. Each of these research projects has generated a body of valuable knowledge about early childhood experience which could become a basis for family history. Yet the revised Freudian model presented here offers the most comprehensive theoretical basis for family studies. Other approaches might certainly be added to it in specific studies. But none of them offers as suggestively as

Freud a model that points to major changes in family experience.

A case could be made for anthropological theories. Traditionally anthropology has been sensitive to issues concerned directly with the role of the family in the formation of social solidarity. Lévi-Strauss' position on this question has already been discussed and Malinowski has been mentioned in passing. The dominant school of anthropological theory has been the structural-functionalists, whose major figures (A. R. Radcliffe-Brown, Raymond Firth, Edmond Leach and others) have contributed much to social science. Yet this school is not sufficiently different at the theoretical level from Parsons to warrant special consideration.[2] Within this school there have been efforts to generate theories similar to the one offered here. Francis Hsu has theorized the family by focusing on the dominant dyadic relation in each family structure.[3] But these efforts have all been directed at small-scale, pre-industrial societies which are for the most part outside the modern world system. A critical theory of the family, by contrast, must concern issues that derive from advanced industrial societies and their precursors. The type of anthropology that does relate directly to this study is that of ethnologists, who study peasant communities within the modern world system. These efforts will be discussed in the next chapter.

Objections might be raised to the choice of authority and love as indices to study in relation to the oral, anal and genital stages. Since the object of family studies is the interactional pattern at the emotional level between family members, the types and degrees of love and affection presented by the adults to the child are the best avenue to approach the question. Also, arguments for the value of the present family form center on the question of the necessity of maternal love for child development. Similarly, the category of authority was chosen because it is a major aspect of the adult presence in confrontation with children. The index of authority allows the student of the family to investigate the vital question of freedom, its limits and possibilities. The categories of authority and love are essential as well in drawing attention away from the individual psyche of the child and Freud's energy problematics. These categories help to focus empirical studies clearly on the family as an interactional unit.

There are three theoretical questions which must be clarified at this point: (1) To what extent is the domination of children a biological necessity? (2) To what extent are masculine and feminine roles biologically inevitable? (3) To what extent is the structural model of the family conscious or unconscious? The answer to all three questions is loaded with political significance and determines the extent to which an ideal family form can be based on equality. The answer to these questions defines the limits of domination necessary for the existence of society. Moreover, these questions are inherent in any treatment of the family, and they are best handled theoretically by self-consciously and explicitly articulating answers to them. The difficulty, of course, is that they cannot be answered fully because (1) biological knowledge is rudimentary, (2) the biological and social levels are inextricably mixed, and (3) self-conscious social experiments to test the extent to which domination can be eliminated have not been carried out. Furthermore, answers to these questions are often dependent on the theorist's own society, in particular on his society's norms about what women and men are and what degree and type of authority and love is necessary for children.

The case in favor of biological arguments on issues of family organization has been made recently by Alice Rossi. She contends that in certain areas, like neuro-endocrinology, science has progressed beyond its older notion of closed bio-systems, which had been the basis for arguments of biological determinism. Current research shows that biological systems and social systems mutually influence each other. The flow of hormones and the family are part of the same system. The use of biological arguments, Rossi reasons, no longer presents an alternative to social explanations; rather the two positions are complementary. After demonstrating that certain hormonal changes in the mother attendant to the birth process lead the mother to experience deep feelings of care for the infant, Rossi concludes that there is a biological imperative for "the bonding of the mother and the newborn"[4] which society ought not disrupt. She presents an auxiliary argument that, in the case of maternal care, physiological factors facilitate "species survival." With the population of the earth nearing the four billion mark, "species survival" does not seem threatened by social arrangements that minimize maternal care. Instead, survival is a question of radioactive contamination of nuclear energy. Rossi's contention that species survival is closely connected with furthering biological impulses for mothering appears far-fetched.

Rossi also argues from empirical evidence that the long evolution of the human species confirms the hormonal impulse toward mothering. In making her case, she dismisses unfavorable evidence from the European nobility and upper bourgeoisie. From the Renaissance to the nineteenth century these groups placed a low value on mothering, preferring to send infants to wet nurses for feeding. For Rossi, the elite's behavior was "an extreme aberration in human history."[5] Yet she makes no case that the women or children suffered from such treatment. In addition, Erikson and others have described the feeding practice of the Sioux, in which infants were fed by any lactating female, not just the mother. Hence social arrangements provide a variety beyond the limits imposed by biology.

For the past two centuries Western society has imposed on women an ideology of maternalism that has worked to restrict the opportunities for women to participate in the economy. After women completed their reproductive duties they were not able to compete equally with men in professional and business careers. If the revised biological argument of Rossi were accepted, the options of women in choosing or rejecting maternalism would be restricted. Rossi's general argument that society should be "more attuned to the natural environment, in touch with, and respectful of, the rhythm of our own body processes"[6] cannot be gainsaid. Nor can objections be sustained against her plea for social scientists to integrate new biological research into their studies. However, when she makes a specific case for the biological pressures for maternalism her position supports an arbitrary restriction on women's place in society.

The proper attitude to take in relation to these questions is a thoroughgoing agnosticism. Simply because men and women are defined and have been defined in certain ways or because children have been subject to and are subject to certain patterns of authority and love provides no certainty that things must continue that way. Anthropological evidence, indeed, suggests an enormous variability in all these questions.[7] Neither liberal nor socialist theory provides indisputable grounds for legitimating a specific pattern of domination. Technological advances tend to undercut traditional restrictive norms (such as the value of chastity related to the prevention of unwanted conceptions). What is more, modern societies of both liberal and socialist types claim to support a maximum degree of equality and undercut traditional arguments for domination. Hence the most reasonable position the theorist can take on epistemological grounds is that biological limitations do not provide a basis for justifying any particular pattern of domination of children or restrictive sex role.

To some degree—a degree which cannot be defined at this point in history—children must be subject to adult authority. This is so because (1) children are born into a world not of their choice to which they must become socialized, and (2) children cannot have the same knowledge or consciousness of this world as adults while they are interacting with adults and growing up. Neither of these limitations, however, legitimates any historical family structure. All known family types fall far short of reducing domination to the bare essentials necessary for these requirements. A third reason for adult authority over children which is normally invoked is that children are biologically dependent on adults. While this is true (adults are also dependent on other adults) dependence does not necessarily lead to domination, although it often does. To conclude this discussion, it can be posited that the construction of a theory

of the family must not provide grounds for privileging abso-
lutely any particular historical form of the family. Quite the
contrary, the theorist must be careful to avoid elaborating
categories that justify the existence of a family structure on
grounds that reduce ultimately to biology.

The theoretical task of defining the family contains addi-
tional difficulties. The theorist must not pretend that his definition reveals the true essence of the family. Families vary
widely in different societies and they may be approached in
countless ways depending on the purposes of the investigator.
Family theory is circumscribed in particular by the need to
conceptualize an internal structure of the family that will
allow researchers to compare various historical families, to
render intelligible concrete forms of interaction among family
members, and to open up for research structures by which age
and sex are internalized by family members. These are the
kinds of knowledge that the study of the family can bring to
social science and that can constitute the family as a relatively
autonomous object of study.

With these requirements in mind, theory must specify the
categories which enable researchers to discover emotional patterns accompanying particular family structures. These categories will not define the only elements of family life that can
be studied but they must provide a central foundation upon
which other studies can build. The argument proposed here
in favor of Freud's three stages in relation to patterns of authority and love must not be taken restrictively. The strength
of Freud's insight and its utility for family studies rests on the
ubiquity of the family's response to oral, anal and genital
stages of experience. All family organizations develop strategies to feed the child, to train the child to dispose of its wastes
and to cope with the child's exploration of its genitals. In so
doing, families present to the child a pattern of love and authority which helps form the child's psyche. The child develops emotional patterns that are enduring and concern major
questions of social life. These emotional patterns establish a
general set of feelings toward the body; they internalize sexual

identity; they form an ego defining the ways in which the self will relate to society; and they institute a pattern of responding to external authority. The understanding of these issues for a given society will tell the social scientist much about relative sexual roles, degrees of authoritarianism, degrees of individualization and, in general, psycho-social strengths. The aim of such knowledge is not, as it was for Freud, the comprehension of the individual psyche but the pattern of emotions specific to the family.

Child-rearing practices and attitudes are of central importance for this theory of the family. Child-rearing practices are an excellent highway into the dark countryside of family relations.[8] When properly theorized, they provide relatively easy access to a great field of recalcitrant materials. But these attitudes and practices must not be studied in relation to the values they leave behind in the individual psyche. Since the problem under consideration is family structure and not individual character traits, child rearing must be examined as part of an interactional process between adults and children. When the nexus of child rearing is studied in this way, each society can be seen as constituting a particular pattern of relations encompassing both the parents and the children. These relations, conceptualized at the emotional level, constitute a unique pattern which defines family life.

The degree of permissiveness in a family is an important issue but not the central one. Types of control of the child's behavior, from physical punishment to threats of withdrawal of love, are only part of the problem. Adults in a family constitute a pattern of love and authority that provides an emotional context for a child which goes beyond the direct strategies of limiting and sanctioning the child's behavior. This pattern is always there for the child, even when the parents are not involved in child care.

An important component in this matrix is the availability of adult models for the child to identify with. Freud's classic definition of identification distinguishes it from other forms of emotional attachment. In identification, the relation between the lover and the loved is so deep that the distinction between the two individuals is erased. The lover, in this case the child, takes the other as himself, incorporating the other into his psyche at an unconscious level. In the context of the family, the child identifies with an adult, normally one of the same sex, so that for psychological purposes he is that adult. Freud's analysis, however, does not conceptualize the process of identification in a way that can account for the variety of types of identification and for different degrees of identification. Typical of his theory in general, Freud understands identification only as a process going on in the child, leaving family structure out of the account. If one reinserts the concept of identification in the family context, the number of adults and their pattern of love and authority take on their proper significance. Where a great variety of adults appear, identification might be more diffuse; where authority figures are separate from loving figures, identification might be less ambivalent and less profound. In some cases adult figures might not be incorporated by the child as persons but only as functions. Just this result is obtained in the kibbutz, where the major adult authority figure is the nurse, who is internalized as a function or socializing agent and not as an individual personality.[9] Hence the category of identification must be studied in relation to the concrete constellation of adults in a given society so that the particular type of identification can be illuminated.

One danger for the researcher associated with analyses such as these concerns the researcher's own family patterns. Historians have learned that child beating was common in preindustrial Europe. Their initial response was to treat this practice with indignation as representing an inferior form of child rearing. Child beating is certainly not praiseworthy, but an attitude of moral righteousness does not help uncover emotional patterns of the past. In a middle-class family of today beating a child might mean something different from what it meant in other family forms. Studying feelings of rejection, psychologists have learned that everything depends on the established pattern of the emotions. In a contemporary middle-class family, child beating represents rejection by the parents and the child takes it as such. In the context of a preindustrial European peasant family, child beating no doubt did not represent rejection. Of course the child was still beaten and the blows caused pain; at the emotional level, however, there would be a difference in the two situations. The middleclass child would experience the beating as an unusual event, signifying great hostility by the parents. For the peasant child, it would be a normal occurrence, not to be taken too seriously.[10] When the family is studied at the emotional level, an unusual sensitivity is required on the part of the scientist. Because the same behavior can mean different things in two settings, the careful elaboration of the full family pattern is all the more important.

A recent effort by a Freudian historian of childhood, Lloyd de Mause, to generate a model for the psychological history of the family is flawed by just such an insensitivity to emotional differences. De Mause conceptualized the history of childhood optimistically: in Western history parenting begins with brutal forms of child abuse which have gradually but inexorably been overcome until the present stage is reached, where children enjoy true empathy by their parents. Concerned with the history of childhood as distinct from family history, de Mause suggests that there are three ways parents can relate to children:

1. They can use the child as a vehicle for projecting the contents of their own unconscious (projective reaction).
2. They can use the child as a substitute for an adult figure important in their own childhood (reversal reaction).
3. They can empathize with the child's needs and act to satisfy them (empathic reaction).[11]

De Mause then applies this model by looking at child-rearing practices, beginning with the ancients. He finds a movement from infanticide (a combination of the first two forms of reaction) to the "helping mode" of modernity based on empathic reaction.

There are several problems with de Mause's paradigm. First, it remains an individualistic model, seeing only individual parental reactions without indicating the general context of socializing figures or sources of identification, and accounting for variations at this level. In short, it takes the conjugal family as the norm. Second, it theorizes the "evolution of parent-child relations" outside of family history and social history. In de Mause's worthy effort to stress the independence of parent-child relations he obscures the interaction of child rearing and social structure. Third, his model is optimistic in nature, viewing the history of children as an upward march toward the present. Hence de Mause's model is incapable of demonstrating the limits of parent-child interactions in the modern nuclear family. Finally, the psychic mechanisms of the model are too limited. They are not flexible enough to account for the wide variety of parental responses to children, nor for the relative intensity, as opposed to the form, of the response.

Scientists engaged in studies of the present might register some skepticism about the accessibility of the past to the kind of psychological analysis proposed here. There are good reasons for doubts. The dead do not easily reveal their feelings and their traces, especially at the level of the popular classes, who are almost invisible in any case. Indeed, one cannot expect the distant past to reveal its emotional patterns with the degree of subtlety that is found since Freud's time and in particular at the present time. Nevertheless, knowledge of pre-industrial family forms is crucial for establishing a critical distance from present family forms. Even if knowledge of the past is less nuanced it is more valuable just for its differences. Also, the categories offered in these pages are designed to take the inaccessibility of the past into account and establish the concept of family structure at a level for which comparable data can be obtained. Granting these difficulties, students of the family also have reasons to be optimistic. Emotional life in pre-industrial times was not shrouded in the cloak of privacy that has covered it since the emergence of the nuclear family.

There is reason to expect that, with ingenuity on the researcher's part, much information about *la vie intime* can become available. Sexual practices, for example, is one area often thought to be beyond the historian's grasp. Yet Roland Mousnier has looked at reports of meetings between village priests and the church hierarchy in France, where problems of the church's stance on sexual promiscuity were discussed. The local priests revealed much about village sexual life, as well as the church's attitude toward it. Mousnier found that the priests were reluctant to enforce heavy penances for such sins as adultery and fornication because these practices were in some villages so widespread that regulation was impossible.[12]

In summary, the family is here conceptualized as an emotional structure, with relative autonomy, which constitutes hierarchies of age and sex in psychological forms. The family is conceived as a system of love objects. Child-rearing patterns are theorized as interactional processes, focusing on the first three stages of development (oral, anal and genital). In these interactions, a pattern of authority and love is instituted by the adults forming a background to the strategies for raising children. Finally, a pattern of identification can be discerned which cements the bonds between the adults and the children. When these categories are studied in detail a concrete family structure becomes intelligible.

In addition to the psychological level, the theory of the family requires two other kinds of analyses. They are the everyday life of the family and the relation of the family to society. Before the pattern of authority and love during the first three stages of development can be determined with precision, the social scientist must have a clear sense of who the family members are as characters in the social drama. Knowledge of the family's daily life and its relation to society is the background for the analysis at the psychological level.

The categories for the analysis of everyday life are derived from studying the routines of family activity. They are not difficult to generate and those offered below are simply suggestions. The criterion to use in selecting categories in this context is: What information is necessary to determine the concrete configuration of social life for the family in question? The historian and social scientist should approach the study of everyday life with an ethnographer's sense for the mundane. Without a picture of the daily life of the family the epistemological danger of myopia cannot be checked. Current psychological tendencies are too easily projected onto different family structures. By looking carefully at daily life, one can obtain a vivid sense of alien customs and practices. In this way, hopefully, the widespread tendency of attributing contemporary motives to all societies will be minimized.

The analysis of daily life must provide a rudimentary sense of what kind of group one is dealing with. It must provide a clear sense of the types of relations that exist between family members, the types of buildings the family inhabits, architecturally and in terms of design. How the edifice helps to organize the functions of everyday life needs to be learned. Other questions are: What are the typical norms and behaviors of the family members in relation to their attitude toward each other, toward the family as a whole, and toward non-family members? What is the relation between kinship and presence in the family group?

The broadest way to define the daily life of the family, one which least distorts the definition of the family by contemporary forms, is to look loosely at the households in the society under study without anticipating at all that they will be composed solely of kinship or "family" relations. If kinship is defined first, the question is loaded in favor of the definitions of the family of the present period and of "primitive" societies. It is not necessarily true that the people who live together and interact daily are tied together by blood or kin status. For this reason anthropological studies of kinship cannot be taken as models. If households consist, in a given society, of large numbers of non-kin, they must be included in the picture of the family's daily life.

The general environment of the household must be known. Where is it geographically? Does the household exist in a metropolitan area or in a rural setting? Population density and geographical features are appropriate information here. Next, the composition of the household must be ascertained. Demographic studies are most helpful as a start, but they must include a sensitivity to kin and non-kin members as well as to the stability of the composition. Recent demographic work has studied the life cycle of the family to learn how the composition of the family varies over time. In some families three generations cohabit, but only for a short time due to the early average age of death. In other places, children are sent out of the family to be breast-fed and then again later to be apprenticed, so that they live with their family for short, intermittent periods only. The simple statistic of the overall average number in a family is a deceptive piece of information.

The study of the composition of the household should also include the functions, roles and hierarchies of the members. It is not enough to note that there is a wife in the house. The role of wife does not mean the same thing in a peasant family in the seventeenth century in Burgundy and in a bourgeois family in Los Angeles in 1910 or in 1970. By studying the tasks of members of a household and the relative authority of members one can see how the family operates as a system in everyday life. It might be the case that in some family structures servants are closer to the wife than is the husband. Again, there can be no presumption that an alliance between husband and wife, as Parsons and Lidz maintain, is necessary, inevitable or desirable in "normal" families.

Next, the relations among households must be studied to get a general sense of the relative isolation of each household. It might be that daily interactions concern mixtures of people from different households who are closer to each other than members of the same household. Also, relatives might live close to one another or far away, interact frequently or infrequently. In each case research must determine what obligations families can exact from relatives.

The material structure of the household is also important. How big is the structure? How close is it to the nearest neighbor? How does its design embody the social position of the family? How does its internal arrangement regulate or limit the interactions among family members? How are the rooms arranged, and what is the degree of functional differentiation of the rooms? What is the nature of the furniture in the residence, its degree of opulence and its functionality? Who built the structure, and out of what materials? How old is it?

The question of the establishment of the household and family can be treated by studying the nature of marriage and courtship customs. Who can marry whom? At what age is marriage appropriate? What financial and emotional obligations does it entail? Does the man or the woman determine the line of the family? Which spouse moves into the other's family? The answer to this question reveals much about the relative power of the two sexes in the society. For what reasons does one marry and who decides that the couple can marry? What is the meaning of marriage in the society—a permanent bond or a relatively unimportant and transitory alliance? What is the emotional significance of marriage? Does it provide the sole love object for the partners or no love object at all? At what age do people marry? On purely logical grounds, sexual patterns have no fixed relation to marriage or to the establishment of family and household.

Concerning sexuality, demographers provide data about the age of menarche and fertility and fecundity rates. Also important is information about contraceptive devices, abortion and infanticide practices. Does the woman give birth by herself, with the aid of a midwife or a doctor, at home, in the woods or in a hospital? What social networks are established through the regulation of sexuality? Are women bound together through knowledge of abortion and midwifery? Are young people formed into groups to control pre-marital sexuality or is this in the hands of the state? Is the society bound together through orgies or religious rituals? Is sex limited to the marriage partners? In the broadest sense sexuality concerns the bodily contacts of people, so that the physical closeness of members of the family, household and society is important.

Sexuality does not necessarily accompany love or intimacy—witness the practices of bourgeois males in the late nineteenth century who, in many cases, loved their wives but had their sexual needs gratified with prostitutes and servants. Social and familial limits and values concerning sexual practices are germane to the study of the family. Also, one must study the life cycle of sexuality: At what ages are different forms of sexuality customary? Do old people have intercourse, are children sexually active? And how is sexual knowledge transmitted?

Much about family life is revealed by the diet. The kinds of food eaten, their nutritional value, the times of day meals are taken, the ordering of family members around the table, the ceremonies of the table—all these are essential for understanding the family. Scientists have determined, for example, that the contraceptive value of breast-feeding is limited to those societies with certain dietary deficiencies. For nutritional reasons, in some pre-industrial societies, lactating women were not able to ovulate. Until this was determined, medical opinion was puzzled by demographic data which confirmed the widespread belief among European peasants that conception was not possible until weaning was completed.

With an analysis of these topics the social scientist should have a good picture of the structure of the family at the level of everyday life. The nature of this knowledge will be descriptive, not explanatory. Yet the psychological analysis of the family cannot proceed very far without a firm sense of the family's daily life. One example should suffice. Until the nineteenth century, peasant women swaddled their infants, who then required only minimal care during the day. It might be assumed that swaddling was an indication of neglect for children, with deep psychological significance. A study of the mother's daily work routine indicates that she could not spend her time either changing the wrappings when they were soiled or keeping a constant eye on the baby to protect it. In this way, the comprehension of daily life guards against projection.

The analysis of the relation between society and the family is carried out for another set of reasons. The argument was made earlier that the family is relatively autonomous, that it must be taken as such in order to make intelligible how age and sex hierarchies are internalized. Now the other side of the question must be faced, that is, to what extent the family is not an autonomous unit. Unless the determinations of the family by society are taken into account, a false conclusion may be drawn that the family is self-contained. In other words, although every family structure contains its own psychological pattern, sociologically family structures vary in the extent to which they are integrated with larger social units. This complexity in family theory was not accounted for in the sociological traditions reviewed earlier in this book. The purpose of studying the relation of the family to society is not to reduce the intelligibility of the family as a psychological unit to some broader determination, such as modernization or the mode of production. Instead, this relation must be explored to enrich the understanding of the psychological level itself. By defining how political, economic, religious and urban institutions encroach upon family space, the degree of conflict or equilibrium between family and society can be studied empirically. Hierarchies of age and sex might be more prevalent, or less prevalent, or the same in society and in the family. These conjunctions or disjunctions will affect the stability of the pattern of authority and love within the family. As a reminder, it is worth repeating that the analysis remains at the synchronic level, not the diachronic. There is no attempt here to explain theoretically changes in family structure. Such an effort cannot be made until the history of the family is written in greater detail. Nevertheless, as this history is being written, the structural relations between the family and society need to be taken into account. In sum, while the family generates a psychological pattern of internalized age and sex hierarchies, it also participates in larger social institutions. The types of this participation must be made intelligible.

Different economic systems are based on different types of wealth (land in feudalism, money in capitalism) and different relations of people to wealth. Family structure must be understood in relation to the control of wealth: What kind of ownership does the family have (landed property for the aristocracy, forms of tenancy for the peasantry, ownership of labor power for workers)? Which member or members of the family maintains this control? The pattern of inheritance (primogeniture, to all sons equally, to all children) will indicate much about the underlying conditions of the family's internal relations. A good way to focus on the analysis of property is to describe the mechanisms through which those in control of property maintain that control. A peasant vintner in early modern France might pass on his land and his skills in making wine to his sons while a coal miner in early nineteenth-century England might employ his own children in his work team.

The analysis of work roles and schooling systems concentrates on a slightly different question, that is, to see how the work activity done by various members of the family fits into the general economic structure. In peasant villages families are bound together in work activities in numerous ways. A strong degree of collective dependence exists (at harvest time, if a barn or house has to be rebuilt, and so forth), undercutting the family's autonomy. Although the household is a productive unit, it cannot survive separate from other families. In contemporary families, on the contrary, work is separate from the household, and the family has no immediate economic dependence on neighboring households. In addition to the extent of collective dependence, family work roles are determined by the extent of the development of the market. Whereas the family once produced almost entirely for its own use, now work is done for the market, leaving housework in a secondary position as a remnant of an older system which has a low social value. Work done in the home today concerns the social status of the family and the reproduction of labor value in the children. Housework is no longer a directly economic activity. With the clear picture of family structure derived from the previous analyses, the meshing of the family and the economy can be specified. Questions of contradictions between economic structure and family structure can be analyzed with precision.

The most important index of collective dependence is the

form of social authority over the family. Here one is dealing with a variable that has changed enormously over the past three centuries. To what extent are the daily activities of the family, from work to sex, controlled by institutions and figures outside the family? We need to have a history of the privatization of the family, noting carefully which sectors of the population, which family structures, were affected at different times. The extent of privacy of family relations is a crucial determinant of the psychological life of the family, one which Freud did not take into account. When there is little secrecy in family relations, when the larger community can intervene in what are today regarded as intimate matters, then the emotional quality of family relations will have an entirely different character from that of families where these conditions do not prevail. It is very difficult to appreciate the meaning of the recent isolation of family relations from a broader community or to appreciate a system where privacy has no value. A legend from Africa tells of a husband and wife, arriving at a village in search of a home. The couple engaged in a mock family quarrel at night to see if other villagers would intervene. They left the village in the morning because no one came to arbitrate their conflict. Such intervention would occur, they thought, in a good village.

The analysis of religion, ideology, festivals and games (leisure, sports, and the entertainment media for the modern period) also helps to define the autonomy of the family. Community authority is most visible at these moments of family life. One can contrast a modern family on a weekday evening gathered around the TV with an early modern peasant family huddled together in someone's barn along with many other families. The dialogues and gestures in these two cases imply entirely different family relations. One can study the interlocking of family and society in ceremonies surrounding birth, marriage and death. Philip Slater contends, for example, that the custom of the honeymoon, normally seen as an opportunity for the newlyweds to establish their private bond, is really a means society uses to curtail this privacy and set up the dominance of the wider family over the couple.[13]

Conceptions of the family by religious, political and legal institutions do much to determine relations between family and society. The policy of the state toward the family is affected by the ideology of the family. Theological ideas about the family have had a deep impact in European history. Puritanism, for instance, encouraged the emerging nuclear family. Obviously, the Bible is a basic document for family history. A study of the attitudes of European communist parties toward the family would probably reveal surprisingly conservative tendencies. The history of the idea of the family largely remains to be written.

Conventional wisdom in the social sciences tends to assume that the family fits into the society like a hand in a glove. But this is not always the case. Women in the United States have been severely handicapped by economic institutions in obtaining credit and loans, in competing equally for jobs, and so forth. Patriarchal mechanisms were entrenched in many sectors of the economy. Seclusion in the home was women's fate. Family and society worked hand in hand in this case to reproduce sexual hierarchy. The women's movement has challenged economic inequality, and it began by questioning the restriction of women to the family. In this instance, an egalitarian movement was initiated within the context of the family and came to influence and reform the economy. Numerous examples to the same effect can be found. A critical theory of the family must leave open the possibility that the family may not be in tune with the society. The hierarchies generated within the family may be out of phase or in discontinuity with other social hierarchies. The impact of the psychological structure of the family may work, as Freud thought, to reproduce archaic ideologies and retard social change, or, on the contrary, to move society forward toward eliminating modes of domination. Because, at the synchronic level, the family produces its own psychological forms of hierarchy, there is no way to predict the results of the interaction between the family and society.

This chapter has presented the outlines of a critical theory of the family in which the analysis proceeds at three levels. At the first level, the family was conceived as a psychological structure. This level defined the family and indicated what contribution the study of the family can make to social science. The second and third levels, those of daily life and the relation to society, were conceptualized as supplementary to the first. They filled in and enriched the grasp of emotional structure. The theory was critical in the sense that it led to a comprehension of the limits to which any family structure reinforces or eliminates hierarchies of age and sex. Implicit in the theory was judgment that family structure should be so reformed that age and sex hierarchies are minimized if not eliminated completely.

Given the present state of research on the family, the theory could only proceed at the synchronic level. The explanation for changes in family structure must await the fuller comprehension of family history. One must know what it is that is changing before one explains the change. Although this seems elementary, historians and sociologists, as we have seen, have not hesitated to offer grand explanatory schemes to account for the total history of the family. Such schemes assume a linear, continuous, evolutionary quality in family history that cannot be sustained. When the theory offered in these pages is employed in empirical studies, it will become clear that there have been numerous, distinct family structures, each with its own psychological pattern. At that point it will be recognized that family history has been discontinuous. It encompasses many unique structures whose changes cannot be explained in a linear fashion. Family history cannot be conceived as an evolution toward small, conjugal units, as an increasing differentiation of instrumental and expressive functions, or as an increasing form of patriarchy tied to the mode of production. Instead, family history should be conceived in the plural, as the history of distinct structures of age and sex hierarchies. The change from one structure to another will require different explanatory strategies, each suited to its own case.

Although the critical theory of the family is limited to the synchronic level, it should not be assumed that an argument for objectivism is being made in which the goal is to discover alternate combinations of the same structure of authority and love through the oral, anal and genital stages. Family members must be studied as subjects who internalize structures, but not necessarily in a passive way. Family structures have been oppressive in varying degrees; they have always involved domination. The history of these structures must be written in a tragic mode. It has had its share of brutalities, sacrifices and repressions. But the story also has its moments of conflict. Women and children have not always internalized their inferior roles quietly and obediently. One can assume that, in dealing with human subjects, when there is domination there is also resistance. The history of family will have to include this side of the story along with that of outlining the psychological patterns.

Finally, the shape of the critical theory of the family offered in this chapter has been influenced by the need for clarification about the condition of the family today. Prominence has been given to the psychological level and to age and sex hierarchies because these determinations, when studied in a broad historical scope, can help make sense of today's concerns with the family. The scientific study of the value of the modern family can proceed only on a firm historical base.

Chapter 7

MODELS OF FAMILY STRUCTURE

> *There came a time when the middle class could no longer bear the pressure of the multitude or the contact of the lower class. It seceded: it withdrew from the vast polymorphous society to organize itself separately, in a homogeneous environment, among its families, in homes designed for privacy, in new districts kept free from all lower class contamination.*
>
> PHILIPPE ARIES

IN THE CONTEXT of present-day concerns with the family, the critical theory of the family must contribute to answering the following questions. When did the modern family emerge and what is its historical significance? What family structures predominated in society before the modern family? In response to each question, the issue at hand is the psychological pattern of the family. In order to evaluate the modern family, which is praised for the emotional solace it promises, social scientists must examine its original psychological pattern, as well as changes in this pattern up to the present. One can then raise the question of the desirability of the modern family. In order to indicate how the critical theory of the family can contribute to illuminating these questions, the critical theory will be used to generate four models of family structure. The four models are the bourgeois family in the mid-nineteenth century, the aristocratic family of the sixteenth and seventeenth centuries, the peasant family of the sixteenth and seventeenth centuries, and the working-class family of the early industrial revolution.[1] These models have been selected because they contribute best toward comprehending the situation of the family today. The four models are also presented here because they illustrate the use to which the critical theory of the family can be put. Other models could just as well be developed, based, for example, on ethnic differences. But these would not serve as well in illuminating the fundamental issues of the fate of the family today.

The data used to outline the four models comes primarily from the history of the European family. Data could be drawn from other sources, like American history, Chinese history, anthropology and so forth. My knowledge of European history is the limiting factor here. Family history, in any case, is a relatively new field of empirical study, and the body of data for Europe is still small. Generalizations offered about the four models must necessarily be taken as most tentative. The four models are offered heuristically, to provide a concrete guide for further research. This chapter is presented in a spirit of intellectual conjecture: If the four models are accurate, what can be said about the fate of the contemporary family?

The argument of the chapter presupposes that the modern family arose among the bourgeoisie in Europe around 1750, later in some places, earlier in others. The bourgeoisie developed a family form in sharp contrast to that of the aristocracy and the peasantry, indeed, in sharp contrast to what this group itself experienced before the eighteenth century. During the early stages of the industrial revolution the working class had a unique family structure which, in the course of the next two centuries, became more and more like that of the bourgeoisie. During the same time period, much of the old bourgeoisie lost its control of property, becoming skilled salaried labor and hence resembling the working class. Thus, in the present conjuncture, the family presents a blend of historical elements. This encapsulated history of the European family suggests why the four models are necessary for understanding the modern family.

The bourgeois (nuclear) family affords, thanks to Freud, the clearest picture of an emotional structure. Emerging as the dominant family structure in twentieth-century, advanced capitalist society, the bourgeois family also raises the most pressing historical questions. In the literature of family history the bourgeois family is frequently taken as the norm for all other family structures. One of the chief goals of my model will be to avoid this faulty practice.

The bourgeois family by definition is located in urban areas. From the late Middle Ages and early Renaissance until the mid-eighteenth century (for France, but a little earlier for England and later for central Europe), it is not essentially different from contemporaneous family forms. Evidence for a history of the emergence of the bourgeois family is thin.[2] It is known that from 1750 to the present the bourgeois family's demographic pattern moved progressively toward a pattern of low fertility, low mortality.[3] Family planning on a large scale first began in this group. In everyday life, relations among the members of the bourgeois family took on a distinct pattern of emotional intensity and privacy. Marriage entailed a conflict for this group between the needs of parents, not so much to uphold traditional customs or lineage but to preserve their capital accumulation and the value of individual choice. Selection of partners over the course of the nineteenth and twentieth centuries more and more became the choice of the young themselves, but only as the bourgeoisie was progressively proletarianized into white-collar jobs based on salaried labor.

Sexuality among this class, until recent changes, is one of the more astonishing features of modern history. Like no other class before, the bourgeoisie made a systematic effort to delay gratification. This led to sexual incapacities for both men and women. Freud called this the "high watermark" of sexual repression.[4] Among the bourgeoisie, women were viewed as asexual beings, as angelic creatures beyond animal lust. When internalized, this image of women led to profound emotional conflicts.[5] In 1850 the *Westminister Review* recommended an ideal of asexuality for women; they should, it said, go through life without ever being aware of "the promptings of the senses." For men of this class, sex was divorced from feelings of tenderness and performed as a conquest of lower-class women. Prostitution was required by bourgeois males, as Keith Thomas has shown,[6] because the "double standard," which originated with this class, made sexual fulfillment impossible for both spouses. Literary evidence points consistently to the view that sex was the model of impulsive, incautious action to the Victorian businessman. A gospel of thrift was applied to semen as well as to money. The act of sex, with its connotations of lust, rapture and uncontrolled passion, was the epitome of unbusinesslike behavior. The bourgeoisie defined itself morally against the promiscuous proletariat and the sensual nobility as the class with virtuous self-denial. Bourgeois respectability[7] led to a most unique separation of marriage and love on the one hand, from sexuality on the other.

Bourgeois marriage bound the couple forever. Social and financial interests tended to predominate in these alliances, especially in the early part of the period, as the soundest reason for marriage. Almost from the beginning, however, bourgeois youth was impelled by a drive of romantic love. The couple was smitten from the first moment of meeting with deep feelings of attachment. As the nineteenth century wore on, romantic love became the purest reason for marriage. The strange thing about the sentimental pattern of the middle class is that romantic love rarely outlasted the first few years, or even months, of the union. "Happily ever after" meant living together not with intense passion but with restrained respectability.

Relations within the bourgeois family were regulated by strict sex-role divisions. The husband was the dominant authority over the family and he provided for the family by work in the factory or market. The wife, considered less rational and less capable, concerned herself exclusively with the home, which she cleaned and decorated, sometimes with the aid of servants, to suit the social status of the husband. The husband was considered an autonomous being, a free citizen, upon

whom the wife was dependent. Bourgeois women were relative creatures whose sense of self was derived from their husbands' place in the world. The major interest of the wife for
a good part of the marriage concerned the children: she was
to raise them with the utmost attention, a degree of care new
in family history. Children were re-evaluated by the bourgeoisie, becoming important beings for the parents. A new degree
of intimacy and emotional depth characterized the relations
between parents and children of this class. A novel form of
maternal love was thought natural to women. Women were
not simply to tend to the survival of their children, but to train
them for a respectable place in society. More than that, they
were encouraged to create a bond between themselves and the
children so deep that the child's inner life could be shaped to
moral perfection. Thus for a large part of their lives bourgeois
women were confined to the home as never before; they were
to nurture their children, maintain the home, and cater to
their husbands, leaving aside the great transformations of politics and economics going on around them.[8]

Internal relations of the bourgeois family were regarded as
beyond the province of society. The family was a private micro-world, a sanctum into whose hallowed chambers no out-
sider had a right of entry. The privacy of the bourgeois family,
however, depended on the capitalist economy in two important ways. In quest for profit, the bourgeois needed to devote
his entire attention to economic affairs. The early modern
household, where family and economy were fused in one location, was inadequate in this situation. Men had to leave their
homes and establish separate, functionally differentiated
places of business. Ariès describes how this process took place
even among professional men like lawyers, and not only
among merchants and craftsmen. The home was no longer a
place of production, but one of leisure, of time outside the
work world. Second, activity in the market was carried out "at
arm's length," on the basis of written contracts, as if total
anonymity existed. Men treated others as things, each calculat-
ing his own self-interest. The hostile tone of competitive capi-

talism defined the family as a negative opposite, as a place of close, warm, emotive relations. The shop was now a place of reason and action and the home a place of feeling, with a segmented personality required to go from one to the other.

As it eschewed the productive function, the bourgeois home also divorced itself from external authority. Within the family's clearly defined boundaries, authority over the relations of parents and children was now limited to the parents alone. Bourgeois children of pre-school age would often encounter no other children and few adults besides their parents. The power of parents over children rose considerably as other authority figures in the community lost the ability to intervene in family relations. What happened in the family was no one else's concern. From 1830 onward the liberal state began to formulate policy on family matters, but generally it intervened only in the affairs of proletarian families; no one monitored the treatment of bourgeois children. Similarly, no youth groups were available to chastise the adults if any aspect of family life went astray. Norms for family relations no longer were set in the context of community traditions. The emergence of books and journals devoted to defining family relations was an index of the collapse of traditional norms.

The rise of private authority within the family is usually applauded by liberal writers as a contribution to the emancipation of the individual from social constraint. While the liberating aspect of the bourgeois family cannot be ignored, one must also assess its limitations, especially as they affected women (who thereby lost the support of the community in relations with their husbands, since women's networks no longer operated) and children. The cozy domestic nest of the bourgeois family forms in addition the structure without which one cannot analyze the emotional configuration of the modern psyche. It provides just that social context absent in Freud's thought.

With new forms of love and authority, the bourgeois family generated a new emotional structure. Child-rearing methods of this family were sharply different from those of the earlier

aristocracy and peasantry. During the oral stage the mother
was deeply involved with the child, probably breast-feeding it
herself. She was deeply committed to giving her infant all the
tenderness and attention she could muster. Swaddling was
now out of the question, and constant attention, regular feeding and meticulous cleaning were the rule. In the oral stage,
the child was immersed in a heaven of sensual and emotional
gratification as compared with anything that went before. Yet
along with these beneficent practices came new sources of
anxiety and tension. Increasingly isolated and without support from a community of women, bourgeois women were
burdened by considerable pressures. Whatever befell the infant was considered the fault of the mother. God's will and
blind fate could no longer be held responsible for any inadver-
tence, either physical or moral. In this context, the interactions between mother and infant were found to be frought
with anxiety.

During the anal phase the same constant attention continued accompanied by a sharp element of denial, like rigid
schedules during the oral stage. Along with higher levels of
cleanliness in bourgeois apartments went a new dread of
human wastes. The child was compelled to exchange anal
gratification for maternal love, denying radically the pleasure
of the body in favor of sublime forms of parental affection.
Some indication of the severity of bourgeois toilet-training
practices is provided by Friedrich Scholz, writing in 1891:

Toilet training should be carried out in such a way that the child
cannot bear to have any dirt on his body or dress or in his surroundings for even the briefest time. It should be instilled in his unconscious that dirt is improper and that the lack of it is the most natural
and most desirable condition. The child's physical sensibility should
be heightened so that dirt on or about him causes discomfort.[9]

Reasons of health were no doubt prominent in the minds of
bourgeois parents and medical advisers, with good reason. Yet
the emotional burden on the child of severe bodily denial was
present as well. Furthermore, toilet training was begun at a

very early age before the child could control its sphincters. Strapping the child to the potty was not uncommon. The child was asked to master ruthlessly its own body and to regard its body as a container and producer of filth. Bourgeois parents in the Victorian era treated their children with empathy, as de Mause contends; equally one could characterize this treatment as persecutory.

Freud considered emotional ambivalence, so crucial for the whole of psychic development, as resting on the foundation of opposing cosmic forces, eros and thanatos. Whatever value this mythology might have in other respects, for family history it serves only to obscure what is happening. Far from depending on cosmic forces, ambivalence must be seen as a direct creation of the bourgeois family structure. Ambivalence is the central emotional context of the bourgeois child. Physical punishment for signs of autonomy by the child were absent, or tended to diminish; indeed, autonomy was encouraged and not seen as a threat by bourgeois parents. But in the context of the mother's ever watchful and deeply concerned eye the child had to learn the difficult emotional lesson that its own body was disgusting.

The third, genital stage saw equally profound innovations in child-rearing ·methods. Concern with childhood genital play was minimal, as far as historians can tell, in earlier family forms.[10] In the middle of the eighteenth century there was a sudden and profound awareness and horror of childhood masturbation. If early modern aristocrats were amused by precocious childhood sex play, the Victorian middle classes could not tolerate it.[11] The phrases about cutting off "widdlers" found in Freud's reports of case studies are accurate evidence, by no means the most bizarre or telling, of a new effort to desexualize children. In the nineteenth century, medical opinion unequivocally warned parents of the dangers of self-abuse, which included acne, mental torpor, hemmorhoids, tumors, homosexuality, insanity and, finally, death. Inventions were developed and sold on the market designed to aid parents in their war on child masturbation. There were sharp-toothed rings to prevent erection and devices that set off an alarm when the penis hardened. The final solution in this mad politics of repression was surgery. Doctors in the United States, France, Germany and England, at least for a short time, performed on boys and girls circumcisions, cauterizations, infibulations of the labia majora, all to curtail masturbation.[12] Again the child was caught in a deeply ambivalent situation: he had to give up bodily pleasure in favor of parental affection.

During the anal, oral and genital stages, the bourgeois child experienced a new emotional configuration in which a sharp choice was presented between its body and parental love. It is not a matter of simple repression, because surely early modern family structures brutalized children and dominated them as much or even more than the bourgeois family. Instead it is a question of a new emotional structure, with its own character- istics. What made the bourgeois structure so unique for the child was that the ambivalent pulls of body and parental love were so absolute, so inescapable. One can only comprehend the bourgeois child's emotional plight when one remembers the general structure of love and authority in the privatized family. Parental authority was absolute for the child and *equally* parental love was deep. The child had to give up bodily gratification to an extreme degree but at the same time it enjoyed much affection. There was a double-bind situation here. The child could not question or rebel overtly against parental strictures because their authority was unlimited, in- deed, terrifying to a small child. If the child insisted upon bodily pleasure it would be tormented continuously with threats of castration. If it relinquished bodily pleasure, it found itself accepting the love of someone who controlled it completely, surely not a "free" choice for the child.

In fact, Freud noted, bourgeois children reared in such a context developed extraordinarily aggressive impulses. When a child was denied genital pleasure it responded with anger. But the anger could not be acted out in the situation because the denial was commanded out of love. So the child was forced to suppress its anger; it could not face hating someone who loved it and whom it loved so deeply. Where did the anger go? Freud provided the answer: it was internalized (as the super-ego) and directed against the child itself, so that when the child felt anger at its mother, who so obviously felt such deep love for it, the child could only regard itself as worthless and evil, in short, as guilty. Hence the important result of the child's drama of ambivalence was that it internalized deeply a pattern of rules which summed up its authority-love relation with its parents. The secret of the bourgeois family structure was that, without conscious intention on the part of the parents, it played with intense feelings of love and hate which the child felt both for its body and for its parents in such a way that parental rules became internalized and cemented in the un-conscious on the strength of both feelings, love and hate, each working to support and reinforce the other. Love (as ego-ideal) and hate (as super-ego) both worked to foster the attitudes of bourgeois respectability. In this way the family generated an "autonomous" bourgeois, a modern citizen who needed no external sanctions or supports but was self-motivated to con-front a competitive world, make independent decisions and battle for capital.

The emotional structure of the bourgeois family helps ex-plain how a psychic structure can be implanted which enables individuals to act on their own authority. With Freud's help this new level of "individualization" is revealed not as a tri-umph of a better morality, but as the product of the bourgeois family structure. However, even the ambivalent condition of the child and its presence in a unique context of love and authority is not enough to explain what happens. In addition, it must be noted that the bourgeois family structure restricted as never before the sources of identification for the child. The child's parents alone were available as adult models, so that emotional structure took on an added and crucial intensity. Because the child tended to take as itself (or identify with) adult figures, whatever went on between parents and children became all the more important. The child took the adult of the same sex as its ego-ideal, providing positive values and directions for later life. But with only two sources of identification (really only one, since there was sexual specialization) the child was dependent on the parents to an extraordinary degree. The dependence of the child in bourgeois families was not a natural consequence of biology or social life, as many writers assume. All people depend on others in many ways, so children are not the only beings who are dependent. Dependence must be studied not as an inevitability but in terms of its concrete, distinguishing features in different situations. Dependence of children in bourgeois families was heightened by the family's isolation. Children had fewer figures for identification and were therefore dependent in a new way.

Finally, the psychic structure must be differentiated by sex. At the same time that sexuality was denied to children, they were confronted by the parents' attitude toward the two genital types. Encouraged to identify with the parent of the same sex, the child already learned its boyness or girlness. It also learned that the distinction was based on the presence or absence of the penis, since female genital and reproductive organs were unmentionable secrets. Moreover, it learned that the penis was a sign of power, since father had one and father was all powerful. The role of the bourgeois father in child rearing was minimal: he was the last resort, the reference point anchoring the mother's authority, the highest power the child experienced. It was not Freud who diminished the value of female reproductive organs; he was simply complicitous with his time and class, registering and exploring the consequences of the sex division in the bourgeois family.

In sum, the attributes of the bourgeois family structure were for the child the conditions for the development of the type of psychic structure which Freud was the first to articulate. The specificity of his notion of the Oedipus complex becomes truly intelligible only when seen in terms of the family structure outlined above. To be caught up in an emotional dynamic (for boys) of loving one's mother and resenting father's interference, of resolving the resentment by developing an unconscious need to imitate the father and find a replacement-substitute for the mother all at the deep level of an internalized authority was the special consequence of the bourgeois family. Aristocratic sons may have had hostile feelings toward their fathers but without the same intensity, without the same play of love against the body, without the same reliance on the father for support and identification, without the same value to the mother, without her deep concern and tenderness, without therefore needing to internalize the father as deeply. Surely peasants and aristocrats had unconscious structures, but only the bourgeoisie generated an unconscious that was defined in terms of the denial of the body.

To recapitulate my argument, I have attempted to set Freud's insights into the context of the emergence of the bourgeois family, and I have come up with the peculiar mixture of social and psychic elements that characterized this family structure. The bourgeois family should be understood not simply as a progressive, morally beneficial nest of love, domesticity, the "wish to be free" and individualism, but as constituting a particular emotional pattern which served to promote the interests of the new dominant class and to register in a unique way the conflicts of age and sex. In the bourgeois family, new forms of the oppression of children and women arose which were dependent upon critical mechanisms of authority and love, of intense ambivalent emotions.

Stated succinctly, the emotional pattern of the bourgeois family is defined by authority restricted to parents, deep parental love for children and a tendency to employ threats of the withdrawal of love rather than physical punishment as a sanction. This pattern, applied to the oral, anal and genital stages, results in a systematic exchange on the child's part of bodily gratification for parental love, which, in turn, produces a deep internalization of the parent of the same sex. Sexual differences become sharp personality differences. Masculinity is defined as the capacity to sublimate, to be aggressive, rational and active; femininity is defined as the capacity to express emotions, to be weak, irrational and passive. Age differences become internalized patterns of submission. Childhood is a unique but inferior condition. Childhood dependency is the basis for learning to love one's superiors. Passage to adulthood requires the internalization of authority. Individuality is gained at the price of unconsciously incorporating parental norms.

I have attempted to cover only the main outlines of an adequate treatment of the bourgeois family. One must study the extent of applicability of this structure, how low in the social hierarchy it descended and how high it went, how it changed. I offer only a static, synchronic summary. The bourgeois family structure is suited preeminently to generate people with ego structures that foster the illusion that they are autonomous beings. Having internalized love-authority patterns to an unprecedented degree by anchoring displaced body energy in a super-ego, the bourgeois sees himself as his own self-creation, as the captain of his soul, when in fact he is the result of complex psycho-social processes. One can appreciate the political and social importance of this phenomenon when one realizes that the proletariat eventually adopts this same family structure.

The second model of family structure is drawn from the European aristocracy. Aristocratic households of the old regime included a mixture of kin, servants, retainers and clients. They could consist of 40 to upwards of 200 people.[13] Demographers have found that aristocrats tended to have more children than the lower classes and a slightly lower infant mortality rate. Yet the demographic pattern of the pre-industrial era applied to them as well as to the peasants: high fertility, high mortality.[14] Aristocrats saw themselves as part of a network of kin relations or lineage whose preservation was of paramount importance. The composition of the household was far from stable: servants and clients came and went; children of both sexes were sent to other aristocratic houses to be reared.

The great chateaux were public and political places. They symbolized in their material grandeur the power of the lord over the surrounding peasantry.[15] No privacy was possible in the chateaux. The buildings had no corridors; to get from one

place to another one had to walk through rooms, disturbing
the occupants. There was little functional differentiation of
rooms until the end of the period. People slept everywhere
using trundle beds. The furniture also tended to be multiple
in function. Relations among members of the household were
exceedingly hierarchical, and roles were fixed by rigid traditions.

Marriage was a political act of the highest order. The fate
of the line depended on marriages which kept the family hold-
ings intact. Matches were the parents' decision and marrying
off daughters was expensive. Dowries at certain periods involved small fortunes. Marriage therefore had little to do with
love, or, in fact, with sex. Lawrence Stone refers to the sexual
pattern of the English nobility before the seventeenth century
as "serial polygamy." Aristocrats made love with servants and
with other aristocrats. Concubines were accepted publicly.[16]
In general the attitude of the nobility was that women were
as much sexual creatures as men and that love and sex were
not secret, private affairs. James I was known to ask his cour-
tiers, especially newlyweds, about their sex lives in full view
of his entire court. In sum, the daily life in aristocratic families
was a bustling, public round of exchanges, whose center was
the status of the house, not the conjugal unit.

The opulence of this small elite (about 1 ½ % of the population in eighteenth-century France) was based on control of the
land and to some degree on the favor of the monarch. Land
was the chief property of the aristocracy, and in general it was
seen not as capital to be invested and exploited but as under
the stewardship of the family line. Wealth was to be inherited
and passed on, not earned or accumulated. During the transition from feudalism to capitalism, only a minority of nobles
behaved as capitalists. The work of the nobles was in war, in
serving the king and in maintaining order in their domains.
Wives were equally lofty figures, but their functions were
primarily to bear sons and arrange the social life. Generally
they were concerned neither with management of the house
nor with child rearing.[17]

Authority in the household was arranged hierarchically and was relatively independent of outside interference. The monarch sought to control his nobles but not, except in rare cases, at the local level of family affairs. Given the transportation facilities of the time, aristocrats, when not at court, lived far from their nearest equals. The chateau was autonomous in its domain, limited only by the power of the centralized state.

The emotional structure of the aristocratic home has been analyzed only by a few historians.[18] Children were in the hands of servants from the moment they came into the world. Fathers and mothers rarely bothered with their children, especially during the early, formative years. Child care was considered beneath the dignity of an aristocratic woman. Children were thought of as little animals, not as objects of love and affection. The essayist Montaigne quipped, "We have loved infants for our own amusement, like monkeys, not like human beings." In this and every other way, the aristocracy presents a marked contrast with the nineteenth-century bourgeoisie.

Noble infants were breast-fed by nurses. Little is known about the care they received. The few hints historians have uncovered indicate a bleak picture. Women's milk was thought to be a form of blood. Babies therefore were in the unwelcome role of vampires. Death at the hands of the nurse was not uncommon, and some nurses were known as "killing nurses." Unwanted children surely found their way to these women. In any case children formed their first attachment to someone outside the family. Aristocratic families did not attempt to focus the child's emotions exclusively on the family. A psychoanalytically informed interpreter might consider nurses to be mother-substitutes. This would be a mistake. Theoretically, the position is reductionist since it takes the bourgeois mother as the norm, discounting alternate emotional configurations where other adults predominate in the child's life. In the case of aristocratic child rearing, neither the nurses nor the mothers themselves related to the child in the bourgeois fashion. The emotional pattern of these families can only be comprehended by recognizing the diffusion of love objects which it instituted.

If the oral stage in aristocratic families bears little resemblance to that of the bourgeoisie, the anal stage is perhaps even less similar. Toilet training was minimal, since sanitation standards were low. Adults urinated just about everywhere in the house, so children were not carefully controlled. The main interest of adults in the child's toilet habits was not in demanding self-control but in examining the feces for signs of humors or demons, which were thought to indicate personality traits and moods. Toilet training was hence carried out with laxity and had an entirely different emotional meaning from that of the modern period. During the anal stage, however, nobles were concerned that the child learn obedience to the social hierarchy. Since children tended to be defiant at this stage, aristocrats responded by attempting to beat humility into the child. Whippings were as normal to these children as forced sitting on the potty was for bourgeois children. Using Erikson's theory, David Hunt, a historian of aristocratic families, discerns in these beatings signs of the inability of adults to cope with the child's striving for autonomy. In this hierarchical social world, adults felt threatened by the willfulness and obstinacy of two-year-olds. Since adults had little sense of the child's needs or stage of growth, they responded to children as they would to any person. When authority was challenged it was met with force. According to Hunt, the consequence of the whippings was to erase all traces of autonomy in the child.

This interpretation of the anal stage among the nobility requires further elaboration in accordance with the theory presented here. Unlike the bourgeois child, the young aristocrat was not required to exchange bodily gratification for parental love. The issue in the bourgeois home was toilet training; the issue in the chateau was obedience to authority. In one case, the child was required to control its body; in the other, to respect social hierarchy. For the aristocratic child, parental love was not at stake in the emotional drama. Although Hunt may be right in maintaining that the result of the whipping was the squelching of autonomy and the weakening of the ego, the Eriksonian model misses other aspects of the emotional pattern. This model does not account for the way in which the aristocratic case fails to strengthen the bond between parent and child. The beatings did not result in the internalization of the parent by the child. Instead they reinforced the social norm of hierarchy. The aristocratic anus was not the locus of pleasure denied. Beatings on the backside contributed not to a secret sense of guilt, not to traits of cleanliness, order and punctuality. Instead, the psychic residue of the whip was a sense of shame at transgressing community norms. The direction of the emotional trauma was not from deep family bonds toward individualism but from public punishment to social obedience.

Equally different from modern practices was the aristocratic training at the genital period. Sexuality was not kept hidden from the child, who was viewed as a sexual pet to be played with for adult amusement. Childhood masturbation was not forbidden or regarded as unusual. It was not uncommon for nurses and other adults to fondle the child's genitalia, to encourage five-year-olds to imitate adult sex acts and to acknowledge publicly childhood sexuality. One of the nurses of the future Louis XIII disapproved of the way adults fooled with her charge. She warned the Dauphin, "Monsieur, do not let anyone touch your nipples or your cock; they'll cut them off."[19] This "castration threat" may be contrasted with that of the mother of Little Hans. In the case of Little Hans the threat was made because he masturbated. In the case of the Dauphin, where powerful aristocratic figures amused themselves at the child's expense and against his will in this instance, the nurse was urging the child not to curtail his masturbation but to insist on treatment due his rank. The "castration threat" was made neither by the Dauphin's parents nor by the nurse. It was presented as a general social threat. The moral and emotional lesson for the Dauphin was to be on guard because powerful but inferior political forces might undercut his authority and position. Hence the emotional tension for the child during the genital stage did not concern profound relations with his parents; nor was there the need to exchange bodily pleasure for love. Instead the noble child was inserted into a complex, public world where the basic lesson concerned knowing one's place.

Through the first three stages the psychic structure of aristocrats was quite divergent from the bourgeois pattern. No sharp antagonism was found between the body and the social world, or between the id and internalized morality. No deep internalizations resulted from an ambivalent play of love and authority. Identifications were not made with parents or with any individuals, but with the family line.[20] Hence, instead of a severe super-ego, the child would develop a keen sense of external, social norms. Rather than a guilt mentality based on internal self-criticism, the likely form of conscience was a shame mentality based on public condemnation of improper acts, on rebukes by the community.

The main interest in the aristocratic family structure derives from its radical difference from the later ones. Even with the same general norms of patriarchy and monogamy, there is enormous variety in family structure. Was there an aristocratic Oedipus complex? Surely there was antagonism between fathers and sons, parents and children, but it took a form so different from that described by Freud that it would be misleading to give it the same name. Indeed the mother symbolized a political alliance rather than a conquest of romantic love and was not the same personage as the bourgeois mother. The struggles between the generations concerned social power rather than sexuality. The body was marked not by sexual ambivalence (pleasure vs. virtue) but by political power: bodies were subject to ordering according to the social hierarchy.

Given the scanty nature of the evidence, a detailed model of aristocratic family structure is not possible. Even so, it can be concluded that aristocratic families placed little value on privacy, domesticity, maternal care, romantic love and intimate relations with children. The emotional life of children was not centered on their parents but was diffused over a wide range of adult figures. One can speculate that the egos of aristocrats were not as strong as those of the bourgeoisie, since self-control was not a goal of child rearing. Perhaps the success of the bourgeoisie in gaining control of the means of production during the early stages of industrialization can be accounted for in part by this difference in ego strength.

Peasant family structure in the old regime was different from that of the ruling class, although it probably had more in common with the aristocracy than with the modern bourgeoisie. The peasantry of Europe included large disparities in economic position and wealth, from sharecroppers and day laborers to independent farmers. It encompassed different modes of production: two- and three-field systems; dispersed and clustered settlements. From the sixteenth to the eighteenth centuries, peasants in some areas were influenced profoundly by modernizing trends like the enclosures and scientific farming. In other areas peasant life went on relatively unchanged. Indeed, pockets of traditionalism still persist in some places, and anthropologists have begun employing ethnographic methods to study these peasants. Since so little is known of the daily life of the peasantry under the old regime, the anthropological evidence, even though it is taken from the twentieth century, is invaluable.[21] For the purpose of a general model of family structure, this study will assume a peasantry living in villages.

Demographers have learned that Old Regime peasants married very late (in their late twenties) and had few children (four or five) alive at any given time. Although there were numerous births, only about one-half survived to adulthood. Over the cycle of the family there was a period when three generations lived in the same house—at least this was so in many areas studied. Yet the norm, demographers have shown, was not an extended family, but a small conjugal family.

This statistical conclusion is misleading for several reasons. First, peasants lived in close proximity to other villagers, and there were numerous relatives close at hand. Second, the family (parents and children) was not a particularly significant social group.[22] The ties of dependence with the village were so strong that survival was not possible at the household level. Third, daily interactions involved the whole village or large parts of it, and the family was not closed off from society as a private world.[23] Hence the impression of statistical similarity with bourgeois families is controverted by the force of collective dependence. European peasant families of the old regime were not nuclear families. Although their numbers were small, the family was intermeshed in a wide circle of sociability. In fact, the basic unit of early modern peasant life was not the conjugal family at all but the village. The village was the peasant's "family."

Social authority was invested not in the father of the house but in the village itself. In some places the lord and the priest were effective authorities. But in the day-to-day regulation of life, the customs and traditions of the village prevailed.[24] Nothing could occur in individual families of any importance that was not known by the village and supervised by it. Marriages, relations between husbands and wives and parents and children were all scrutinized by the villagers and it was they who imposed sanctions. A wife who behaved in a manner not approved by tradition would be ridiculed by other women. Unmarried young people were organized into youth groups which policed the rites of courtship.[25] Since daily interactions, even nightly interactions, were acted out in the presence of the community or a relevant section of it, privacy was unknown and not valued.

Peasant men and women had separate functions to perform and in general women were subordinate, although in their own sphere they had considerable power. Women's work was vital to the survival of the family and the community, and women worked hard and long.[26] Peasant women cooked, cared for children, tended domestic animals and gardens and joined the village in the fields at crucial times, like the harvest. Women regulated births and supervised courtship at evening gatherings. In short, peasant patriarchy was different from aristocratic and bourgeois patriarchy. Its mechanisms need to be studied carefully to avoid the incorrect characterization, by Reich and some feminists, of a blanket, uniform patriarchal pattern in European history.

Emotionally significant events in the villages did not take

place in the conjugal family but in the community as a whole. Festivals (pagan and Christian), patterns of worship and play were all affairs of the community. Every member of the village had a right to attend all weddings, for example. Death also was an event engaging the community. Although in some places parents made the decisions about their children's marriages, most communities had collective forms of courtship in which appropriate matches were made.[27] Beginning in the sixteenth century, the state intervened in marriages, attempting to reinforce patriarchal authority. The rights of parents over their children were increased considerably as the ideology of patriarchalism viewed parental authority as crucial for monarchical authority. Governments attempted to eradicate the peasant practice of marriage based on consent of the partners. The success of state policy is difficult to estimate, although clandestine marriages continued throughout the old regime.[28]

Symbolic and religious life were dominated by public worship of sacred Christian figures. Although the quality of religiosity varied considerably from the Middle Ages to the modern period, and from village to village, in general there was an acceptance of Christian myths as part of a wider set of traditions. Groethuysen writes of a priest who compared the Christianity of a bourgeois, who wrestled with his conscience over the irrationality of certain doctrines and worried about orthodoxy, with that of a peasant, who proclaimed simply but in complete heresy that he liked the Virgin better than Christ.[29] The interest here is not with religiosity per se but with underscoring the communal nature of moral, psychic and emotional life among the peasantry.

The dominance of the village over kinship and the family,[30] even in the context of monogamous marriage, affected the relations of parents and children. Peasant mothers were assisted in child-care duties by relatives, old people, and young women. Women in the village passed on to young mothers traditional knowledge about breast-feeding, swaddling, curing infant maladies, and so forth. Along with this assistance went supervision. Villagers made sure that customs and traditions were upheld in the rearing of the young. The conjugal family was not a privileged and private space, but was integrated into larger networks of sociability. Children were not possessed and controlled by peasant parents as exclusively as they were by bourgeois parents in the modern period.

Within the conjugal family, children were not regarded as the center of life. They were not brought up by parents with devoted attention or shaped by them for moral perfection. Perhaps the high infant and child mortality rates curbed parental affection. In any case, the bonds between parents and children among the peasantry of early modern Europe had none of the intensity and intimacy of the later period. Rather than limited to parents and children, emotional attachments extended outward to the village and backward to earlier generations. The dead were still part of the community, part of the stories and oral traditions of the village. Historians of childhood bemoan the peasant's indifference to his children. Children would be left all day, at early ages, to fend for themselves when matters of survival demanded the women's presence in the fields. People who could afford it sent their babies out to wet nurses, and very poor women sent their children away to free themselves for remunerating work. Babies were swaddled, freeing mothers for the vitally important work of the day. Children were probably undernourished, and they emerged from the first stage of life in all likelihood without much basic trust. Breast-feeding was performed by the mother with little emotional involvement as an annoying and time-consuming burden. Toilet training was also supervised with little of that tense, nervous concern of modern mothers. The control of sexual life during the genital phase was also light. Like young aristocrats, peasant children bore little pressure to repress bodily pleasure in favor of winning parental approval. Although some historians view these peasant practices with concern, there is no conclusive evidence that they were any more deleterious to psychic life than the practices of the bourgeoisie.

In yet other ways childhood for the peasant differed from

that of the nineteenth-century bourgeois. At an early age (from seven to ten) the child would usually be sent away to another peasant's home for a period of apprenticeship. There was a circulation of children[31] in which young people learned to depend not on their parents but on the community. The psychic structure of the child was undoubtedly shame-oriented, not guilt-oriented. Approval for actions was external, based on public sanctions by the whole community. There were numerous sources of identification, since the child from its earliest moments would be present in the wider community. Authority and love did not exist in violent opposition and ambivalence, following instead the aristocratic pattern of submission to hierarchy and communal tradition. The child was not trained to defer its gratifications, to accustom itself to a clocklike schedule of rewards, to face the world alone and be prepared to make autonomous decisions, to regulate emotional energy for a competitive struggle against others. Life for peasants had a fixed pattern, governed by innumerable traditions which were not even to be questioned by individuals. Well-being was regulated more by the inexorable cycle of nature than by individual initiative. The picture of the bourgeois psyche presented by Freud does not capture the dynamics of the peasant's emotional life.

Some historians maintain that the sexual life of the peasants was more repressive than that of modern times, that it was instrumental and not expressive, based on calculations of interest and not spontaneous empathy. I find this position inaccurate. It forgets the important considerations that peasant wives were not sex objects, nor were they intimate companions. They were workmates, judged by their skills and strength and not by the shape of their nose. Furthermore, if child-rearing practices are an indication of sexual norms, peasants were not sexually restrictive. As we have seen, peasants made little effort to curtail childhood forms of bodily gratification through the first three stages. Since peasants lived in one- or two-room dwellings, children became familiar with sexual acts early in life. Often children and adults slept in the same bed. Bourgeois observers, such as folklorists in the nineteenth century, condemned peasant life as promiscuous.[32] Peasant courtship practices, like the maraîchinage and bundling, permitted numerous forms of sexual activity short of intercourse which were prohibited among the urban bourgeoisie. Still, it must be admitted that late marriages and hostility to sex in the Christian Church leave the impression that peasant life was far from ribald and licentious.

Direct evidence on peasant sexuality is difficult to find. In the case of the peasant novelist Restif de la Bretonne,[33] however, evidence is given of loose and frequent sexual practices in a Burgundian village in the eighteenth century. In his autobiography, Restif related the story of his sexual initiation at an early adolescent age by a young woman from the village. The promiscuity of day laborers was dwelt upon by Restif in great detail. He also described the sensuous practices of young women placed in charge of small children. When he was but four years old Restif was seduced by Marie, a babysitter:

I used to be fondled and very ardently by Marie, and carried in her arms to Vespers. I am forced to describe her caresses. . . . Marie used to kiss me on the cheek, and upon my lips. . . . She went further, though in all innocence on her part; she put her hand under my little petticoats and amused herself by gently slapping and tickling me. She went further yet and then she would devour me with kisses.[34]

Restif's experience, if his memory was faithful, matched that of young Louis XIII rather than Little Hans. Given the present state of research, however, one cannot draw solid conclusions about peasant sexuality in the early modern period.

In sum, the peasant family structure appears, however indistinctly, to have been very different from that of the bourgeoisie. Authority was diffused throughout the village, with numerous adults participating in the child's life. This authority was likely to be harsh and indifferent to the child's needs. The pattern of love confronting the child was also spread over a wide variety of relatives and villagers, although nowhere did it resemble the deep maternal concern of the nineteenth-cen-

tury middle class. As Ariès points out, the peasant child par-
ticipated from a very early age in the entire round of village
life. The child enjoyed, therefore, the emotional configuration
of the whole village. Through the first three stages of development, the child was cared for in an expedient, perhaps offhand,
yet traditional way. The condition of his soul was not considered the charge of his mother, but of God or fate. Relations
between parents and children were not characterized by intimacy or emotional intensity. Sanctions were enforced with
physical punishment rather than with threats of the withdrawal of love. The peasant child probably did not internalize
deeply parental figures. Nor was it likely that he built up a
strong ego. Instead the child's emotional life had to be geared
to the rhythms of the village, with its extensive traditions and
customs.

Models of aristocratic and peasant family structure of early
modern Europe serve to highlight the uniqueness of the bourgeois family structure. A model of the family structure of the
working class during the early stages of industrialization can
serve the same end. But in the case of the working class, family
structure has undergone dramatic transformations in a period
of less than two centuries. Recruited from the dislocated peasantry and the lowest levels of urban society, the industrial
working class developed a family structure under conditions
of social and economic distress. Yet in the course of a century
the working-class family began to resemble closely that of the
bourgeoisie. This important change in family structure must
be taken into account.

During the early period of industrialization, demographic
data on the working class indicates a continuation of the pre-
industrial pattern of high fertility, high mortality. Another
demographic indicator, life expectancy, was much lower
among factory workers than among gentry or tradesmen in
England in the mid-nineteenth century.[35] In addition, factory
wages were so low that typically the entire family had to work
in order to maintain subsistence. Very young children worked
in the mines and mills in many instances with their parents.

For this proletariat something like the old domestic economy existed, except that work took place not around the home and farmland but in the factory and mine. Living conditions among the workers were notoriously bad.[36] Historians present a dreadful picture for England, France and Germany. Sanitation facilities were appalling, with only one toilet for 200 people in parts of Manchester. Rooms were often without windows and running water. In the worst cases one room was inhabited by three to eight people, as workers often took in lodgers to help pay the rent. Garbage was thrown into the street or was disposed of only by open sewers. In Liverpool one-sixth of the population lived in dingy cellars accompanied by rats, lice, roaches and bedbugs, the pets of the working class. Add to that the long working hours, at times from 14 to 17 hours a day, and the gloominess of these early industrial cities and one can easily see that the proletarian home was not a nest of domesticity.

Sexual patterns among the workers have scarcely been studied. Shorter argues that a rise in illegitimacy figures for the workers indicates a new, modern rush to sexual emancipation,[37] while other scholars have presented statistics in refutation of this claim.[38] Bourgeois moralists thought that workers were indecently promiscuous. One form of employment available for women coming into the cities from the countryside was prostitution. Studies of workers' autobiographies tend to confirm a continuation of pre-bourgeois sexual patterns along with a lessening of community controls.[39] In the factories and cities many opportunities for sexual encounters outside and before marriage existed both in an offhand way and by the sexual exploitation of working women by foremen and bosses. Masturbation also seems not to have been a great concern. All in all, the sexual pattern does not seem to match that of the bourgeoisie.[40]

Judged by standards of bourgeois respectability and intimacy, the proletarian family did not come off well. The property base, of course, was different, with the father having no capital upon which to base his authority. Also, children could, once in their teens, go off and find work. Young men and women alike asserted early an independence from their parents.[41] Youth groups developed by proletarian teenagers became a great concern of the liberal wing of the ruling class, who invented the term "juvenile delinquency" to define and control them. Workers also tended to marry earlier than the bourgeoisie, with no concern for property to delay their inclinations. Relations between men and women within the family tended to upset patriarchal patterns, since women both earned money outside the home and did housework. Many new jobs were provided for women by the industrial process, from mill work at the beginning of the century to office work later on. Nevertheless, male dominance in the home and factory continued, but it took on new forms.

Industrialization did not produce the private bourgeois family among the working class, at least not in the beginning. Instead the workers attempted to resist capitalist domination by preserving older community ties.[42] The cases that have been studied show that factory workers, whenever feasible, clutched at community forms of dependence and mutual aid in order to ameliorate their harsh conditions of life. In addition to alienation and exploitation at work, the proletariat had to contend with fragmentation and atomization, as the old rural forms of collective life were threatened in the cities. The strike and machine burning were, in their early manifestations, extensions of older forms of communal solidarity to oppressive factory conditions. While the economic structure certainly influenced the structure of the proletarian family it did not do so in any direct way and it certainly did not lead, with the force of a law of nature, to the bourgeois family. Old values, especially that of woman as a productive worker rather than as a genteel guardian of virtue, continued under industrialization.

The emotional pattern of the working-class family in the first half of the nineteenth century in no way resembled that of the bourgeoisie. Children were raised in the older, informal way, without constant attention and supervision by the mother. Children were breast-fed from necessity by under-nourished, exhausted and preoccupied mothers. Both toilet training and genital control were undoubtedly lax. Proletarian children, as it was often said, were raised by the street, not by the family. Left alone much of the time or in the easygoing care of a relative or neighbor, these street urchins learned about life under capitalism quickly and surely. They were confronted not so much by the ever-present authority of parents concerned only with shaping their moral nature, but rather by an indifferent society which treated them roughly and promised them little if anything in return. One cannot expect a strong super-ego, a compulsive anal personality and a repressed body to develop among this generation of working-class youth. Nor, probably, can one expect to find among them the shame-oriented super-ego of the peasantry. Proletarian youths were confronted less by multiple agents of socialization than by an anonymous, cruel world.

Compared to bourgeois children, however, proletarian children faced a wider network of adults. The pattern of authority and love confronting working-class children resembled more the community of the peasants than the private family of the bourgeoisie. Unlike the rural village, however, working-class communities were not self-contained social islands. At least to some degree, forms of authority that emanated from industrial capitalism must have impinged on working-class children. In all likelihood, the relatively stable patriarchal authority of the peasants was not reproduced perfectly among industrial workers. Working-class men were less in control of their lives than their peasant counterparts. Working-class children were in a modern situation where traditional forms of authority were being undermined by the process of industrialization. Hence the process of socializing these children for the discipline of the factory was probably not accomplished in the home, but in the factory itself. The capitalists, then, were not figures with whom the working class could identify. The authority of factory owners must have appeared foreign to these youths. Perhaps the gap between authority in the working-class family and authority in the factory helps to account for the rebellious disposition of the proletariat in the first half of the nineteenth century. At stake in this issue is the way in which the family served to mediate responses to authority during the early stages of industrialization. When the cases of Western Europe and the United States are compared, it appears that the experience of emigration to the United States from peasant societies in southern and eastern Europe paradoxically may have increased paternal authority and family ties and served to mollify the rebelliousness of working-class children. Needless to say, this question requires further study.

In the last decades of the nineteenth century, a working-class "aristocracy" emerged from among the most skilled male workers, such as lathe operators. A family wage was at last achieved by a minority of workers. Bourgeois philanthropists were simultaneously seeking to better the workers' lives by imposing their moral standards upon the lower class. Liberals attempted to limit the working hours of women and children, in part with the intention of securing a proper home environment for children. In Britain, middle-class women visited working-class mothers to instruct them in modern child-rearing techniques. The philanthropic zeal of these liberals needs to be studied as part of an effort to bring aspects of the bourgeois family structure—maternal-care domesticity, privacy—to the working class. In some cases, this inter-class activity brought quite peculiar results. Prime Minister William Gladstone, for example, was a great advocate of the reform of prostitutes. He would bring prostitutes to his home, give them a stern lecture on morality, and then offer to help them financially if they had the courage for self-reform. At other times, however, he would visit prostitutes for different and not at all respectable reasons. Masochistic flagellation was his passion.[43] The fascinating history remains to be written of the effort of the philanthropic bourgeoisie to reform working-class morality by integrating the lower classes into the bourgeois family model. Perhaps the greatest influence on the living conditions of the working class was the trade-union movement in which workers struggled collectively for better wages and conditions. A detailed history of these interrelated developments and their impact on the proletarian family structure remains to be written.

One can see, however, on the basis of a few pioneering studies[44] that this second stage of the proletarian family saw the wife more and more at home with the children. The bourgeois pattern of sex-role differentiation began to take effect. Complete bourgeois domesticity, however, had not yet reached the working class. During this phase, working men tended to form a male society centered around work and the pub, while women established their own community based on the residence. In England, a matriarchal kinship system extending beyond the nuclear family was the norm, with "mum" or the grandmother at the center. Mum arranged for an apartment for her daughter close to her own when her daughter married, and the daughter became integrated into women's social life, which was quite extensive. In the working-class ghettos of East London the women all knew each other, and their daily lives manifested not the isolated bourgeois pattern but something resembling the older village community. A new concern for the fate of the children began to emerge in this setting, but still not to the extent of the bourgeoisie. The children had too much independence for that.

Only during a third stage when the couple moved into the suburbs (in the 1950s for the London group studied by Wilmott and Young) were ties broken somewhat with mum and the community. At this point the proletarian wife was isolated in the home, her husband gave up the pub for domesticity and the children became a prime center of attention. The future of the children was now of utmost concern both to father and mother. Only at this third stage did the working class fully adopt the bourgeois family pattern. The upper levels of the working class began raising their children in the bourgeois pattern, with the same structure of authority and love during the early stages of the child's development. Psychologically, the working-class family resembled closely that of their social superiors. Workers thought of their family as a refuge from society. Working-class wives adopted the values of maternalism and domesticity. Even in the leadership of European communist parties, attitudes toward the family and women were carbon copies of the nineteenth-century bourgeois model.[45] The conservatism of the working class in the twentieth century can be attributed, in part, to the attraction of the bourgeois family model. Unlike the liberal bourgeoisie of an earlier day, which rose up against the aristocracy in part from disgust at its promiscuous family life, the working class, at least important sections of it, acknowledged the moral legitimacy of the bourgeoisie by adopting its family structure. The European and American working class found no better way to raise children, share affection and sexuality between the sexes, and enjoy leisure time than to imitate or aspire to bourgeois patterns. The transformation of working-class family structure is one of the unwritten aspects of the political success of bourgeois democracy.

One significant conclusion that can be drawn from the examination of four models of family structure is that the bourgeois model is decisively distinct from the others. Neither the aristocratic and peasant families of the old regime nor the working-class family of the early industrial period included the limitation of authority over children to the parents, the intense concern and love of the parents for the children, and the systematic attempt by the parents to substitute their love for the child's bodily gratification. Even though the non-bourgeois models remain somewhat indistinct due to the lack of empirical data, the bourgeois family does emerge from this analysis as a historically distinct phenomenon. Thus the critical theory of the family renders the bourgeois model intelligible at the emotional level. It does so without privileging the bourgeois family over all others, and without reducing the intelligibility of the family to other levels of society. With the family presented as a distinct unit of investigation, further studies can explore how the family was intertwined with the economy and with politics. In this way the question of the relationship between the modern family and industrialization can be answered rigorously.

A second conclusion suggested by the four models concerns the assumption of continuity in family history.[46] Most family historians presuppose that there has been one overall pattern, one linear development of the family in time. The Laslett group, studying the quantity of people in the family, concludes that there has been little change in family size over the past four centuries in England. Ariès, looking at France, sees one basic change, occurring in the mid-eighteenth century, in which the family moved from village sociability to isolated privacy. Historians who use modernization theory, like Shorter, try to correlate family change directly with the movement toward modernity. Psychohistorians, like de Mause, see a linear progress toward empathy. All these positions suffer from a fundamental bias of presenting the family as a unitary phenomenon with a continuous, homogeneous pattern of change. The critical theory of the family enables social scientists to reject that false assumption. Family history is now conceptualized as discontinuous, non-linear and non-homogeneous. The four models outlined above suggest that family history consists of distinct family patterns, each with its own history, each requiring its own set of explanations of origin and change. The family in Europe has included multiple forms, distinct structures, and particular histories.

With the four models before us, it is now possible to turn to the contemporary period and examine the question of the fate of the bourgeois model.

Recent developments in advanced capitalism have brought about a fusion between the old factory working class and the new "white-collar" proletariat. A true bourgeois pattern, with the father owning means of production that could be passed on to his children, has become typical only of a tiny minority. Small factories and retail shops have given way to large corporations. The overwhelming majority of the population in advanced industrial society does not control capital. Hence a vast, heterogeneous working population has emerged which tends to follow the bourgeois family pattern. Only racial minorities living in ghettos and islands of severe white poverty, perhaps as much as 25% of the population in the United States, can be said to retain older working-class family patterns. Differences certainly remain in the child-rearing patterns of the white-collar middle class and the blue-collar working class.[47] Nevertheless, it is fair to say that large sectors of the traditional working class live in families that resemble the bourgeois model in fundamental ways.

In the new context, certain needs of the capitalist economy have brought about changes in the family. First, the family has become a unit of consumption. A new ideology of leisure encourages the family to consume more and more.[48] As the primary need of capitalism shifted increasingly to problems of re-investing excess capital, managers responded by attempting to stimulate higher levels of consumption. New products, rapid style changes, built-in obsolescence, product differentiation through advertising—all fostered an ideology of consumerism with profound effects on the home.[49] The automobile and the TV also served to isolate an already privatized family and even to isolate members within the family. It has been shown that a new indifference to children is emerging among some parents, a so-called "Parent Gap," with American fathers spending, on the average, less than twenty minutes a day with their children.[50]

At the same time, through several interrelated influences, sexual patterns have been changing. Originating among the middle class, the old repressive bourgeois ideology has collapsed in favor of a new acceptance of sexual gratification. With wealthier families leading the way, a reversal of sexual patterns has occurred. The factory workers, now integrated into bourgeois family norms, tend to resist the new sexual ethos.[51] In a strange reversal of nineteenth-century positions, the middle class today is the more promiscuous group. Since consumerism implies impulsive buying and instant gratification, it follows that impulsive sexuality or sexual liberation fits well with the psychological trends.[52] New contraceptive devices and legalized abortion further the tendency toward easing sexual restraints. Along with consumerism and the new sexuality, "permissive" child-rearing practices have spread. Psychoanalysis itself, at least in the United States, has influenced child-rearing patterns, discouraging castration threats and rigid anal discipline. In the context of advanced capitalism, parents are increasingly unwilling to uphold Victorian constraints on children's bodily enjoyment. Many parents consider unnecessary or harmful methods of child rearing which prepare the child for a life of deferred gratification. The consequence of these practices on personality formation remains in dispute.

The women's movement may be seen as a response to the pressures placed on the family by late capitalism. Resisting traditional forms of sex-role differentiation which restricted the wife to the home and to subservience to men in general, women have begun to demand an equal chance to work for equal pay. Such a demand threatens patriarchy, especially in the home. Assuming that capitalism can survive a general employment of women on an equal basis with men, the bourgeois family probably cannot survive a threat to sex-role differentiation. The feminist movement has challenged the basic components of the role of women in the family. Among the nineteenth-century bourgeoisie, women were considered asexual; feminists now contend, with the support of medical opinion, that women have sexual drives that are as deep as men's. In the nineteenth century, respectable bourgeois women avoided politics and business; such reticence is now held in disrepute. In the nineteenth century, domestic tranquility and maternal care were women's responsibility; now these are increasingly considered the tasks of both mates. When men share housework and child care with women, important mechanisms of patriarchy are threatened.

Evidence appears as frequently as the daily newspaper that the bourgeois family structure is on shaky ground. The rise in divorce rates and in extra-marital sex bespeak an unwillingness of marriage partners to stay together and remain faithful for a lifetime. And once a variety of love objects is demanded, the bourgeois family appears too constraining. In the same vein, children now seek friendships outside the home in peer groups and school.

But one must not forget that this general drift away from the exclusive domesticity of the home has followed a deep undermining of the economic power of the father. No longer a proprietor with significant property to pass on to his children, the father does not even have skills to teach them, since each generation must adapt to a rapidly changing technology. In substance, the principles of companionship, intimacy and love among marriage partners in the bourgeois family are being questioned as never before.

Nevertheless, in the United States more people marry than ever before and more and more divorced people are remarrying. The ideology of "happily ever after" exerts an enormous attraction. Outside the reified, commodity relations of work, people desperately seek emotional fulfillment, the only avenue for which continues to be the family. In fact a counter-movement to the collapse of the family has arisen. Many couples see their parents quite often, even though more and more move away from relatives. The Total Woman movement stresses the old family virtues.[53] Although the youth culture of the sixties sought alternatives to the bourgeois family in communes and although many people continue to experiment with non-bourgeois family patterns,[54] it cannot be said that the bourgeois family has been abolished.

To what extent, it may be asked, does the nineteenth-century bourgeois family structure persist? The privacy and isolation of the family unit continues, perhaps to a greater degree than before. Romantic love is more than ever the single legitimate ground for marriage. Intimate relations between parents and children, concern for the children's future and recognition of their special needs has, if anything, been intensified. Even though wife beating and child abuse are being recognized in the United States as widespread social problems, bourgeois forms of enforcing parental authority have replaced earlier and more brutal types of domination. The exclusive authority of parents over children remains the social ideal, even if the state increasingly intervenes to curb parental excesses. In the first three stages of development, aspects of the nineteenth-century pattern persist as well. Feeding by mothers, mostly with bottles rather than breasts, remains the norm. Toilet training is still attempted early and is done with scrupulous attention to remove wastes from the child's body. In all of these ways, the bourgeois family remains the norm.

Structural changes have also occurred. Demands made by spouses on each other for emotional and sexual fulfillment have risen dramatically. Husbands and wives are often not willing, as their nineteenth-century predecessors were, to hide their emotional problems in the closet in order to maintain harmony and respectability in the marriage. Increased demands for psychic fulfillment have placed a heavy burden on marriage. The result is that marriage is no longer viewed as an exclusive relationship or a lifetime partnership. This situation leads to great unhappiness both for those who undergo the trauma of divorce and for those who maintain the marriage but feel unsatisfied and frustrated in it. The hesitancy with which marriage is undertaken and the ambivalence that is felt about it is generated perhaps by the unhappy combination of deep needs for emotional fulfillment along with equally deep needs for exclusive relationships. This combination of demands, generated during childhood, today seems to create a contradiction within the family.

In the first three stages of development, partial changes have occurred. The middle class has experimented with LaMaze and Leboyer methods of childbirth. Some people have reintroduced midwives and home births. The birth rate continues to decline, with many couples deciding not to have children at all. This option certainly goes against nineteenth-century attitudes toward women's procreative function. Many parents send their children out of the home to schools and day-care centers at an early age, exposing them to their peers sooner than was common in the nineteenth century. Child-rearing

methods have become more "permissive," more "empathic,"
allowing for the child to develop at its own rate more than in
the past. Above all, the war against childhood sexuality is
slowing down. Less demands are placed on children to deny
the pleasure of their bodies in exchange for parental love.
Nevertheless, even with these changes, the basic structural
features of the bourgeois family persist: the child is confronted
by two adults from whom it must obtain satisfaction for all its
needs for love and nurturance. In this context, the child must
learn to love people who appear far more powerful than it.
Children must seek sources of identification from a narrow
range of adults, one male and the other female. Sexual stereo-
typing and internalized authority are built firmly into this
family structure.

Although the neo-bourgeois family provides many benefits,
it also sustains certain forms of oppression which are being felt
with particular intensity and are being challenged politically.
The domination of women and especially children, the limited
sources for identification for children, the limited sources of
love objects for all family members, the restriction of the satisfaction of all emotional and sexual needs to the couple, the
peculiar combination of total parental authority and intense
love for children, the absence of community dependence and
sociability—all these *structural* features of the bourgeois family
produce emotional effects which undermine the mutual recognition of people in the process of regulating their own affairs.
These are contradictions in the structure of the family, dependent on hierarchies of age and sex, which enter into the wider
social conflicts of today.

Opinions are sharply divided over the ultimate worth of the
contemporary family. The optimistic note, which tends to be
heard among historians, sociologists of the family and family
therapists, is sounded by William Goode:

I see in [the family] and in the industrial system that accompanies it
the hope of greater freedom: from the domination of elders, from
caste and racial restrictions, from class rigidities. Freedom is *for*

something as well: the unleashing of personal potentials, the right to love, to equality within the family, to the establishment of a new marriage when the old has failed. I see the world revolution in family patterns as part of a still more important revolution that is sweeping the world in our time, the aspiration on the part of billions of people to have the right for the first time to *choose* for themselves—an aspiration that has toppled governments both old and new, and created new societies and social movements.[55]

Goode's hopes for the bourgeois family coincide with his advocacy of liberal forms of modernization. The opposite, critical stance is taken by Simone de Beauvoir, a feminist and a socialist:

I think that if people put so much emphasis on family and children, it is because generally they live in great isolation; they have no friends, no love, no affection, nobody. They are alone; therefore they have children in order to have somebody.[56]

De Beauvoir condemns the bourgeois family as a poor solution to problems generated by an evil society. Both positions contain merits. Given the present structure of advanced capitalism, the family does offer escape from elders, individual choice of partners, and so forth. At the same time, the family generates hierarchies of age and sex which undercut the prospects of social democracy.

In the context of such disagreements over the contemporary family, one must recognize that family structure, in Western Europe and the United States, has never been the object of intentional social reform. Changes in family structure have come about in indirect, unconscious ways. Current efforts to politicize issues of family structure, such as the rights of gays to marry, the rights of women to control their reproductive capabilities, and so forth, open up for the first time new levels of social reform. In the past, experiments with family structure have been limited in their appeal to small, sectarian groups. In the present conjuncture, these issues are reaching a wide popular base. It is appropriate, then, for the critical theory of the family to propose a utopian model which eliminates the mechanisms that reproduce age and sex hierarchies and therefore points to directions for change. A democratic ordering of authority and love through the first three stages presupposes the disappearance of class and sex as determinants of social status and power. With this goal in mind, the isolation of the family from other families and from the work structure needs to be reformed. A democratic community is called for in which family relationships can find wide sources of support. Relations between husband and wife and parent and child must be rid of their possessive and devouring character. Multiple patterns of marital relations must be recognized, so that feelings of affection can expand throughout the community. The ideology of romantic love has become a heavy chain around the neck of marriage partners, weighing them down with expectations that are difficult to fulfill. The ideology of domesticity deprives the couple of necessary support from the community and shackles women to the chores of housework. The ideology of maternal care compels women to surrender their own needs in service to their children, discourages men from engaging in the humanizing activity of child rearing, and confronts children with a pattern of intrusive authority. Love, domesticity and empathetic child care are in themselves unobjectionable. When restricted to the contemporary family they work to undermine sociability and distort relations within the family. A democratic community must avoid the terrifying choice confronting people today of commitment to the family or complete loneliness.

Students of child development remain in disagreement about child-rearing practices. If the goal, however, is to diminish hierarchy and augment individual development, it would appear that methods of child rearing instituted by the Kibbutzim are desirable. When children are raised together with their cohorts in separate dwellings they can select figures for identification from a wide group of adults. Family is no longer segmented from society, and children can find love objects throughout the community. In this situation, parents are in a position to enjoy their children without becoming the sole authority figures. Parents can share affection and love with their children without intruding upon the independent psychic life of the younger generation. The utopian model calls for the loosening of parent-child relations so that the dependence of each upon the other becomes less total, extending to wider social networks. The rigid age hierarchy of the current family form would become softened, as both children and adults would have their own peer group. Specific practices concerning the oral, anal and genital stages would be designed to eliminate Oedipal feelings. With the utopian family model the structural limitations of the bourgeois model could be eliminated or reduced.

The critical theory of the family indicates that the bourgeois model is not the only possible family type. It also indicates that age and sex hierarchies can be reduced by alternate family structures. The goal of this book, however, is not to present detailed proposals for reform. Instead, it is to argue that the family has a relatively autonomous history, one which for the most part remains to be written: that this history concerns mechanisms of instituting age and sex hierarchies at the psychological level; and that these hierarchies are found in different forms in all past family structures. The heuristic aim of the critical theory of the family then is to make the family intelligible as a field for research by defining the categories through which it may be studied empirically. It remains for other researchers to test the value of the critical theory in concrete studies of the family.

NOTES

PREFACE

1. Frédéric Le Play, *L'Organisation de la famille selon le vrai modèle signalé par l'histoire de toutes les races et de tous les temps* (Paris, 1871).

2. Peter Laslett, *The World We Have Lost* (New York, 1965); Peter Laslett and Richard Wall, eds., *Household and Family in Past Time* (New York, 1972).

3. Lutz Berkner, "The Stem Family and the Developmental Cycle of the Peasant Household," *American Historical Review* 77 (1972) 398–418; Tamara Hareven, "The Family as Process," *Journal of Social History* 7 (1974) 322–27. See also: Lutz Berkner, "Recent Research on the History of the Family in Western Europe," *Journal of Marriage and the Family* (1973) 395–405; and "The Use and Misuse of Census Data for the Historical Analysis of Family Structure," *Journal of Interdisciplinary History* 5 (1975) 721–38.

4. Roland Mousnier, *La Famille, l'enfant, et l'éducation en France et en Grande-Bretagne du XVIe au XVIII siècle,* vol. 1 (Paris, 1975); Jean-Louis Flandrin, *Familles: parenté, maison, sexualité dans l'ancienne société* (Paris, 1976).

5. Laslett, *World We Have Lost,* p. 1 ff.

6. Philippe Ariès, *Centuries of Childhood: A Social History of Family Life (L'Enfant et la vie Familiale sous l'ancien régime),* trans. R. Baldick (New York, 1965).

7. Edward Shorter, *The Making of the Modern Family* (New York, 1975). For a fine review essay on Shorter and other important works in family history see Christopher Lasch, "The Family and History," *New York Review of Books,* 13 November 1975, pp. 33–38, 27 November 1975, pp. 37–42, 11 December 1975, pp. 50–54.

8. Shorter, *Making of the Modern Family,* pp. 268, 254.

9. Ibid., p. 259.

10. D. H. J. Morgan, in *Social Theory and the Family* (London, 1975), does not attempt a theory of the family.

Chapter 1. FREUD'S CONCEPT OF THE FAMILY

1. "Fragment of a Case of Hysteria," in *The Complete Works of Sigmund Freud,* standard edition (London, 1953), vol. 7, pp. 112, 122.

2. *Group Psychology and the Analysis of the Ego* (New York, 1959), p. 44.

3. Ibid., pp. 89–90.

4. "The Passing of the Oedipus Complex," in *Collected Papers: Sexuality and the Psychology of Love,* ed. P. Rieff (New York, 1963), p. 177.

5. What makes Freud's commentary even more astonishing is the fact that he knew Hans' parents well and thought of the mother, whom he treated separately, as a neurotic and intrusive person. Far from justifying Freud's reporting and analysis of Little Hans, this knowledge confirms Freud's inability to see the interactional basis of psychic development and presses our doubts on the intra-psychic nature of libidinal structure. For an analysis of the case of Little Hans along somewhat similar lines as mine, see Erich Fromm, Fernando Narvaez et al., "The Oedipus Complex: Comments on 'The Case of Little Hans,'" *Contemporary Psychoanalysis* 4 (1968) 178–88. See also: Philip Weissman, "Early Development and Endowment of the Artistic Director." *Journal of American Psychoanalytic Association* 12 (1964) 59–79; J.W. Slap, "Little Hans' Tonsillectomy," *Psychoanalytic Quarterly* 30 (1961) 259–61.

6. "Analysis of a Phobia in a Five-Year-Old Boy," in *Collected Papers: The Sexual Enlightenment of Children,* ed. by P. Rieff (New York, 1963), p. 65.

7. Ibid., p. 49.

8. Ibid., p. 60; emphasis added.

9. Jean Laplanche and J.-B. Pontalis, "Fantasme originaire, fantasmes des origines, origine du fantasme," *Les Temps Modernes* 215 (1964) 1841.

10. "On Narcissism," in *Collected Papers: General Psychological Theory,* ed. by P. Rieff (New York, 1963), pp. 71–72.

11. Cited in Bogna Lorence, "Parents and Children in 18th Century Europe," *History of Childhood Quarterly* 2 (1974) 2.

12. "Letter to Fliess, Sept. 21, 1897," in *Sigmund Freud's Letters,* ed. M. Bonaparte et al., trans. J. Strachey and E. Mosbacher (New York, 19545) pp. 215–16.

13. *New Introductory Lectures on Psychoanalysis,* trans. J. Strachey (New York, 1964), p. 120; emphasis added.

14. *Totem and Taboo,* trans. A. Brill (New York, 1946), p. 205; emphasis added.

15. *Civilization and Its Discontents,* trans. J. Strachey (New York, 1961), p. 51. See also: " 'Civilized' Sexual Morality," in *Collected Papers: Sexuality and the Psychology of Love,* p. 21, and *Studies on Hysteria,* trans. J. Strachey (New York, 1966), p. 171, where rural and urban sexuality are contrasted.

17. *Civilization and Its Discontents,* p. 81.

18. " 'Civilized' Sexual Morality," p. 21.

19. Ibid., 38; emphasis added.

20. *Civilization and Its Discontents,* p. 50.

21. " 'Civilized' Sexual Morality," p. 29.

22. Ibid., p. 21.

23. *New Introductory Lectures,* 164.

24. Ibid., p. 66.

25. "Family Romances," in *Collected Papers: The Sexual Enlightenment of Children,* p. 42.

26. *New Introductory Lectures,* p. 66.

27. Ibid., p. 88.

28. There is an extensive literature on the Oedipus complex, although none of it, so far as I know, approaches the question in terms of a critical theory of the family. See Philip Rieff, *Freud: The Mind of the Moralist* (New York, 1961), esp. ch. 8; Carl Schorske, "Politics and Patricide in Freud's *Interpretation of Dreams,*" *American Historical Review* 78 (1973); Paul Roazen, *Freud: Political and Social Thought* (New York, 1968); Patrick Mullahy, *Oedipus, Myth and Complex* (New York, 1948). For an excellent discussion of the original debate on the universality of Oedipus between Ernest Jones and Bronislaw Malinowski, see Anne Parsons, *Belief, Magic and Anomie: Essays in Psychological Anthropology* (New York, 1969), esp. pp. 3–66.

29. *Totem and Taboo,* p. 24.

30. I do not have adequate space to explore fully the question of Freud's treatment of women. Briefly stated, Freud is not the biological determinist many feminists have made him. His characterizations of women and femininity are theorized at the level of *psychic* development. The problem with his view of women as inherently less able to sublimate than men derives from his universalization of bourgeois patterns. It is the same problem that I have been arguing regarding

his failure to theorize the family. Because the girl has no penis, he says, she does not develop a castration fear that is as deep as it is for boys; therefore, she does not internalize her parent as deeply as boys, and her super-ego is weaker, rendering her less capable of delaying gratification of the instincts. The problem here is not a biological one: it is rather that Freud is blind to the power relationships of the family, seeing them as natural. Thus he assumes that the problem is the material lack of the penis, when it is clearly the valuation placed on the penis and on males in general by parents in Victorian society. It is also the limitations imposed on the mother in male-dominated society, limitations that are both sociological and psychological. For example, one of the differences between masculinity and femininity for Freud results from the fact that women tend to make object choices into identifications (*New Introductory Lectures*, p. 63). In many cases this is true, since women identify with their husband and his career. They feel they have no complete self of their own. But clearly this comes from the limitations imposed on their practice in bourgeois society. Everything is designed to make women live their lives through their husbands and children. Freud's value for feminism is to allow us to see how girls develop psychically in bourgeois society; but he does all he can to prevent us from seeing how this development is related to wider social structures and how it might be changed.

31. *New Introductory Lectures*, p. 86.

32. Ibid., p. 64.

33. Ibid., p. 62.

34. *Civilization and Its Discontents*, p. 74.

35. Ibid., p. 76.

36. Ibid., p. 77n.

37. Peter Cominos, "Late-Victorian Sexual Respectability and the Social System," *International Review of Social History* 8 (1963) 18–48, 216–250.

38. *Civilization and Its Discontents*, p. 79.

39. *Totem and Taboo*, p. 202.

40. Freud states explicitly the importance of the social dimension: "The ego-ideal is of great importance for the understanding of group psychology. Besides its individual side, this ideal has a social side; it is also the common ideal of a family, a class, or a nation" ("On Narcissism," pp. 81–82).

41. *New Introductory Lectures*, p. 110.

42. Ibid., p. 76.

43. Ibid., p. 67.

44. Ibid., p. 179.

45. *Civilization and Its Discontents*, p. 33.

46. Ibid., p. 69.

47. Ibid., pp. 60–61; emphasis added.

48. Ibid., p. 42.

49. Ibid., p. 46.

50. Ibid., p. 23.

51. Ibid., p. 59.

52. *Group Psychology and the Analysis of the Ego*, trans. J. Strachey (New York, 1965), p. 3.

53. Ibid.

54. George Rudé, *The Crowd in History, 1730–1848* (New York, 1964).

55. *Group Psychology*, p. 26.

56. Ibid., p. 25.

57. W.R. Bion, *Experience in Groups* (New York, 1974).

58. Freud always kept the term ego-ideal but used it only for a special aspect of the super-ego. The super-ego became the general term in his metapsychology and the ego-ideal was used to denote those positive aspirations which the child internalized from its parents during the dissolution of the Oedipus complex.

59. Lewis Feuer, *The Conflict of Generations* (New York, 1969); Raymond Aron, *The Elusive Revolution*, trans. G. Clough (New York, 1969).

60. *Group Psychology*, p. 71.

61. Ibid., p. 87.

62. Ibid., p. 88.

63. Ibid., p. 93.

64. Ibid., p. 92.

65. Ibid., p. 93.

66. Ibid.

67. " 'Civilized' Sexual Morality."

68. *Group Psychology*, p. 67

69. *New Introductory Lectures*, p. 80.

Chapter 2. THE RADICALIZATION OF EROS

1. *The Communist Manifesto* (New York, 1955), pp. 27–28.

2. It is true that Engels, in *The Origin of the Family, Private Property and the State* (New York, 1942), suggests an autonomous or substruc-

tural role for the family: "According to the materialistic conception, the determining factor in history is, in the final instance, the production and reproduction of the immediate essentials of life. This, again, is of a twofold character. On the one side, the production of the means of existence, of articles of food and clothing, dwellings, and of the tools necessary for that production; on the other side, the production of human beings themselves, the propagation of the species. The social organization under which the people of a particular historical epoch and a particular country live is determined by both kinds of production: by the stage of development of labor on the one hand and of the family on the other" (p. 5). Unfortunately, in the rest of the text, the family loses this important role and trails badly behind the mode of production.

3. Ibid., pp. 46–47.

4. Ibid., p. 65.

5. Ibid.

6. Ariès, *Centuries of Childhood*.

7. Joan Scott and Louise Tilly, "Women's Work and the Family in Nineteenth-Century Europe," *Comparative Studies in Society and History* 17 (1975) 36–64.

8. Others to attempt the synthesis in the 1920s were Bernfeld, Fenichel, Sapir and Fromm, to mention only the most prominent.

9. *Character Analysis*, trans. T. Wolfe (New York, 1949), p. 145.

10. *Dialectical Materialism and Psychoanalysis*, in *Sex-Pol Essays, 1929–1934*, ed. Lee Baxandall (New York, 1972), pp. 24–25, 46, 49.

11. For two good treatments of Freudo-Marxism see Reuben Osborn, *Marxism and Psychoanalysis* (New York, 1965), and Paul Robinson, *The Freudian Left* (New York, 1969).

12. *Dialectical Materialism*, p. 26.

13. *The Imposition of Sexual Morality*, in *Sex-Pol Essays*, p. 141.

14. Ibid., p. 237.

15. Ibid., p. 135.

16. Ibid., p. 248.

17. *The Mass Psychology of Fascism*, trans. V. Carfagno (New York, 1970), pp. xiii, xv.

18. Ibid., p. 53.

19. Ibid., pp. 54–55.

20. Ibid., p. 63.

21. Ibid., p. 66. See also *Imposition of Sexual Morality*, p. 95.

22. For discussions of the history of the interaction between official

Marxism and Freudians see: Michael Schneider, *Neurosis and Civilization*, trans. M. Roloff (New York, 1975), vol. 1; Hans Jörg Sandkühler, ed., *Psychoanalyse und Marxismus: Dokumentation einer Kontroverse* (Frankfurt, 1970); Hans-Peter Gente, ed., *Marxismus, Psychoanalyse, Sexpol* (Frankfurt, 1970), 2 vols.

23. "What is Class Consciousness?" in *Sex-Pol Essays*, p.294.

24. For a general discussion of the Frankfurt School, see Martin Jay, *The Dialectical Imagination* (Boston, 1973).

25. I have decided, partially for reasons of space, not to deal with the contributions of some members of the Frankfurt School. Adorno's works (specifically, "Sociology and Psychology," *New Left Review* 46 (Nov.-Dec. 1967) 67–80, 47 (Jan.-Feb. 1968) 79–97, and the massive collective work edited by Adorno, *The Authoritarian Personality* (New York, 1950) will not be studied at all. The contributions of Jürgen Habermas and Alfred Lorenzer will be taken up in the discussion of communication theories of the family.

26. In Fromm's own words, "Wilhelm Reich['s] . . . evaluation of the role of the family is in broad agreement with the view developed in this paper" (*The Crisis of Psychoanalysis* [New York, 1970] p. 145n). This volume contains translations of many of Fromm's contributions to the Frankfurt School's journal, *Zeitschrift für Sozialforschung*.

27. Fromm does try to show how the dialectic of authority varies with different social classes, but his account is sketchy and not systematic. See a reprint of Fromm's essay in *Studien über Autorität und Familie* in *Marxismus, Psychoanalyse, Sexpol*, vol. 1, pp. 254–65.

28. "Authority and the Family," a translation from *Studien* in *Critical Theory* (New York, 1972), p. 53.

29. Ibid., p. 98. See also Franco Ferrarotti, "The Struggle of Reason Against Total Bureaucratization," *Telos* 27 (1976) 157–69.

30. "Authority and the Family," p. 106.

31. Ibid., p. 99.

32. The mother plays an entirely secondary role for Horkheimer. She acts to inhibit the libido and strengthen authority only in the service of her husband's economic ambitions (ibid., pp. 119–20).

33. Ibid., p. 107.

34. Ibid., p. 111.

35. Ibid.

36. Ibid.

37. Ibid., p. 71.

38. "The Concept of Man," in *Critique of Instrumental Reason* (New

York, 1974), pp. 11–12; emphasis added. See also Alexander Mitscherlich (a psychoanalyst who continues the Frankfurt School approach), *Society Without the Father*, trans. E. Mosbacher (New York, 1969).

39. His contribution was translated as "A Study of Authority," in *Studies in Critical Philosophy*, trans. J. de Bres (Boston,1972).

40. "Epilogue: Critique of Neo-Freudian Revisionism," in *Eros and Civilization: A Philosophical Inquiry into Freud* (New York, 1962), pp. 217–51. Marcuse's other essays devoted to the question of Freud are "Aggressiveness in Advanced Industrial Society," in *Negations*, trans. J. Shapiro (Boston, 1968) pp. 248–68 and *Five Lectures: Psychoanalysis, Politics and Utopia*, trans. J. Shapiro and S. Weber (Boston, 1970).

41. *Eros and Civilization*, p. 218.

42. For a criticism of the concept of the performance principle see Reimut Reiche, *Sexuality and Class Struggle*, trans. S. Bennett (London, 1970) p. 49.

43. *Crisis in Psychoanalysis*, p. 27.

44. *Eros and Civilization*, p. 46.

45. Ibid., pp. 196–97.

46. For an excellent critique of *Eros and Civilization* see A. Wilden, "Marcuse and the Freudian Model," *Salmagundi*, Winter, 1970, pp. 196–245.

47. *Eros and Civilization*, p. 90.

48. Ibid., pp. 87–88.

49. Reiche, for example, says: "No more satisfactory model for the early socialization of children exists in any of the highly developed capitalist industrial countries than averagely successful family upbringing (whether the success be the result of accident or design). The necessary conditions are: normal and loving parents, moderately favorable subsidiary factors such as secure economic circumstances, reasonable living conditions, satisfactory division of roles between the parents, and time for the mother to devote herself to the child" (*Sexuality and Class Struggle*, p. 155). Schneider's book is *Neurosis and Civilization*.

50. One other book of note on Marxist psychology by Lucien Sève (*Marxisme et la théorie de la personnalité* [Paris, 1969]) deals not with the family but with the work situation. Noteworthy also are two other Marxist treatments of the family: Eli Zaretsky, *Capitalism, the Family and Personal Life* (New York, 1973); and Heidi Rosenbaum, *Familie als Gegenstruktur zur Gesellschaft: Kritik grundlegender theoretischer Ansätze der westdeutschen Familiensoziologie* (Stuttgart, 1973).

Chapter 3. EGO PSYCHOLOGY, MODERNIZATION AND THE FAMILY

1. Heinz Hartmann, *Ego Psychology and the Problem of Adaptation* (New York, 1958) and *Essays on Ego Psychology: Selected Problems in Psychoanalytic Theory* (New York, 1964).

2. *Essays on Ego Psychology*, p. xiv.

3. Ibid., pp. 90–98.

4. *Childhood and Society* (New York, 1950), p. 35.

5. Ibid., p. 282. Erikson's reasons are slightly different from the ones I have given.

6. Erikson's categories play down the importance of work for the individual. He considers only school age as a time for "industry." Yet, especially under capitalism, work has a psychological meaning that is very deep. Similarly, he does not account for consumption.

7. *Identity: Youth and Crisis* (New York, 1968), pp. 24, 46.

8. Ibid., p. 221.

9. Ibid., p. 47.

10. The most important statement in this regard by a psychoanalytic theorist is W. R. Fairburn, *An Object-Relations Theory of Personality* (New York, 1954).

11. *Childhood and Society*, p. 184.

12. *Identity: Youth and Crisis*, p. 50.

13. *Parents and Children in History: The Psychology of Family Life in Early Modern France* (New York, 1970).

14. This is especially clear in Erikson's studies of Luther and Gandhi, which unfortunately I do not have the space to explore in detail.

15. *Insight and Responsibility: Lectures on the Ethical Implications of Psychoanalytic Insight* (New York, 1964) p. III.

16. *Childhood and Society*, p. 138.

17. Ibid., p. 250; *Identity: Youth and Crisis*, p. 105.

18. *Identity: Youth and Crisis*, p. 263.

19. *Childhood and Society*, p. 156.

20. *Identity and the Life Cycle*, Psychological Issues Monograph no. I (New York, 1959).

21. *Childhood and Society*, pp. 294–95.

22. Jean Strouse, ed., *Women and Analysis: Dialogues on Psychoanalytic Views of Femininity* (New York, 1974), p. 372, and "Womanhood and Inner Space," in *Identity: Youth and Crisis*, pp. 261–94.

23. *Women and Analysis*, p. 368.

24. Robert Stoller, "Facts and Fancies: An Examination of Freud's Concept of Bisexuality," in *Women and Analysis*, pp. 391–416.

25. *Young Man Luther: A Study in Psychoanalysis and History* (New York, 1958); *Gandhi's Truth: On the Origins of Militant Nonviolence* (New York, 1969); "The Legend of Hitler's Childhood," in *Childhood and Society*, pp. 326–58.

26. Lee Rainwater, "Crucible of Identity: The Negro Lower-Class Family," in Gerald Handel, ed., *The Psycho-Social Interior of Families* (Chicago, 1967) pp. 362–400.

27. Parsons adopted the project of discovering the universal attributes of the family from Murdock. For a discussion and refutation of the notion of the universality of the nuclear family in American sociology see Rolf Eickelpasch, "Ist die Kernfamilie universal?" *Zeitschrift für Soziologie* 3 (1974) 323–38.

28. Talcott Parsons et al., *Family, Socialization and Interaction Process* (New York, 1955) pp. 45–47, and *Social Structure and Personality* (New York, 1964), p. 58.

29. *Social Structure and Personality*, p. 44n.

30. Morris Zelditch, in *Family, Socialization and Interaction Process*, pp. 307, 334.

31. *Social Structure and Personality*, pp. 66–67; Robert Bales and Philip Slater, in *Family, Socialization and Interaction Process*, p. 306.

32. *Social Structure and Personality*, p. 20.

33. *Family, Socialization and Interaction Process*, pp. 17, 31.

34. *Social Structure and Personality*, p. 23.

35. Ibid., p. 27.

36. *Family, Socialization and Interaction Process*, p. 54.

37. Ibid., pp. 12–19.

38. See the following examples of Parsonian treatments of the family: S.N. Eisenstadt, *From Generation to Generation* (New York, 1965); Ernest Burgess and Harvey Locke, *The Family: From Institution to Companionship* (New York, 1945); W. Ogburn and M. Nimkoff, *Technology and the Changing Family* (New York, 1955); Frank Furstenberg, "Industrialization and the American Family: A Look Backward," *American Sociological Review* 31 (1966); Bert Adams, "Isolation, Function and Beyond: American Kinship in the 1960s," *Journal of Marriage and the Family* 32 (1970). Above all see the works of Gerald Platt and Fred Weinstein, *The Wish to Be Free* (Los Angeles, 1969) and *Psychoanalytic Sociology* (Baltimore, 1973). The latter is an attempt to syn-

thesize Freud and Parsons and comes closest to my effort to present a historical theory of the family.

39. *Social Structure and Personality*, p. 52.

40. The best-known and most comprehensive of these efforts is William Goode, *World Revolution and Family Patterns* (New York, 1963). The first effort at a family history of Europe also relies on Parsonian theory; see Shorter, *Making of the Modern Family*. For a review of work by historians of the family who use Parsons' modernization theory, see Tamara Hareven, "Modernization and Family History: Perspectives on Social Change," *Signs* 2 (1976) 190–206.

Chapter 4. THE LANGUAGE OF THE FAMILY

1. For a discussion of the various trends in Lacanian psychoanalysis see the excellent article by Sherry Turkle, "Contemporary French Psychoanalysis," *The Human Context* (1975) 333–42, 561–69. See also Anne Fabre-Luce, "Paris Letter," *Partisan Review* 41 (1974) 77–81 and Antoine Compagnon and Michael Schneider, "Economie et marche de la psychanalyse en France," *Critique*, no. 333 (1975), p. 120 ff. for an explanation of the rise in popularity of Freud in France.

2. "The Function of Language in Psychoanalysis," in *The Language of the Self*, trans. Anthony Wilden (New York, 1968), p. 7. See also "Some Reflections on the Ego," *International Journal of Psychoanalysis*, no. 343 (1953) pp. 11–17. Wilden's commentary in *The Language of the Self* is an excellent introduction to Lacan.

3. "The Function of Language in Psychoanalysis," p. 3.

4. See his *Course in General Linguistics*, trans. W. Baskin (New York, 1959).

5. Lacan holds "seminars" with hundreds in attendance. "Students" speak of the experience in religious terms.

6. For a critique of these concepts see Jacques Derrida, "Le facteur de la verité," *Poetique* 21 (1975) 96–147.

7. "The Mirror-phase as Formative of the Function of the I," *New Left Review* 51 (1968) 71–77.

8. For a clear, excellent description of this process in great detail see Françoise Dolto, "Au jeu du désir les dés sont pipés et les cartes truquées," *Bulletin de la Société française de Philosophie*, 67 (1972) 101–71. I have also consulted in this regard Serge Leclaire, *Démasquer le réel* (Paris,1971), and Moustapha Safouan, *Etudes sur l'Oedipe* (Paris, 1974).

9. For a discussion of Hegel's concept of desire see Mark Poster,

Existential Marxism in Postwar France (Princeton, 1975), ch. 1.

10. *Le Séminaire* (Paris, 1975), vol. 1, p. 189.

11. A theorist who comes close to Lacan in this regard is Alfred Lorenzer, who argues that connections and relations which are distorted in the family are "desymbolized and excommunicated from language" (*Uber den Gegenstand der Psychoanalyse, oder: Sprache und Interaktion* [Frankfurt am Main, 1973] p. 165). He goes on to define the id as the concrete bodily needs which emerge from the interactional structure of the child and his *Umwelt* (ibid., p. 166). Unlike Lacan, Lorenzer places the emphasis more on the social interactions than on language structure.

12. For an example of Lacan's understanding of the role of the family in the individual's symptoms from his pre-linguistic period, see Jacques Lacan, "La Famille," in *Encyclopédie Française de Monzie*, vol. 8, *La Vie mentale* (1938), pp. 403–28.

13. *The Backward Child and His Mother*, trans. A.M.S. Smith (New York, 1972), p. 45.

14. *The Child, His "Illness" and the Others* (New York, 1970), pp. vii–viii.

15. *Dominique: Analysis of an Adolescent*, trans. I. Kats (New York, 1973), pp. 170–71.

16. *The Child, His "Illness" and the Others*, pp. 123–24.

17. *Dominique*, p. 82.

18. *Backward Child*, pp. 36, 196.

19. *Speculum de l'autre femme* (Paris, 1974), p. 58.

20. Catherine Baliteau, "La Fin d'une parade misogyne: la psychanalyse lacanienne," *Les Temps Modernes* 30 (1975) 1948.

21. *Speculum de l'autre femme*, p. 41.

22. "The Function of Language in Psychoanalysis," p. 39. See also Jean Joseph Goux, *Economie et symbolique* (Paris, 1973).

23. "The Function of Language in Psychoanalysis," p. 40. Numerous historians have called for the application of anthropological theory to the historical study of the family. (See, for example, Keith Thomas, "History and Anthropology," *Past and Present* 24 [1963] 3–24.) In light of the recognized importance of anthropology for history, it might appear strange that I am not treating the concept of the family in Lévi-Strauss on its own account. My reason is that he concentrates so exclusively on the universal structures of the family that his results are of limited use to the historian. He tells us that the elements of the modern nuclear family have always existed, a perception close to that

of Parsons (see "The Family," in H. Shapiro, ed., *Man, Culture and Society* [New York, 1956], pp. 261–85). More specifically, he discovers a universal set of relations, whose rules of combination yield the total possible family structures. These relations are (1) consanguinity, (2) alliance, and (3) descent (*Structural Anthropology*, trans. Jacobson and Schoepf [New York, 1967], p. 43). While these systems of relations are certainly important to the study of the family, I do not think Lévi-Strauss has elaborated them in a manner complex enough for further historical study.

24. *The Elementary Structures of Kinship*, trans. Bell, Sturmer and Needham (Boston, 1969), p. 493.

25. *Structural Anthropology*, pp. 44–45.

26. "Introduction à l'oeuvre de M. Mauss," in *Marcel Mauss, Sociologie et anthropologie* (Paris, 1950), p. xxxii.

27. *Elementary Structures of Kinship*, pp. 24–25.

28. *Elementary Structures of Kinship*, pp. 129–30.

29. *Oedipe africain* (Paris, 19073), p. 9

30. Ibid., pp. 383–84.

31. *Sex and Repression in Savage Society* (New York, 1964), p. 76. In the 1920s Jones answered Malinowski by claiming that the uncle-son relation is only a "defense" against the primacy of the father-son relation —hardly an adequate response (see Jones, "Mother-Right and Sexual Ignorance of Savages," *Essays in Applied Psychoanalysis* 2[1924] 145–73). Anne Parsons clarifies the issue by separating it into two parts: (1) the level of instinct and fantasy which she says does not change in different family structures, and (2) the level of identification and object choice, which is dependent on social structure and norms. She then argues that each society has its own "nuclear complex" as a variation of the universal (see *Belief, Magic and Ritual* [New York, 1969], p. 8.) As an example, see her discussion of southern Italian family structure, in which she finds a "madonna complex." Parsons, however, is not convincing about why the first level of instinct and fantasy does not change. For a less successful use of the concept of Oedipus by an anthropologist see William Stephens, *The Oedipus Complex: Cross-Cultural Evidence* (New York, 1962).

32. *Oedipe africain*, pp. 9–10.

33. Ibid., p. 369.

34. Ibid., p. 371.

35. Ibid., p. 340.

36. Ortigues denies the applicability of psychodynamics to the

study of "particular family institutions" (see Edmond Ortigues, "La Psychanalyse et les institutions familiale," *Annales* 27 [1972] 1091–1104). For an argument similar to mine in criticizing the notion of the universality of the Oedipus complex, see Jean Baudrillard, *L'Exchange symbolique et la mort* (Paris, 1976), pp. 202–35. Goux, in *Economie et symbolique*, tries to show how Marx's dialectic of the formation of money is directly parallel with Lacan's (and Freud's) notion of the formation of the psyche. Also see Fredric Jameson, "Imaginary and Symbolic in Lacan: The Place of the Subject and the Problem of Psychoanalytic Criticism," *Yale French Studies* (forthcoming); Jameson argues that Lacan's concept of the imaginary is important for literary and historical studies, a topic which I have not dealt with directly.

37. Jean-François Lyotard, in *Discours, Figure* (Paris, 1971), *Dérive à partir de Marx et Freud* (Paris, 1973), *Des Dispositifs pulsionnels* (Paris, 1973), and *Economie libidinale* (Paris, 1974), makes a similar argument, although I do not have the space to discuss his thought.

38. *L'Anti-oedipe* (Paris, 1972), p. 136. A partial translation by Seem and Hurly appears in *Sub-Stance* 11–12 (1975) 170–97.

39. *L'Anti-oedipe*, p. 115.

40. Ibid. p. 209.

41. Ibid.

42 Ibid., p. 123.

43. Ibid., p. 116.

Chapter 5. FAMILY THERAPY AND COMMUNICATION THEORY

1. J. C. Flügel, *The Psychoanalytic Study of the Family* (London, 1921) provides an astonishingly early but not very successful exception in the Freudian tradition. Even at a rudimentary level, Flügel finds it necessary, once he has taken the perspective of the family, to relativize Freud's model of the psyche. He points to the importance of limited objects for identification in the constitution of the modern psyche (p. 178), an issue which I shall take up in later chapters.

2. Jurgen Ruesch and Gregory Bateson, *Communication: The Social Matrix of Psychiatry* (New York, 1951), p. v.

3. W. R. Bion, *Experiences in Groups* (London, 1959).

4. See "Towards a Theory of Schizophrenia," *Behavioral Science* 1:251 (1956). Work was also going on at NIMH by Lyman Wynne and at Yale by Theodore Lidz. In addition, Nathan Ackerman had concur-

rently broken from psychoanalysis to develop a theory of family therapy; See *The Psychodynamics of Family Life* (New York, 1958).

5. Ruesch and Bateson, p. 5.

6. Ibid., p. 168ff.

7. Ibid. p. 17.

8. The list is taken from Terry Kupers, "Schizophrenia and Reification," *Socialist Revolution* 29 (1976), 116–17.

9. Ibid.

10. *Steps to an Ecology of Mind* (New York, 1972), pp. 202–03.

11. Ibid., p. 208.

12. Ibid., p. 217.

13. Ibid., p. 212.

14. Ibid., p. 243.

15. Quoted in Paul Watzlawick, Janet Beavin, and Don Jackson, *Pragmatics of Human Communication: A Study of Interactional Patterns, Pathologies and Paradoxes* (New York, 1967), p. 153.

16. *Steps to an Ecology of Mind*, p. 243.

17. Ibid., p. 242, and Watzlawick, pp. 131, 214–15, present a similar problem.

18. Watzlawick, p. 241.

19. See Maud Mannoni, *Psychiatrie, son "fou" et la psychanalyse* (Paris, 1970), p. 179, and Michel Plon, *La Théorie des jeux: une politique imaginaire* (Paris, 1976). Far a more favorable view of the relation of Lacan and Bateson see Wilden, *Language of the Self.*

20. It might be mentioned, however, that there is virtually no family therapy at present going on in France. The one exception is Jacques Hochmann of Lyon; see his *Pour une psychiatrie communautaire* (Paris, 1971). He studied with the Palo Alto group. In Germany, Jürgen Habermas of the Frankfurt School has attempted to use communication theory in his social theory. He postulates an "ideal speaking situation" underlying all communications. Thereby he avoids behaviorism, but falls into an opposite idealist danger. See his "Toward a Theory of Communicative Competence," in H. Dreitzel, *Recent Sociology*, no. 2 (New York, 1970), pp. 114–48. Habermas does not relate his communication theory to the family in particular.

21. For an account of how therapists came to work with families, see Andrew Ferber, Marilyn Mendelsohn, and Augustus Napier, *The Book of Family Therapy* (New York, 1972).

22. For a sense of this diversity one has only to look at some of the anthologies on family therapy. See, for example, Peter Lomas, ed., *The Predicament of the Family* (London, 1967); Gerald Handel, ed., *The*

Psycho-Social Interior of the Family (New York, 1967); Nathan Ackerman, ed., *Family Therapy in Transition* (Boston, 1970); and Gerald Erickson and Terrence Hogan, eds., *Family Therapy: An Introduction to Theory and Technique* (Belmont, Cal., 1972). See also Ross Speck and Carolyn Attneave, *Family Networks* (New York, 1973) for an attempt to extend family therapy beyond the nuclear family to more distant relatives and friends.

23. See Virginia Satir, *Conjoint Family Therapy* (Palo Alto, Cal., 1964).

24. James Framo, "Symptoms from a Family Transaction Viewpoint," in Ackerman, *Family Therapy in Transition,* p. 162.

25. Robert Hess and Gerald Handel, *Family Worlds* (Chicago, 1959), p. 1.

26. "Pseudo-Mutuality in the Family Relations of Schizophrenics," (with Irving Rycoff, Juliana Day, and Stanley Hirsch) in Handel, *Psycho-Social Interior,* pp. 443–65.

27. Ibid., p. 445.

28. Ibid., pp. 448–57.

29. For psychoanalytic family therapy, see Ivan Boszormenyi-Nagy, "Intensive Family Therapy as Process," in Ivan Boszormenyi-Nagy and James Framo, eds., *Intensive Family Therapy* (New York, 1965), pp. 87–142; Adelaide Johnson, "Sanctions for Superego Lacunae of Adolescents," in K. Eissler, ed., *Searchlights on Delinquency* (New York, 1949), pp. 225–45; David Mendell and Seymour Fisher, "An Approach to Neurotic Behavior in Terms of a Three-Generational Family Model," *Journal of Nervous and Mental Disease* 123 (1956) 171– 80; Helen Borke, "Continuity and Change in the Transmission of Adaptive Patterns over Two Generations," *Marriage and Family Living* 25 (1963) 294–99; and "A Family Over Three Generations," *Journal of Marriage and the Family* 29 (1967) 638–55.

30. August Hollingshead and Fredrick Redlich, *Social Class and Mental Illness* (New York, 1967), and J. Meyers and B. Robert, *Family and Class Dynamics in Mental Illness* (New York, 1964).

31. Theodore Lidz, *The Family and Human Adaptation* (New York, 1963), p. 9.

32. Theodore Lidz, Stephen Fleck, and Alice Cornelison, *Schizophrenia and the Family* (New York, 1965), p. 101.

33. *Family and Human Adaptation,* p. 8.

34. Ibid., pp. 8–9; emphasis added.

35. "The Contemporary Treatment of Psychosis," in *Salmagundi,* Spring 1971, p. 135.

36. *Family and Human Adaptation,* p. 65.

37. Ibid., p. 72.

38. *The Divided Self* (London, 1959), p. 9.

39. See *Madness and Civilization*, trans. Richard Howard (New York, 1965), and *The Birth of the Clinic*, trans. A. M. S. Smith (London, 1973).

40. For discussions of Laing's thought see *Salmagundi*, Spring 1971, devoted to "Laing and Anti-Psychiatry," especially the contribution of Peter Sedgwick. Juliet Mitchell devotes a long and uneven section to Laing in *Psychoanalysis and Feminism* (New York, 1974). She inaccurately views Laing as a philosopher and as an anti-Freudian, barely discussing his family therapy. Mitchell's polemic, while at times interesting, suffers from one-sidedness and an absolute concern with preserving Freud's thought intact. For a similar critique of Laing see Russell Jacoby, *Social Amnesia* (Boston, 1975).

41. *The Divided Self*, pp. 39–61.

42. Ibid., p. 12.

43. *The Myth of Mental Illness* (New York, 1961).

44. *The Divided Self*, pp. 29–30.

45. Ibid.

46. *The Politics of the Family* (London, 1969), p. 9.

47. See also Jules Henry, *Pathways to Madness* (New York, 1965).

48. *Politics of the Family*, p. 24 ff.

49. *Sanity, Madness and the Family* (with Aaron Esterson) (London, 1964), p. 21, and *The Politics of Experience* (London, 1967), p. 86 ff.

50. Laing, with David Cooper, had written a summary of Sartre's positions in *Reason and Violence: A Decade of Sartre's Philosophy* (London, 1964).

51. *Politics of Experience*, p. 87.

52. *Politics of the Family*, p. 13.

53. Ibid., p. 285 ff.

54. Ibid., p. 78 ff.

55. Ibid., pp. 78–79.

56. Ibid., p. 99.

57. Ibid., p. 31.

58. *Politics of Experience*, p. 127.

59. See Mary Barnes, "Two Memoirs," *Salmagundi*, Spring 1971, pp. 193–98.

60. *The Death of the Family* (New York, 1970), pp. 22–25.

61. Ibid., p. 45.

Chapter 6. ELEMENTS OF A CRITICAL THEORY OF THE
FAMILY

1. "Science and the Future of the Family," *Science,* 29 April 1977, p.
1.

2. For a general overview see Marvin Harris, *The Rise of Anthropological Theory* (New York, 1968).

3. Francis Hsu, "Kinship and Ways of Life," in F. Hsu, ed., *Psychological Anthropology* (Illinois, 1961), pp. 400–56.

4. Alice Rossi, "A Biosocial Perspective on Parenting," *Daedalus,*
Spring 1977, p. 24.

5. Ibid., p. 26.

6. Ibid., p. 25. Rossi warns that if men are expected to care for
infants they would require special training to compensate for hormonal deficiencies. She overlooks the obvious fact that women already receive that training in so many ways during socialization—
role modeling from their mothers and the media, cultural indoctrination from the ideology of motherhood and femininity, and so forth.
Apparently, society does not trust mother nature and her hormones.

7. For example see Gayle Rubin, "The Traffic in Women," in
Rayna Reiter, ed., *Toward an Anthropology of Women* (New York, 1975),
pp. 157–210.

8. There are many difficult methodological questions in studying
child-rearing practices. Some of these were brought up earlier in the
discussion of Erikson's *Childhood and Society.* Since this study is not
concerned directly with methodological issues, I can only refer interested readers to appropriate sources. For research on the contemporary family the best guide I have found is Robert Sears, Eleanor
Maccoby and Harry Levin, *Patterns of Child Rearing* (New York, 1957).
For research on historical families see Abigail Stewart, David Winter,
and David Jones, "Coding Categories for the Study of Child-Rearing
from Historical Sources," *Journal of Interdisciplinary History* (1975) 687–
701.

9. See Melford Spiro, *Children of the Kibbutz* (New York, 1958), and
Bruno Bettelheim, *Children of the Dream* (New York, 1969).

10. For a more detailed discussion of this issue see Jerome Kagan,
"The Child in the Family," *Daedalus,* Spring 1977, pp. 33–56.

11. "The Evolution of Childhood," *History of Childhood Quarterly* 1
(1974) 508.

12. Mousnier, *La Famille, l'enfant, et l'éducation,* vol. 1, p. 179.

13. Philip Slater, "Social Limitations on Libidinal Withdrawal," in Rose Coser, ed., *The Family: Its Structures and Functions* (New York, 1974), pp. 111–33.

Chapter 7. MODELS OF FAMILY STRUCTURE

1. In what follows I will cite the relevant studies from family history but I will not attempt an exhaustive bibliography. For further references on European family history see, Lutz Berkner, "Recent Research on the History of the Family in Western Europe," *Journal of Marriage and the Family* (1973) 395–405.

2. See James Ross, "The Middle Class Child in Urban Italy: 14th to Early 16th Century," in De Mause, pp. 183–228. Puritan influence on the origins of the bourgeois family has been much studied; see R. V. Schnucker, "The English Puritans and Pregnancy, Delivery and Breast Feeding," *History of Childhood Quarterly*, 1(1974) 637–58, and Lawrence Stone, "The Rise of the Nuclear Family in Early Modern England," in C. Rosenberg, ed., *The Family in History* (Philadelphia, 1975). For the German *petite bourgeoisie* see Helmut Möller, *Die Kleinbürgerliche Familie im 18. Jahrhundert: Verhalten und Gruppenkultur* (Berlin, 1969) and for insights on the French family see Elinor Barber, *The Bourgeoisie in 18th Century France* (Princeton, 1955).

3. J.A. and Olive Banks, *Feminism and Family Planning in Victorian England* (New York, 1964), and P. and O. Ranum, eds., *Popular Attitudes toward Birth Control in Pre-Industrial France and England* (New York, 1972).

4. This view of the sexual repression of the bourgeoisie has been challenged most interestingly by Michel Foucault, in *Histoire de la sexualité*, vol. 1, *La Volonté de savoir* (Paris, 1976). Foucault contends that the bourgeois, far from repressing sexuality, talked about it, invented discourses about it, and created mechanisms (psychoanalysis) for changing it all to a far greater extent than what had occurred previously. Repression, for Foucault, is therefore a poor concept to use in analyzing sexuality. Instead, he proposes that the history of sexuality be written from the standpoint of power. Foucault goes on to suggest that sex played the role for the bourgeoisie that blood played for the aristocracy; that is, as a means of defining the body. The bourgeoisie defined the body as an object to be known, controlled, and in general made use of in order to maximize life. The bourgeois family, to Foucault, serves to locate sexuality, to confine it and to intensify it.

My discussion of the bourgeois family leads in general to the same conclusions, although in different theoretical terms. Foucault misunderstands Freud's definition of repression. Repression for Freud was not, as Foucault thinks, the elimination of sexuality from the psyche. This would be impossible. Instead bourgeois sexual repression, as I am using the term, blocked the direct forms of sexual expression and diverted the drive to other avenues. This is consonant with Foucault's argument that the bourgeoisie increased the incidence and scope of discourse on sex. In a sense, sex has been a great preoccupation of the middle class just because it was forbidden or "repressed."

5. François Basch, *Relative Creatures: Victorian Women in Society and the Novel,* trans. A. Rudolf (New York, 1974), pp. 3–15. For contradictory evidence see Carl Degler, "What Ought To Be and What Was: Women's Sexuality in the 19th Century," *American Historical Review* 79 (1974) 1467–1490.

6. "The Double Standard," *Journal of the History of Ideas* 20 (1959) 195–216.

7. Peter Cominos, "Late Victorian Sexual Respectability and the Social System," *International Review of Social History,* 8 (1963) 18–48, 216–50.

8. For remarks on the mundane but revealing aspects of daily life see R. W. Chapman, ed., *The Novels of Jane Austen* (London, 1923).

9. Cited in Stephen Kern, "Freud and the Discovery of Child Sexuality," *History of Childhood Quarterly* 1 (1973) 130.

10. René Spitz, "Authority and Masturbation," *Psychoanalytic Quarterly* 21 (1952) 490–527. Also see R. P. Newman, "Masturbation, Madness and the Modern Concepts of Childhood and Adolescence," *Journal of Social History,* Spring 1975, pp. 1–27.

11. For a discussion of this incredible response see Mary Hartman, "Child-Abuse and Self-Abuse: Two Victorian Cases," *History of Childhood Quarterly* (1974) 221–48. Also see Stephen Kern, "Explosive Intimacy: Psychodynamics of the Victorian Family," *History of Childhood Quarterly* 1 (1974) 437–62; note the pictures of gadgets used to prevent masturbation.

12. See G. J. Barker-Benfield, *The Horrors of the Half-Known Life: Male Attitudes Toward Women and Sexuality in 19th-Century America* (New York, 1976).

13. Mousnier, *La Famille, l'enfant, et l'éducation,* vol. 1, p. 24 ff.

14. For a summary of demographic research see Pierre Goubert,

"Historical Demography and the Reinterpretation of Early Modern French History," in Rabb and Rotburg, eds., *The Family in History* (New York, 1971), pp. 16–27.

15. Lawrence Stone, *The Crisis of the Aristocracy* (New York, 1967), pp. 269–302.

16. Flandrin, p. 176 ff.

17. Bogna Lawrence, "Parents and Children in 18th Century Europe," *History of Childhood Quarterly* 2 (1974) 1–30; Elizabeth Marvick, "Nature Versus Nurture: Patterns and Trends in 17th Century French Child-Rearing," in L. de Mause, ed., *History of Childhood* (New York 1974), pp. 259–302; J.H. Plumb, "The New World of Children in 18th Century England," *Past and Present* 67 (1965) 64–95; and Ivy Pinchbeck and Margaret Hewitt, *Children in English Society*, 2 vols. (London, 1969–73).

18. David Hunt, *Parents and Children in History: The Psychology of Family Life in Early Modern France* (New York, 1970); E. Marvick, "Childhood History and Decisions of State," *History of Childhood Quarterly* 2 (1974) 135–80 and references in note 17.

19. Hunt, p. 169.

20. Philippe Ariès makes similar suggestions in "La Famille d'Ancien Régime," *Revue de l'Académie des sciences morales et politiques* (1956) 46–55 and in "The Family," *Encounter*, August 1975, pp. 7–12.

21. See Laurence Wylie, *Village in the Vaucluse: An Account of Life in a French Village* (New York, 1957); Julian Pitt-Rivers, *The People of the Sierra* (Chicago, 1954); and J.K. Campbell, *Honour, Family and Patronage: A Study of Institutions and Moral Values in a Greek Mountain Community* (New York, 1964). Also, anthropologists have been studying "the culture of poverty" in modern societies, using to advantage methods derived from studies of "primitive societies." See, for example, Oscar Lewis, *Five Families* (New York, 1959).

22. Ariès, *Centuries of Childhood*, p. 10.

23. Anthropologists claim that this is not uniformly true of contemporary peasants.

24. See Shorter, *Making of the Modern Family*, for a description of village life. See also Keith Thomas, *Religion and the Decline of Magic* (New York, 1971).

25. For a discussion of the charivari see Natalie Davis, "The Reasons of Misrule," *Past and Present* 50 (1971) 41–75.

26. Shorter, *Making of the Modern Family*, p. 68.

27. See Natalie Davis, "Ghosts, Kin and Progeny: Some Features

of Family Life in Early Modern France," *Daedalus*, Spring 1977, pp. 87–114.

28. For a long period marriages were outside the church, contracted by oral agreement. See, C. Lasch, "The Suppression of Clandestine Marriage in England," *Salmagundi*, Spring 1974, pp. 90–109.

29. Bernhard Groethuysen, *The Bourgeois: Catholicism vs. Capitalism in 18th Century France*, trans. M. Ilford (New York, 1968).

30. See Flandrin's discussion of the weight of kin relations among the peasants, p. 28 ff.

31. John Gillis, *Youth in History* (New York, 1974).

32. Flandrin, pp. 93–94.

33. See E. Le Roy Ladurie, "Ethnologie rurale du XVIIIe siècle: Restif à la Bretonne," *Ethnologie française* 2 (1971) 215–52, and Jean-Louis Flandrin, *Les Amours paysannes* (Paris, 1975).

34. Cited in Mark Poster, *The Utopian Thought of Restif de la Bretonne* (New York, 1971), p. 30.

35. E. P. Thompson, *The Making of the English Working Class* (New York, 1963), p. 330.

36. See Lewis Mumford, *The City in History* (New York, 1961), and A. and L. Lees, eds., *The Urbanization of European Society in the 19th Century* (New York, 1976) for excerpts from standard works by Michael Anderson, Sidney Pollard and Hsi-Huey Liang.

37. "Illegitimacy, Sexual Revolution and Social Change in Modern Europe," in Rabb and Rotburg, pp. 48–84.

38. D. Smith and M. Hindus, "Premarital Pregnancy in America, 1640–1971." *Journal of Interdisciplinary History* 4 (1975) 537–70.

39. R.P. Newman, "Industrialization and Sexual Behavior: Some Aspects of Working-Class Life in Imperial Germany," in R. Bezucha, ed., *Modern European Social History* (New York, 1972), pp. 270–300.

40. For a comparison with non-European working classes see Lee Rainwater, "Marital Sexuality in Four Cultures of Poverty," *Journal of Marriage and the Family* (1964) 457–66.

41. See Gillis, *Youth in History*.

42. Joan Scott and Luise Tilly, "Women's Work and the Family in 19th Century Europe," *Comparative Studies in Society and History* 17 (1975) 36–64, and Virginia McLaughlin, "Patterns of Work and Family Organization: Buffalo's Italians," in Rabb and Rotburg, pp. 111–126.

43. See the review of Gladstone's diaries in the *Los Angeles Times* (13 March 1975).

44. Most notably, M. Young and P. Wilmott, *Family and Kinship in East London* (New York, 1957).

45. Dominique Desanti, *Les Staliniens* (Paris, 1975).

46. For a review of studies in family history see Arlene Skolnick, "The Family Revisited: Themes in Recent Social Science Research," *Journal of Interdisciplinary History* 4 (1975) 702–19.

47. For studies of these differences in the United States, see A. D. Hollinghead and F. C. Redlich, *Social Class and Mental Illness* (New York, 1958).

48. Ruth Cowan, "The 'Industrial Revolution' in the Home," *Technology and Culture* 17 (1976) 1–23, and Dorothy Smith, "Women, The Family and Corporate Capitalism," *Berkeley Journal of Sociology* 20 (1975–76) 55–90.

49. See M. Marrus, ed., *The Emergence of Leisure* (New York, 1970).

50. *Newsweek*, 22 September 1975, pp. 48–56.

51. See Hans Dreitzel, ed., *Family, Marriage and the Struggle of the Sexes* (New York, 1972).

52. M. Schneider (*Neurosis and Civilization*, trans. M. Roloff [New York, 1975]) sees this impulsive orality in conflict with the older compulsive anality as the major psychic conflict of advanced capitalism.

53. Joyce Maynard, "The Liberation of the Total Woman," *New York Times Magazine*, 28 September 1975, p. 9 ff.

54. For changing child-rearing patterns see Hans Dreitzel, ed., *Childhood and Socialization* (New York, 1973).

55. William Goode, *World Revolution and Family Patterns* (New York, 1970), p. 380.

56. "Interview," *Ms.*, July 1977, p. 15.

INDEX

Adler, Alfred, xviii, 145
anal character, 40, 75
anti-psychiatry, 113, 125
Ariès, Philippe, xi, xii, 170, 190,
  197
aristocratic family, 37, 166, 180, 181,
  183, 190, 196
Aron, Raymond, 33

Bachofen, Johann, 43, 148
Baliteau, Catherine, 95
Bateson, Gregory, 110, 112–19, 130,
  134
Beauvoir, Simone de, 203
behaviorism, 118, 119
Berkner, Lutz, x
Bion, W. R., 32, 110
Bleuler, Eugene, 112
Bolshevism, 47
bourgeois family, xiv, xv, 3, 8, 12,
  16, 22–24, 36, 37, 42, 55–57, 166–
  68, 170, 173–76, 178, 196, 200,
  202
Burgundy, 157

capitalism, xiii, xvi, xvii, 2, 19, 22,
  29, 36, 40, 45, 47–50, 57, 60, 62,
  64, 65, 74, 79, 81, 82, 105–107,
  113, 121, 127, 137, 141, 161, 170, 179,
  193, 198, 199, 203

castration threat, 5–7, 18, 19, 21, 22,
  91, 92, 99, 100, 182
Christ, 186
communication theory, 111, 123
communism, 28, 42, 48, 52
condensation, 88
conjugal family, x, 101, 185, 187
Cooper, David, 137, 138
counter-transference, 86
critical theory, xix, 40, 41, 46, 62,
  63, 70, 85, 139, 140, 146, 163–67,
  197, 205
cybernetics, 111

Deleuze, Gilles, 1, 105–109, 138
demography, 144
developmental psychology, 145
displacement, 88
Dolto, Françoise, 92–95
double bind, 113–15, 118
double standard, 44, 45, 169
Durkheim, Emile, 144

ego psychology, 58, 64, 65, 76, 86,
  89, 123
England, 125, 161, 168, 174, 190, 191,
  194, 195, 197
Enlightenment, 30, 31, 38
Engels, Friedrich, xviii, 42–46,
  48, 49

DATE DUE

CARR McLEAN, TORONTO FORM #38-297